SECOND EDITION

PostgreSQL: Up and Running

Regina O. Obe and Leo S. Hsu

Beijing · Cambridge · Farnham · Köln · Sebastopol · Tokyo

PostgreSQL: Up and Running, Second Edition

by Regina O. Obe and Leo S. Hsu

Copyright © 2015 Regina Obe and Leo Hsu. All rights reserved.

Printed in the United States of America.

Published by O'Reilly Media, Inc., 1005 Gravenstein Highway North, Sebastopol, CA 95472.

O'Reilly books may be purchased for educational, business, or sales promotional use. Online editions are also available for most titles (*http://safaribooksonline.com*). For more information, contact our corporate/institutional sales department: 800-998-9938 or *corporate@oreilly.com*.

Editors: Andy Oram and Meghan Blanchette	**Indexer:** Lucie Haskins
Production Editor: Melanie Yarbrough	**Cover Designer:** Karen Montgomery
Copyeditor: Eileen Cohen	**Interior Designer:** David Futato
Proofreader: Amanda Kersey	**Illustrator:** Rebecca Demarest

July 2012:	First Edition
December 2014:	Second Edition

Revision History for the Second Edition:

2014-12-05:   First release

See *http://oreilly.com/catalog/errata.csp?isbn=9781449373191* for release details.

ISBN: 978-1-449-37319-1

[LSI]

Table of Contents

Preface... ix

1. The Basics... 1
   Where to Get PostgreSQL   1
   Administration Tools   1
       psql   2
       pgAdmin   2
       phpPgAdmin   3
       Adminer   3
   PostgreSQL Database Objects   4
   What's New in Latest Versions of PostgreSQL?   9
       Why Upgrade?   9
       What's New in PostgreSQL 9.4?   10
       PostgreSQL 9.3: New Features   11
       PostgreSQL 9.2: New Features   12
       PostgreSQL 9.1: New Features   13
   Database Drivers   14
   Where to Get Help   15
   Notable PostgreSQL Forks   15

2. Database Administration.. 17
   Configuration Files   17
       postgresql.conf   18
       pg_hba.conf   21
       Reloading the Configuration Files   23
   Managing Connections   23
   Roles   24
       Creating Login Roles   25
       Creating Group Roles   25

Database Creation   27
   Template Databases   27
   Using Schemas   27
Privileges   29
   Types of Privileges   30
   Getting Started   30
   GRANT   30
   Default Privileges   31
   Privilege Idiosyncrasies   32
Extensions   32
   Installing Extensions   34
   Common Extensions   36
Backup and Restore   38
   Selective Backup Using pg_dump   38
   Systemwide Backup Using pg_dumpall   40
   Restore   40
Managing Disk Storage with Tablespaces   42
   Creating Tablespaces   42
   Moving Objects Between Tablespaces   42
Verboten Practices   43
   Don't Delete PostgreSQL Core System Files and Binaries   43
   Don't Give Full OS Administrative Rights to the Postgres System Account
      (postgres)   44
   Don't Set shared_buffers Too High   44
   Don't Try to Start PostgreSQL on a Port Already in Use   44

3. psql.   47
Environment Variables   47
Interactive versus Noninteractive psql   48
psql Customizations   49
   Custom Prompts   50
   Timing Executions   51
   Autocommit Commands   51
   Shortcuts   51
   Retrieving Prior Commands   52
psql Gems   52
   Executing Shell Commands   52
   Watching Statements   52
   Lists   53
Importing and Exporting Data   54
   psql Import   54
   psql Export   55

Copy from/to Program   55
Basic Reporting   56

4. Using pgAdmin... 59
    Getting Started   59
        Overview of Features   59
        Connecting to a PostgreSQL Server   60
        Navigating pgAdmin   61
    pgAdmin Features   63
        Accessing psql from pgAdmin   63
        Editing postgresql.conf and pg_hba.conf from pgAdmin   63
        Creating Database Assets and Setting Privileges   64
        Import and Export   66
        Backup and Restore   69
    pgScript   72
    Graphical Explain   74
    Job Scheduling with pgAgent   75
        Installing pgAgent   75
        Scheduling Jobs   76
        Helpful pgAgent Queries   78

5. Data Types... 81
    Numerics   81
        Serials   82
        Generate Series Function   82
    Characters and Strings   83
        String Functions   84
        Splitting Strings into Arrays, Tables, or Substrings   84
        Regular Expressions and Pattern Matching   85
    Temporals   86
        Time Zones: What They Are and Are Not   88
        Datetime Operators and Functions   90
    Arrays   92
        Array Constructors   92
        Referencing Elements in an Array   93
        Array Slicing and Splicing   93
        Unnesting Arrays to Rows   94
    Range Types   95
        Discrete Versus Continuous Ranges   95
        Built-in Range Types   96
        Defining Ranges   96
        Defining Tables with Ranges   97

	Range Operators	98
	JSON	98
	Inserting JSON Data	99
	Querying JSON	99
	Outputting JSON	101
	Binary JSON: jsonb	101
	XML	103
	Inserting XML Data	103
	Querying XML Data	104
	Custom and Composite Data Types	105
	All Tables Are Custom Data Types	105
	Building Custom Data Types	106
	Building Operators and Functions for Custom Types	107
6.	**Tables, Constraints, and Indexes.**	**109**
	Tables	109
	Basic Table Creation	109
	Inherited Tables	110
	Unlogged Tables	111
	TYPE OF	111
	Constraints	112
	Foreign Key Constraints	112
	Unique Constraints	113
	Check Constraints	113
	Exclusion Constraints	114
	Indexes	114
	PostgreSQL Stock Indexes	115
	Operator Classes	116
	Functional Indexes	118
	Partial Indexes	118
	Multicolumn Indexes	119
7.	**SQL: The PostgreSQL Way.**	**121**
	Views	121
	Single Table Views	122
	Using Triggers to Update Views	123
	Materialized Views	125
	Handy Constructions	126
	DISTINCT ON	127
	LIMIT and OFFSET	127
	Shorthand Casting	128
	Multirow Insert	128

    ILIKE for Case-Insensitive Search   128
    Returning Functions   129
    Restricting DELETE, UPDATE, SELECT from Inherited Tables   129
    DELETE USING   130
    Returning Affected Records to the User   130
    Composite Types in Queries   130
    DO   132
  FILTER Clause for Aggregates   133
  Window Functions   134
    PARTITION BY   135
    ORDER BY   136
  Common Table Expressions   138
    Basic CTEs   138
    Writable CTEs   139
    Recursive CTE   140
  Lateral Joins   141

8. Writing Functions. **145**
  Anatomy of PostgreSQL Functions   145
    Function Basics   145
    Triggers and Trigger Functions   147
    Aggregates   148
    Trusted and Untrusted Languages   149
  Writing Functions with SQL   150
    Basic SQL Function   150
    Writing SQL Aggregate Functions   152
  Writing PL/pgSQL Functions   154
    Basic PL/pgSQL Function   154
    Writing Trigger Functions in PL/pgSQL   154
  Writing PL/Python Functions   155
    Basic Python Function   156
  Writing PL/V8, PL/CoffeeScript, and PL/LiveScript Functions   157
    Basic Functions   159
    Writing Aggregate Functions with PL/V8   160

9. Query Performance Tuning. **163**
  EXPLAIN   163
    EXPLAIN Options   163
    Sample Runs and Output   164
    Graphical Outputs   167
  Gathering Statistics on Statements   168
  Guiding the Query Planner   169

Strategy Settings	169
How Useful Is Your Index?	170
Table Statistics	171
Random Page Cost and Quality of Drives	172
Caching	173
Writing Better Queries	174
Overusing Subqueries in SELECT	175
Avoid SELECT *	177
Make Good Use of CASE	178
Using Filter Instead of CASE	179

10. Replication and External Data. **181**

Replication Overview	181
Replication Jargon	181
Evolution of PostgreSQL Replication	183
Third-Party Replication Options	183
Setting Up Replication	184
Configuring the Master	184
Configuring the Slaves	185
Initiating the Replication Process	186
Foreign Data Wrappers	186
Querying Flat Files	187
Querying a Flat File as Jagged Arrays	188
Querying Other PostgreSQL Servers	189
Querying Nonconventional Data Sources	190

A. Installing PostgreSQL. **193**

B. PostgreSQL Packaged Command-Line Tools. **197**

Index. **205**

Preface

PostgreSQL (*http://www.postgresql.org*) is an open source relational database management system that began as a research project at the University of California, Berkeley. It was originally released under the BSD license but now uses the PostgreSQL License (TPL). For all intents and purposes, it's BSD-licensed. It has a long history, dating back to 1985.

PostgreSQL has enterprise-class features such as SQL windowing functions, the ability to create aggregate functions and also utilize them in window constructs, common table and recursive common table expressions, and streaming replication. These features are rarely found in other open source databases but are common in newer versions of proprietary databases such as Oracle, SQL Server, and DB2. What sets PostgreSQL apart from other databases, including the proprietary ones we just mentioned, is how easily you can extend it, usually without compiling any code. Not only does it include advanced features, but it also performs them quickly. It can outperform many other databases, including proprietary ones, for many types of database workloads.

In this book, we'll expose you to the advanced ANSI SQL features that PostgreSQL offers and the unique features it contains. If you're an existing PostgreSQL user or have some familiarity with it, we hope to show you some gems you may have missed along the way or features found in newer PostgreSQL versions that are not in the version you're using. This book assumes you've used another relational database before but may be new to PostgreSQL. We'll show some parallels in how PostgreSQL handles tasks compared to other common databases, and we'll demonstrate feats you can achieve with PostgreSQL that are difficult or impossible to do in other databases. If you're completely new to databases, you'll still learn a lot about what PostgreSQL has to offer and how to use it; however, we won't try to teach you SQL or relational theory. You should read other books on these topics to take the greatest advantage of what this book has to offer.

This book focuses on PostgreSQL versions 9.2, 9.3, and 9.4, but we will cover some unique and advanced features that are also present in prior versions of PostgreSQL.

Audience

We hope that both working and budding database professionals will find this book to be of use. We specifically target the following ilk:

- We hope that someone who's just learning about relational databases will find this book useful and make a bond with PostgreSQL for life. In this second edition, we have expanded on many topics, providing elementary examples where possible.

- If you're currently using PostgreSQL or managing it as a DBA, we hope you'll find this book handy. We'll be flying over familiar terrain, but you'll be able to pick up a few pointers and shortcuts introduced in newer versions that could save time. If nothing else, this book is 20 times lighter than the PostgreSQL manual.

- Not using PostgreSQL yet? This book is propaganda—the good kind. Each day that you're wedded to a proprietary system, you're bleeding dollars. Each day you're using a less powerful database, you're making compromises with no benefits.

If your work has nothing to do with databases or IT, or if you've just graduated from kindergarten, the cute picture of the elephant shrew on the cover should be worthy of the price alone.

What Makes PostgreSQL Special, and Why Use It?

PostgreSQL is special because it's not just a database: it's also an application platform, and an impressive one at that.

PostgreSQL allows you to write stored procedures and functions in several programming languages. In addition to the prepackaged languages, you can enable support for more languages via the use of extensions. Example built-in languages that you can write stored functions in are SQL and PL/pgSQL. Languages you can enable via extensions are PL/Perl, PL/Python, PL/V8 (aka PL/JavaScript), and PL/R, to name a few. Many of these are packaged with common distributions. This support for a wide variety of languages allows you to solve problems best addressed with a domain-specific or more procedural or functional language; for example, using R statistics and graphing functions, and R succinct domain idioms, to solve statistics problems; calling a web service via Python; or writing map reduce constructs and then using these functions within an SQL statement.

You can even write aggregate functions in any of these languages, thereby combining the data-aggregation power of SQL with the native capabilities of each language to achieve more than you can with the language alone. In addition to using these languages, you can write functions in C and make them callable, just like any other stored function. Functions written in several different languages can participate in one query. You can even define aggregate functions containing nothing but SQL. Unlike in MySQL and

SQL Server, no compilation is required to build an aggregate function in PostgreSQL. So, in short, you can use the right tool for the job even if each subpart of a job requires a different tool. You can use plain SQL in areas where most other databases won't let you. You can create fairly sophisticated functions without having to compile anything.

The custom type support in PostgreSQL is sophisticated and very easy to use, rivaling and often outperforming most other relational databases. The closest competitor in terms of custom type support is Oracle. You can define new data types in PostgreSQL that can then be used as a table column type. Every data type has a companion array type so that you can store an array of a type in a data column or use it in an SQL statement. In addition to having the ability to define new types, you can also define operators, functions, and index bindings to work with these new types. Many third-party extensions for PostgreSQL take advantage of these features to achieve performance speedups, provide domain-specific constructs to allow shorter and more maintainable code, and accomplish tasks you can only fantasize about in other databases.

If building your own types and functions is not your thing, you have a wide variety of built-in data types, such as json (introduced in version 9.2), and extensions that provide more types to choose from. Many of these extensions are packaged with PostgreSQL distributions. PostgreSQL 9.1 introduced a new SQL construct, CREATE EXTENSION, that allows you to install an extension with a single SQL statement. Each extension must be installed in each database you plan to use it in. With CREATE EXTENSION, you can install in each database you plan to use any of the aforementioned PL languages and popular types with their companion functions and operators, such as the hstore key-value store, ltree hierarchical store, PostGIS spatial extension, and countless others. For example, to install the popular PostgreSQL key-value store type and its companion functions, operators, and index classes, you would run:

```
CREATE EXTENSION hstore;
```

In addition, there is an SQL command you can run (see "Extensions" on page 32) to list the available and installed extensions.

Many of the extensions we mentioned, and perhaps even the languages we discussed, may seem uninteresting to you. You may recognize them and think, "Meh, I've seen Python, and I've seen Perl.... So what?" As we delve further, we hope you experience the same "wow" moments we've come to appreciate with our many years of using PostgreSQL. Each update treats us to new features, increases usability, brings improvements in speed, and pushes the envelope of what is possible with a relational database. In the end, you will wonder why you ever used any other database, because PostgreSQL does everything you could hope for and does it for free. No more reading the licensing-cost fine print of those other databases to figure out how many dollars you need to spend if you have 8 cores on your server and you need X,Y, and Z functionality, and how much it will cost to go to 16 cores.

On top of this, PostgreSQL works fairly consistently across all supported platforms. So if you're developing an app you need to resell to customers who are running Unix, Linux, Mac OS X, or Windows, you have no need to worry, because it will work on all of them. Binaries are available for all platforms if you're not in the mood to compile your own.

Why Not PostgreSQL?

PostgreSQL was designed from the ground up to be a multiapplication, high-transactional database. Many people do use it on the desktop in the same way they use SQL Server Express or Oracle Express, but just like those products, PostgreSQL cares about security management and doesn't leave this up to the application connecting to it. As such, it's not ideal as an embeddable database for single-user applications—unlike SQLite or Firebird, which perform role management, security checking, and database journaling in the application.

Sadly, many shared hosts don't have PostgreSQL preinstalled, or they include a fairly antiquated version of it. So, if you're using shared hosting, you might be forced to use MySQL. This situation has been improving and has gotten much better since the first edition of this book. Keep in mind that virtual, dedicated hosting and cloud-server hosting are reasonably affordable and getting more competitively priced. The cost is not that much higher than for shared hosting, and you can install any software you want. Because you'll want to install the latest stable version of PostgreSQL, choosing a virtual, dedicated, or cloud server for which you are not confined to what the ISP preinstalls is more suitable for running PostgreSQL. In addition, Platform as a Service (PaaS) offerings have added PostgreSQL support, which often offers the latest released versions of PostgreSQL: four notable offerings are SalesForce Heroku PostgreSQL, Engine Yard, Red Hat OpenShift, and Amazon RDS for PostgreSQL.

PostgreSQL does a lot and can be daunting. It's not a dumb data store; it's a smart elephant. If all you need is a key-value store or you expect your database to just sit there and hold stuff, it's probably overkill for your needs.

Where to Get Data and Code Used in This Book

You can download this book's data and code from the book's site (*http://bit.ly/1tZXANx*). If you find anything missing, please post any errata on the book's errata page (*http://bit.ly/postgresql-errata*).

For More Information on PostgreSQL

This book is geared toward demonstrating the unique features of PostgreSQL that make it stand apart from other databases, as well as how to use these features to solve real-world problems. You'll learn how to do things you never knew were possible with a

---

database. Aside from the cool "eureka!" stuff, we will also demonstrate bread-and-butter tasks, such as how to manage your database, set up security, troubleshoot performance problems, improve performance, and connect to your database with various desktop, command-line, and development tools.

PostgreSQL has a rich set of online documentation. We won't endeavor to repeat this information, but we encourage you to explore what is available. There are more than 2,250 pages in the manuals (*http://www.postgresql.org/docs/manuals*) available in both HTML and PDF formats. In addition, fairly recent versions of these online manuals are available for hard-copy purchase if you prefer paper form. Since the manual is so large and rich in content, it's usually split into a three- to four-volume book set when packaged in hard-copy form.

Other PostgreSQL resources include:

- *Planet PostgreSQL* (*http://planet.postgresql.org*) is an aggregator of PostgreSQL blogs. You'll find PostgreSQL core developers and general users showcasing new features and demonstrating how to use existing ones.
- *PostgreSQL Wiki* (*http://wiki.postgresql.org*) provides lots of tips and tricks for managing various facets of the database and migrating from other databases.
- *PostgreSQL Books* (*http://www.postgresql.org/docs/books/*) is a list of books about PostgreSQL.
- *PostGIS in Action Books* (*http://www.postgis.us*) is the website for the books we've written about PostGIS, the spatial extender for PostgreSQL.

Code and Output Formatting

For elements in parentheses, we gravitate toward placing the open parenthesis on the same line as the preceding element and the closing parenthesis on a line by itself to satisfy columnar constraints for printing:

```
function ( Welcome to PostgreSQL
);
```

We also remove gratuitous spaces in screen output, so if the formatting of your results doesn't match ours exactly, don't fret.

We recommend adding a single space after a serial comma, but we do omit them at times in this book to fit to page width.

The SQL interpreter treats tabs, new lines, and carriage returns as white space. In our code, we generally use white spaces for indentation, not tabs. Make sure that your editor doesn't automatically remove tabs, new lines, and carriage returns or convert them to something other than spaces.

After copying and pasting, if you find your code not working, check the copied code to make sure it looks like what we have in the listing.

Some examples use Linux and some use Windows. For examples such as foreign data wrappers that require full-path settings, you may see a path such as /postgresql_book/ somefile.csv. These are always relative to the root of your server. If you are on Windows, you must include the drive letter: C:/postgresql_book/somefile.csv. Even on Windows, you need to use the standard Linux path slash /, not \.

Conventions Used in This Book

The following typographical conventions are used in this book:

Italic
> Indicates new terms, URLs, email addresses, file names, and file extensions.

`Constant width`
> Used for program listings. Used within paragraphs, where needed for clarity, to refer to programming elements such as variables, functions, databases, data types, environment variables, statements, and keywords.

`Constant width bold`
> Shows commands or other text that should be typed literally by the user.

`Constant width italic`
> Shows text that should be replaced with user-supplied values or by values determined by context.

 This icon signifies a tip, suggestion, or general note.

 This icon indicates a warning or caution.

Using Code Examples

Supplemental material (code examples, exercises, etc.) is available for download at *http://www.postgresonline.com/downloads/postgresql_book_2e.zip*.

This book is here to help you get your job done. In general, you may use the code in this book in your programs and documentation. You do not need to contact us for permission unless you're reproducing a significant portion of the code. For example, writing a program that uses several chunks of code from this book does not require permission. Selling or distributing a CD-ROM of examples from O'Reilly books does require permission. Answering a question by citing this book and quoting example code does not require permission. Incorporating a significant amount of example code from this book into your product's documentation does require permission.

We appreciate, but do not require, attribution. An attribution usually includes the title, author, publisher, and ISBN. For example: "*PostgreSQL: Up and Running, Second Edition* by Regina Obe and Leo Hsu (O'Reilly). Copyright 2015 Regina Obe and Leo Hsu, 978-1-4493-7319-1."

If you feel your use of code examples falls outside fair use or the permission given above, feel free to contact us at *permissions@oreilly.com*.

Safari ® Books Online

 Safari Books Online (*www.safaribooksonline.com*) is an on-demand digital library that delivers expert content in both book and video form from the world's leading authors in technology and business.

Technology professionals, software developers, web designers, and business and creative professionals use Safari Books Online as their primary resource for research, problem solving, learning, and certification training.

Safari Books Online offers a range of product mixes and pricing programs for organizations, government agencies, and individuals. Subscribers have access to thousands of books, training videos, and prepublication manuscripts in one fully searchable database from publishers like O'Reilly Media, Prentice Hall Professional, Addison-Wesley Professional, Microsoft Press, Sams, Que, Peachpit Press, Focal Press, Cisco Press, John Wiley & Sons, Syngress, Morgan Kaufmann, IBM Redbooks, Packt, Adobe Press, FT Press, Apress, Manning, New Riders, McGraw-Hill, Jones & Bartlett, Course Technology, and dozens more. For more information about Safari Books Online, please visit us online.

How to Contact Us

Please address comments and questions concerning this book to the publisher:

O'Reilly Media, Inc.
1005 Gravenstein Highway North
Sebastopol, CA 95472
800-998-9938 (in the United States or Canada)
707-829-0515 (international or local)
707-829-0104 (fax)

We have a web page for this book, where we list errata, examples, and any additional information. You can access this page at:

http://bit.ly/postgresql-up-and-running-2e

To comment or ask technical questions about this book, send email to:

bookquestions@oreilly.com

For more information about our books, courses, conferences, and news, see our website at *http://www.oreilly.com*.

Find us on Facebook: *http://facebook.com/oreilly*

Follow us on Twitter: *http://twitter.com/oreillymedia*

Watch us on YouTube: *http://www.youtube.com/oreillymedia*

## CHAPTER 1

The Basics

In this chapter, we'll get you started with PostgreSQL. We begin by pointing you to resources for downloading and installing it. Next we provide an overview of indispensable administration tools and review PostgreSQL nomenclature. At the time of writing, PostgreSQL 9.4 is awaiting release, and we'll highlight some of the new features you'll find in it. We close the chapter with resources to turn to when you need help.

Where to Get PostgreSQL

Years ago, if you wanted PostgreSQL, you had to compile it from source. Thankfully, those days are long gone. Granted, you can still compile the source if you so choose, but most users nowadays use packaged installers. A few clicks or keystrokes, and you're on your way.

If you're installing PostgreSQL for the first time and have no existing database to upgrade, you should install the latest stable release version for your OS. The downloads page for the PostgreSQL Core Distribution (*http://www.postgresql.org/download*) maintains a listing of places where you can download PostgreSQL binaries for various OSes. In Appendix A, you'll find useful installation instructions and links to additional custom distributions.

Administration Tools

There are four tools we commonly use to manage and use PostgreSQL: psql, pgAdmin, phpPgAdmin, and Adminer. PostgreSQL core developers actively maintain the first three; therefore, they tend to stay in sync with PostgreSQL releases. Adminer, while not specific to PostgreSQL, is useful if you also need to manage other relational databases: SQLite, MySQL, SQL Server, or Oracle. Beyond the four that we cover, you can find plenty of other excellent administration tools, both open source and proprietary.

psql

psql is a command-line interface for running queries. It is included in all distributions of PostgreSQL. psql has some unusual features, such as an import and export command for delimited files (CSV or tab), and a minimalistic report writer that can generate HTML output. psql has been around since the beginning of PostgreSQL and is the tool of choice for many expert users, for people working in consoles without a GUI, or for running common tasks in shell scripts. Newer converts favor GUI tools and wonder why the older generation still clings to the command line.

pgAdmin

pgAdmin (*https://github.com/phppgadmin/phppgadmin*) is a widely used free GUI tool for PostgreSQL. You can download it separately from PostgreSQL if it isn't already packaged with your installer.

pgAdmin runs on the desktop and can connect to multiple PostgreSQL servers regardless of version or OS.

Even if your database lives on a console-only Linux server, go ahead and install pgAdmin on your workstation, and you'll find yourself armed with a fantastic GUI tool.

An example of pgAdmin appears in Figure 1-1.

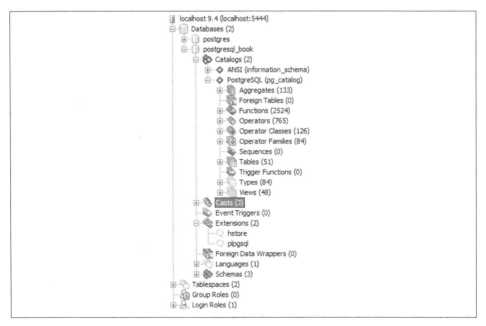

Figure 1-1. pgAdmin

If you're unfamiliar with PostgreSQL, you should definitely start with pgAdmin. You'll get a bird's-eye view and appreciate the richness of PostgreSQL just by exploring everything you see in the main interface. If you're deserting from the SQL Server camp and are accustomed to Management Studio, you'll feel right at home.

phpPgAdmin

phpPgAdmin (*http://phpPgAdmin.sourceforge.net*), pictured in Figure 1-2, is a free, web-based administration tool patterned after the popular phpPgMyAdmin from phpMyAdmin. PostgreSQL differs from phpPgAdmin by including additions to manage schemas, procedural languages, casts, operators, and so on. If you've used phpMyAdmin, you'll find phpPgAdmin to have the same look and feel.

Figure 1-2. phpPgAdmin

Adminer

If you manage other databases besides PostgreSQL and are looking for a unified tool, Adminer (*http://www.adminer.org/*) might fit the bill. Adminer is a lightweight, open source PHP application with options for PostgreSQL, MySQL, SQLite, SQL Server, and Oracle, all delivered through a single interface.

One unique feature of Adminer we're impressed with is the relational diagrammer that can produce a graphical layout of your database schema, along with a linear representation of foreign key relationships. Another hassle-reducing feature is that you can deploy Adminer as a single PHP file.

Figure 1-3 is a screenshot of the login screen and a snippet from the diagrammer output. Many users stumble in the login screen of Adminer because it doesn't include a separate text box for indicating the port number. If PostgreSQL is listening on the standard 5432 port, you need not worry. But if you use some other port, append the port number to the server name with a colon, as shown in Figure 1-3.

Adminer is sufficient for straightforward querying and editing, but because it's tailored to the lowest common denominator among database products, you won't find management applets that are specific to PostgreSQL for such tasks as creating new users, granting rights, or displaying permissions. If you're a DBA, stick to pgAdmin but make Adminer available.

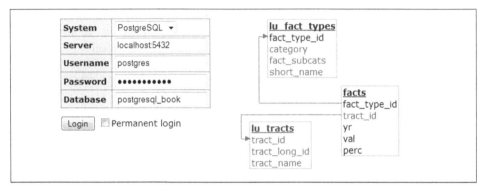

Figure 1-3. Adminer

PostgreSQL Database Objects

So you installed PostgreSQL, fired up pgAdmin, and expanded its browse tree. Before you is a bewildering display of database objects, some familiar and some completely foreign. PostgreSQL has more database objects than most other relational database products (and that's before add-ons). You'll probably never touch many of these objects, but if you dream up something new, more likely than not it's already implemented using one of those esoteric objects. This book is not even going to attempt to describe all that you'll find in a standard PostgreSQL install. With PostgreSQL churning out features at breakneck speed, we can't imagine any book that could possibly do this. We'll limit our discussion to those objects that you should be familiar with:

service
> PostgreSQL installs as a service (daemon) on most OSes. More than one service can run on a physical server as long as they listen on different ports and don't share data storage. In this book, we use the terms *server* and *service* interchangeably, because most people stick to one service per physical server.

database
> Each PostgreSQL service houses many individual databases.

schema

Schemas are part of the ANSI SQL standard. They are the immediate next level of organization within each database. If you think of the database as a country, schemas would be the individual states (or provinces, prefectures, or departments, depending on the country.) Most database objects first belong in a schema, which belongs in a database. PostgreSQL automatically creates a schema named `public` when you create a new database. PostgreSQL puts everything you create into `public` by default unless you change the `search_path` of the database (discussed in an upcoming item). If you have just a few tables, this is fine. But if you have thousands of tables, you'll need to put them in different schemas.

catalog

Catalogs are system schemas that store PostgreSQL built-in functions and metadata. Each database is born containing two catalogs: `pg_catalog`, which has all the functions, tables, system views, casts, and types packaged with PostgreSQL; and `information_schema`, which consists of ANSI standard views that expose PostgreSQL metainformation in a format dictated by the ANSI SQL standard.

PostgreSQL practices what it preaches. You will find that PostgreSQL itself is built atop a self-replicating structure. All settings to fine-tune servers are kept in system tables that you're free to query and modify. This gives PostgreSQL a level of flexibility (or hackability) impossible to attain by proprietary database products. Go ahead and take a close look inside the `pg_catalog` schema. You'll get a sense of how PostgreSQL is put together. If you have superuser privileges, you have the right to make updates to the schema directly (and to screw up your installation royally).

The `information_schema` catalog is one you'll also find in MySQL and SQL Server. The most commonly used views in the PostgreSQL `information_schema` are col umns, which lists all table columns in a database; `tables`, which lists all tables (including views) in a database; and `views`, which lists all views and the associated SQL to build rebuild the view. Again, you will also find these views in MySQL and SQL Server, with a subset of columns that PostgreSQL has. PostgreSQL adds a couple more columns, such as `columns.udt_name`, to describe custom data type columns.

Although `columns`, `tables`, and `views` are all implemented as PostgreSQL views, pgAdmin shows them in an *information_schema→Catalog Objects* branch.

variable

Part of what PostgreSQL calls the Grand Unified Configuration (GUC), variables are various options that can be set at the service level, database level, and other levels. One option that trips up a lot of people is `search_path`, which controls which schema assets don't need to be prefixed with the schema name to be used. We discuss `search_path` in greater detail in "Using Schemas" on page 27.

extension

Introduced in PostgreSQL 9.1, this feature allows developers to package functions, data types, casts, custom index types, tables, GUCs, etc. for installation or removal as a unit. Extensions are similar in concept to Oracle packages and are the preferred method for distributing add-ons. You should follow the developer's instructions on how to install the extension files onto your server. This usually involves installing the extension binaries and scripts. Once done, you must enable the extension for each database separately.

You don't need to enable every extension you use in all databases. For example, if you need advanced text search in only one of your databases, enable `fuzzystr match` just for that database. When you add extensions, you have a choice of the schemas they will go in. If you take the default, extension objects will litter the `public` schema. This could make that schema unwieldy, especially if you store your own database objects in there. We recommend that you create a separate schema that will house all extensions and even create a separate schema to hold each large extension. Include the new schemas in the `search_path` variable of the database so you can use the functions without specifying which schema they're in. Some extensions dictate which schema they should be installed in. For those, you won't be able to change the schema. For example, many language extensions, such as plv8, must be installed in `pg_catalog`.

table

Tables are the workhorses of any database. In PostgreSQL, tables are first of all citizens of their respective schemas, before being citizens of the database.

PostgreSQL tables have two remarkable talents. First, they recognize parents and children. This hierarchy streamlines your database design and can save you endless lines of looping code when querying similar tables. We cover inheritance in Example 6-2.

Second, creating a table automatically results in the creation of an accompanying custom data type. In other words, you can define a complete data structure as a table and then use it as a column in another table. See "Custom and Composite Data Types" on page 105 for a thorough discussion of composite types.

foreign table *and* **foreign data wrapper**

Foreign tables showed their faces in version 9.1. These are virtual tables linked to data outside a PostgreSQL database. Once you've configured the link, you can query them like any other tables. Foreign tables can link to CSV files, a PostgreSQL table on another server, a table in a different product such as SQL Server or Oracle, a NoSQL database such as Redis, or even a web service such as Twitter or Salesforce. Configuring foreign tables is done through *foreign data wrappers* (FDWs). FDWs contain the magic handshake between PostgreSQL and external data sources. Their implementation follows the standards decreed in SQL/Management of External Data (MED) (*http://en.wikipedia.org/wiki/SQL/MED*).

Many programmers have already developed FDWs for popular data sources that they freely share. You can try your hand at creating your own FDWs as well. (Be sure to publicize your success so the community can reap the fruits of your toil.) Install FDWs using the extension framework. Once they're installed, pgAdmin will show them listed under a node called Foreign Data Wrappers.

tablespace
A tablespace is the physical location where data is stored. PostgreSQL allows tablespaces to be independently managed, so you can easily move databases or even single tables and indexes to different drives.

view
Most relational database products offer views for abstracting queries and allow for updating data via a view. PostgreSQL offers the same features and allows for auto-updatable single-table views in versions 9.3 and later that don't require any extra writing of rules or triggers to make them updatable. For more complex logic or views involving more than one table, you still need triggers or rules to make the view updatable. Version 9.3 introduced materialized views, which cache data to speed up commonly used queries. See "Materialized Views" on page 125.

function
Functions in PostgreSQL can return a scalar value or sets of records. You can also write functions to manipulate data; when functions are used in this fashion, other database engines call them stored procedures.

language
Functions are created in procedural languages (PLs). Out of the box, PostgreSQL supports three: SQL, PL/pgSQL, and C. You can install additional languages using the CREATE EXTENSION or CREATE PRODCEDURAL LANGUAGE commands. Languages currently in vogue are Python, JavaScript, Perl, and R. You'll see plenty of examples in Chapter 8.

operator
Operators are symbolic, named functions (e.g., =, &&) that take one or two arguments and that have the backing of a function. In PostgreSQL, you can invent your own. When you define a custom type, you can also define operators that work with that custom type. For example, you can define the = operator for your type. You can even define an operator with operands of two disparate types.

data type *(or just* type*)*
Every database product has a set of data types that it works with: integers, characters, arrays, etc. PostgreSQL has something called a *composite type*, which is a type that has attributes from other types. Imaginary numbers, polar coordinates, and tensors

are examples of composite types. If you define your own type, you can define new functions and operators to work with the type: `div`, `grad`, and `curls`, anyone?

cast

Casts are prescriptions for converting from one data type to another. They are backed by functions that actually perform the conversion. What is rare about PostgreSQL is the ability to create your own casts and thus change the default behavior of casting. For example, imagine you're converting zip codes (which in the United States are five digits long) to `character` from `integer`. You can define a custom cast that automatically prepends a zero when the zip is between 1000 and 9999. Casting can be *implicit* or *explicit*. Implicit casts are automatic and usually expand from a more specific to a more generic type. When an implicit cast is not offered, you must cast explicitly.

sequence

A sequence controls the autoincrementation of a serial data type. PostgresSQL automatically creates sequences when you define a serial column, but you can easily change the initial value, increment, and next value. Because sequences are objects in their own right, more than one table can use the same sequence object. This allows you to create a unique key value that can span tables. Both SQL Server and Oracle have sequence objects, but you must create them manually.

row *or* record

We use the terms *rows* and *records* interchangeably. In PostgreSQL, rows can be treated independently from their respective tables. This distinction becomes apparent and useful when you write functions or use the row constructor in SQL.

trigger

You will find triggers in most enterprise-level databases; triggers detect data-change events. When PostgreSQL fires a trigger, you have the opportunity to execute trigger functions in response. A trigger can run in response to particular types of statements or in response to changes to particular rows, and can fire before or after a data-change event.

Trigger technology is evolving rapidly in PostgreSQL. Starting in version 9.0, a `WITH` clause lets you specify a Boolean `WHEN` condition, which is tested to see whether the trigger should be fired. Version 9.0 also introduced the `UPDATE OF` clause, which allows you to specify which column(s) to monitor for changes. When the column changes, the trigger is fired, as demonstrated in Example 8-11. In version 9.1, a data change in a view can fire a trigger. In version 9.3, data definition language (DDL) events can fire triggers. The DDL events that can fire triggers are listed in the Event Trigger Firing Matrix (*http://bit.ly/12sbQI8*). In version 9.4, triggers for foreign tables were introduced. See CREATE TRIGGER (*http://bit.ly/12sbOzV*) for more details about these options.

rule

Rules are instructions to substitute one action for another. PostgreSQL uses rules internally to define views. As an example, you could create a view as follows:

```
CREATE VIEW vw_pupils AS SELECT * FROM pupils WHERE active;
```

Behind the scenes, PostgresSQL adds an `INSTEAD OF SELECT` rule dictating that when you try to select from a table called `vw_pupils`, you will get back only rows from the `pupils` table in which the `active` field is `true`.

A rule is also useful in lieu of certain simple triggers. Normally a trigger is called for each record in your update/insert/delete statement. A rule, instead, rewrites the action (your SQL statement) or inserts additional SQL statements on top of your original. This avoids the overhead of touching each record separately. For changing data, triggers are the preferred method of operation. Many PostgreSQL users consider rules to be legacy technology for action-based queries because they are much harder to debug when things go wrong, and you can write rules only in SQL, not in any of the other PLs.

What's New in Latest Versions of PostgreSQL?

The PostgreSQL release cycle is fairly predictable, with major releases slated for each September. Each new version adds enhancements to ease of use, stability, security, performance, and avant-garde features. The upgrade process gets simpler with each new version. The lesson here? Upgrade, and upgrade often. For a summary chart of key features added in each release, check the PostgreSQL Feature Matrix (*http://www.post gresql.org/about/featurematrix*).

Why Upgrade?

If you're using PostgreSQL 8.4 or below, upgrade now! Version 8.4 entered end-of-life (EOL) support in July 2014. Details about PostgreSQL EOL policy can be found at the PostgreSQL Release Support Policy (*http://www.postgresql.org/support/versioning/*). EOL is not a place you want to be. New security updates and fixes to serious bugs will no longer be available. You'll need to hire specialized PostgreSQL core consultants to patch problems or to implement workarounds—probably not a cheap proposition, assuming you can even locate someone willing to do the work.

Regardless of which major version you are running, you should always try to keep up with the latest micro versions. An upgrade from, say, 8.4.17 to 8.4.21, requires just binary file replacement and a restart. Micro versions only patch bugs. Nothing will stop working after a micro upgrade, and performing a micro upgrade can in fact save you grief.

What's New in PostgreSQL 9.4?

At the time of writing, PostgreSQL 9.3 is the latest stable release, and 9.4 is in beta with binaries available for the brave. The following features have been committed and are available in the beta release:

- Materialized views are improved. In version 9.3, refreshing a materialized view locks it for reading for the entire duration of the refresh. But refreshing materialized views usually takes time, so making them inaccessible during a refresh greatly reduces their usability in production environments. Version 9.4 removes the lock so you can still read the data while the view is being refreshed. One caveat is that for a materialized view to utilize this feature, it must have a unique index on it.

- The SQL:2008 analytic functions `percentile_disc` (percentile discrete) and `per centile_cont` (percentile continuous) are added, with the companion `WITHIN GROUP (ORDER BY...)` SQL construct. Examples are detailed in Depesz ORDERED SET WITHIN GROUP Aggregates (*http://bit.ly/12sbTnq*). These functions give you a built-in fast median function. For example, if we have test scores and want to get the median score (median is 0.5) and 75 percentile score, we would write this query:

```
SELECT subject, percentile_cont(ARRAY[0.5, 0.75])
  WITHIN GROUP (ORDER BY score) As med_75_score
 FROM test_scores GROUP BY subject;
```

  PostgreSQL's implementation of `percentile_cont` and `percentile_disc` can take an array or a single value between 0 and 1 that corresponds to the percentile values desired and correspondingly returns an array of values or a single value. The `ORDER BY score` says that we are interested in getting the `score` field values corresponding to the designated percentiles.

- `WITH CHECK OPTION` syntax for views allows you to ensure that an update/insert on a view cannot happen if the resulting data is no longer visible in the view. We demonstrate this feature in Example 7-2.

- A new data type—`jsonb`, a JavaScript Object Notation (JSON) binary type replete with index support—was added. `jsonb` allows you to index a full JSON document and speed up retrieval of subelements. For details, see "JSON" on page 98, and check out these blog posts: "Introduce jsonb: A Structured Format for Storing JSON (*http://bit.ly/1yo0Tp9*)," and "jsonb: Wildcard Query (*http://bit.ly/12sbZv4*)."

- Query speed for the Generalized Inverted Index (GIN) has improved, and GIN indexes have a smaller footprint. GIN is gaining popularity and is particularly handy for full text searches, trigrams, `hstores`, and `jsonb`. You can also use it in lieu of B-Tree in many circumstances, and it is generally a smaller index in these cases. Check out GIN as a Substitute for Bitmap Indexes (*http://hlinnaka.iki.fi/2014/03/28/gin-as-a-substitute-for-bitmap-indexes*).

- More JSON functions are available. See Depesz: New JSON functions (*http://bit.ly/1wFr0Yc*).

- You can easily move all assets from one tablespace to another using the syntax ALTER TABLESPACE old_space MOVE ALL TO new_space;.

- You can use a number for set-returning functions. Often, you need a row number when extracting denormalized data stored in arrays, hstore, composite types, and so on. Now you can add the system column ordinality (an ANSI SQL standard) to your output. Here is an example using an hstore object and the each function that returns a key-value pair:

```
SELECT ordinality, key, value
  FROM each('breed=>pug,cuteness=>high'::hstore) WITH ordinality;
```

- You can use SQL to alter system-configuration settings. The ALTER system SET ... construct allows you to set global-system settings normally set in *postgresql.conf*, as detailed in "postgresql.conf" on page 18.

- Triggers can be used on foreign tables. When someone half a world away edits data, your trigger will catch this event. We're not sure how well this will perform with the expected latency in foreign tables when the foreign table is very far away.

- A new unnest function predictably allocates arrays of different sizes into columns.

- A ROWS FROM construct allows the easy use of multiple set-returning functions in a series, even if they have an unbalanced set of elements in each set:

```
SELECT * FROM ROWS FROM (
jsonb_each('{"a":"foo1","b":"bar"}'::jsonb),
jsonb_each('{"c":"foo2"}'::jsonb)) x
(a1,a1_val,a2_val);
```

- You can code dynamic background workers in C to do work as needed. A trivial example is available in the version 9.4 source code in the *contrib/worker_spi* directory.

PostgreSQL 9.3: New Features

The notable features that first appeared in version 9.3 (released in 2013) are:

- The ANSI SQL standard LATERAL clause was added. A LATERAL construct allows FROM clauses with joins to reference variables on the other side of the join. Without this, cross-referencing can take place only in the join conditions. LATERAL is indispensable when you work with functions that return sets, such as unnest, generate_series, regular expression table returns, and numerous others. See "Lateral Joins" on page 141.

- Parallel `pg_dump` is available. Version 8.4 brought us parallel restore, and now we have parallel backup to expedite backing up of huge databases.

- Materialized view (see "Materialized Views" on page 125) was unveiled. You can now persist data into frequently used views to avoid making repeated retrieval calls for slow queries.

- Views are updatable automatically. You can use an `UPDATE` statement on a single view and have it update the underlying tables, without needing to create triggers or rules.

- Views now accommodate recursive common table expressions (CTEs).

- More JSON constructors and extractors are available. See "JSON" on page 98.

- Indexed regular-expression search is enabled.

- A 64-bit large object API allows storage of objects that are terabytes in size. The previous limit was a mere 2 GB.

- The postgres_fdw driver, introduced in "Querying Other PostgreSQL Servers" on page 189, allows both reading and writing to other PostgreSQL databases (even on remote servers with lower versions of PostgreSQL). Along with this change is an upgrade of the FDW API to implement writable functionality.

- Numerous improvements were made to replication. Most notably, replication is now architecture-independent and supports streaming-only remastering.

- Using C, you can write user-defined background workers for automating database tasks.

- You can use triggers on data-definition events.

- A new `watch` psql command is available. See "Watching Statements" on page 52.

- You can use a new `COPY DATA` command both to import from and export to external programs. We demonstrate this in "Copy from/to Program" on page 55.

PostgreSQL 9.2: New Features

The notable features released with version 9.2 (September 2012) are:

- You can perform index-only scans. If you need to retrieve columns that are already a part of an index, PostgreSQL skips the unnecessary trip back to the table. You'll see significant speed improvement in key-value queries as well as aggregates that use only key values such as `COUNT(*)`.

- In-memory sort operations are improved by as much as 20%.

- Improvements were made in prepared statements (*http://bit.ly/1tZZQUP*). A prepared statement is now parsed, analyzed, and rewritten, but you can skip the planning to avoid being tied down to specific argument inputs. You can also now save the plans of a prepared statement that depend on arguments. This reduces the chance that a prepared statement will perform worse than an equivalent ad hoc query.

- Cascading streaming replication supports streaming from a slave to another slave.

- SP-GiST, another advance in GiST index technology using space filling trees, should have enormous positive impact on extensions that rely on GiST for speed.

- Using `ALTER TABLE IF EXISTS`, you can make changes to tables without needing to first check to see whether the table exists.

- Many new variants of `ALTER TABLE ALTER TYPE` commands that used to require dropping and recreating the table were added. More details are available at More Alter Table Alter Types (*http://bit.ly/1tZZVrB*).

- More `pg_dump` and `pg_restore` options were added. For details, read our article "9.2 pg_dump Enhancements" (*http://bit.ly/1q2bLpS*).

- PL/V8 joined the ranks of procedural languages. You can now use the ubiquitous JavaScript to compose functions.

- JSON rose to the level of a built-in data type. Tagging along are functions like `row_to_json` and `array_to_json`. This should be a welcome addition for web developers writing Ajax applications. See "JSON" on page 98 and Example 7-16.

- You can create new range data type classes composed of two values to constitute a range, thereby eliminating the need to cludge range-like functionality, especially in temporal applications. The debut of range type was chaparoned by numerous range operators and functions. Exclusion contraints joined the party as the perfect guardian for range types.

- SQL functions can now reference arguments by name instead of by number. Named arguments are easier on the eyes if you have more than one.

PostgreSQL 9.1: New Features

With version 9.1, PostgreSQL rolled out enterprise features to compete head-on with stalwarts like SQL Server and Oracle:

- More built-in replication features, including synchronous replication.

- Extension management using the new `CREATE EXTENSION` and `ALTER EXTENSION` commands. The installation and removal of extensions became a breeze.

- ANSI-compliant foreign data wrappers for querying disparate, external data sources.

- Writable CTEs. The syntactical convenience of CTEs now works for UPDATE and INSERT queries.

- Unlogged tables, which makes writes to tables faster when logging is unnecessary.

- Triggers on views. In prior versions, to make views updatable, you had to resort to DO INSTEAD rules (*http://bit.ly/1wFrBc9*), which could be written only in SQL, whereas with triggers, you have many PLs to choose from. This opens the door for more complex abstraction using views.

- Improvements added by the KNN GiST index to popular extensions, such as full-text searchs, trigrams (for fuzzy search and case-insensitive search), and PostGIS.

Database Drivers

If you're using or plan to use PostgreSQL, chances are that you're not going to use it in a vacuum. To have it interact with other applications,you need a database driver. PostgreSQL enjoys a generous number of freely available drivers supporting many programming languages and tools. In addition, various commercial organizations provide drivers with extra bells and whistles at modest prices. Several popular open source drivers are available:

- PHP is a common language used to develop web applications, and most PHP distributions come packaged with at least one PostgreSQL driver: the old pgsql driver and the newer pdo_pgsql. You may need to enable them in your *php.ini*, but they're usually already installed.

- For Java development, the JDBC driver keeps up with latest PostgreSQL versions. Download it from PostgreSQL (*http://jdbc.postgresql.org*).

- For .NET (both Microsoft or Mono), you can use the Npgsql (*http://npgsql.projects.pgfoundry.org*) driver. Both the source code and the binary are available for .NET Framework 3.5 and later, Microsoft Entity Framework, and Mono.NET.

- If you need to connect from Microsoft Access, Office productivity software, or any other products that support Open Database Connectivity (ODBC), download drivers from PostgreSQL (*http://www.postgresql.org/ftp/odbc/versions/msi*). The link leads you to both 32-bit and 64-bit ODBC drivers.

- LibreOffice 3.5 (and later) comes packaged with a native PostgreSQL driver. For OpenOffice and older versions of LibreOffice, you can use the JDBC driver or the SDBC driver. You can learn more details from our article OO Base and PostgreSQL (*http://www.postgresonline.com/journal/categories/23-oobase*).

- Python has support for PostgreSQL via various Python database drivers (*http://wiki.postgresql.org/wiki/Python*); at the moment, psycopg (*http://initd.org/*

psycopg/) is the most popular. Rich support for PostgreSQL is also available in the Django (*http://bit.ly/1w5GbtX*) web framework

- If you use Ruby, connect to PostgreSQL using rubygems pg (*http://bit.ly/1vXsUSk*).
- You'll find Perl's connectivity support for PostgreSQL in the DBI and the DBD::Pg drivers. Alternatively, there's the pure Perl DBD::PgPP driver from CPAN (*http://bit.ly/1u00tOc*).
- Node.js is a framework for running scalable network programs written in JavaScript. It is built on the Google V8 engine. There are three PostgreSQL drivers currently: Node Postgres (*https://github.com/brianc/node-postgres*), Node Postgres Pure (*https://github.com/brianc/node-postgres-pure*) (just like Node Postgres but no compilation required), and Node-DBI (*https://github.com/DrBenton/Node-DBI*).

Where to Get Help

There will come a day when you need additional help. Because that day always arrives earlier than expected, we want to point you to some resources now rather than later. Our favorite is the lively mailing list specifically designed for helping new and old users with technical issues. First, visit PostgreSQL Help Mailing Lists (*http://www.post gresql.org/community/lists/*). If you are new to PostgreSQL, the best list to start with is PGSQL-General Mailing List (*http://archives.postgresql.org/pgsql-general*). If you run into what appears to be a bug in PostgreSQL, report it at PostgreSQL Bug Reporting (*http://www.postgresql.org/docs/current/interactive/bug-reporting.html*).

Notable PostgreSQL Forks

The MIT/BSD-style licensing of PostgreSQL makes it a great candidate for forking. Various groups have done exactly that over the years. Some have contributed their changes back to the original project.

Netezza (*http://www.netezza.com*), a popular database choice for data warehousing, was a PostgreSQL fork at inception. Similarly, the Amazon Redshift (*http://aws.amazon.com/redshift/*) data warehouse is a fork of a fork of PostgreSQL. Green-Plum, used for data warehousing and analyzing petabytes of information, was a spinoff of Bizgres, which focused on Big Data. PostgreSQL Advanced Plus by EnterpriseDB (*http://enterprisedb.com*) is a fork of the PostgreSQL codebase that adds Oracle syntax and compatibility features to woo Oracle users. EnterpriseDB ploughs funding and development support to the PostgreSQL community. For this, we're grateful. Their Postgres Plus Advanced Server is fairly close to the most recent stable version of PostgreSQL.

All the aforementioned clones are proprietary, closed source forks. tPostgres (*http://www.tpostgres.org*), Postgres-XC (*http://postgres-xc.sourceforge.net*), and Big SQL (*http://www.bigsql.org*) are three budding forks with open source licensing that we find interesting. These forks all garner support and funding from OpenSCG (*http://www.openscg.com/*). The latest version of tPostgres is built on PostgreSQL 9.3 and targets Microsoft SQL Server users. For instance, with tPostgres, you use the packaged pgtsql language extension to write functions that use T-SQL. The pgtsql language extension is compatible with PostgreSQL proper, so you can use it in any PostgreSQL 9.3 installation. Postgres-XC is a cluster server providing write-scalable, synchronous multimaster replication. What makes Postgres-XC special is its support for distributed processing and replication. It is now at version 1.0. Finally, BigSQL is a marriage of the two elephants: PostgreSQL and Hadoop with Hive. BigSQL comes packaged with `hadoop_fdw`, an FDW for querying and updating Hadoop data sources.

Another recently announced PostgreSQL open source fork is Postgres-XL (*http://www.postgres-xl.org/*) (the XL stands for eXtensible Lattice), which has built-in Massively Parallel Processing (MPP) capability and data sharding across servers.

## CHAPTER 2

Database Administration

This chapter covers what we deem to be the most common activities for basic administration of a PostgreSQL server: role and permission management, database creation, add-on installation, backup, and restore. We assume you've already installed PostgreSQL and have administration tools at your disposal.

Configuration Files

The main configuration files that control basic operations of a PostgreSQL server instance are:

postgresql.conf

> Controls general settings, such as memory allocation, default storage location for new databases, the IP addresses that PostgreSQL listens on, location of logs, and plenty more. Version 9.4 introduced an additional file called *postgresql.auto.conf*, which is created or rewritten whenever you use the new ALTER SYSTEM SQL command. The settings in that file override the *postgresql.conf* file.

pg_hba.conf

> Controls security. It manages access to the server, dictating which users can log in to which databases, which IP addresses or groups of addresses can connect, and which authentication scheme to expect.

pg_ident.conf

> If present, maps an authenticated OS login to a PostgreSQL user. People sometimes map the OS root account to the postgres superuser account. Each authentication line in *pg_hba.conf* can dictate usage of a different *pg_ident.conf* file.

If you accepted the default installation options, you find these files in the main PostgreSQL data folder. You can edit them using any text editor, or using the Admin Pack in pgAdmin. Download instructions are in "Editing postgresql.conf and pg_hba.conf from pgAdmin" on page 63. If you are ever unsure where these files are, run the Example 2-1 query as a superuser while connected to any of your databases.

Example 2-1. Location of configuration files

```
SELECT name, setting FROM pg_settings WHERE category = 'File Locations';
```

```
        name         |                    setting
---------------------+-----------------------------------------------
 config_file         | /etc/postgresql/9.3/main/postgresql.conf
 data_directory      | /var/lib/postgresql/9.3/main
 external_pid_file   | /var/run/postgresql/9.3-main.pid
 hba_file            | /etc/postgresql/9.3/main/pg_hba.conf
 ident_file          | /etc/postgresql/9.3/main/pg_ident.conf
```

postgresql.conf

postgresql.conf controls the life-sustaining settings of the PostgreSQL server instance as well as default settings for new databases. You can override many settings at the database, user, session, and even function levels. You'll find many details on how to fine-tune your server by tweaking settings in the article Tuning Your PostgreSQL Server (*http://wiki.postgresql.org/wiki/Tuning_Your_PostgreSQL_Server*).

An easy way to check the current settings is to query the `pg_settings` view, as we demonstrate in Example 2-2. We provide a synopsis of key setting and description of the key columns, but to delve deeper, we suggest you check the official documentation, pg_settings (*http://bit.ly/1vnIlhH*).

Example 2-2. Key settings

```
SELECT name, context ❶, unit ❷,
    setting, boot_val, reset_val ❸
FROM pg_settings
WHERE name IN ( 'listen_addresses', 'max_connections', 'shared_buffers', 'effec
tive_cache_size', 'work_mem', 'maintenance_work_mem'
)
ORDER BY context, name;
```

name	context	unit	setting	boot_val	reset_val
listen_addresses	postmaster		*	localhost	*
max_connections	postmaster		100	100	100
shared_buffers	postmaster	8kB	131584	1024	131584
effective_cache_size	user	8kB	16384	16384	16384
maintenance_work_mem	user	kB	16384	16384	16384
work_mem	user	kB	5120	1024	5120

❶ If context is set to postmaster, changing this parameter requires a restart of the PostgreSQL service. If it's set to user, changes just require a reload to take effect globally. Restarting terminates active connections, whereas reloading does not.

❷ unit tells you the measurement unit reported by the settings. This is sometimes confusing when it comes to memory because, as you can see in Example 2-2, some are reported in 8 KB units and some just in KB. In *postgresql.conf*, usually, you deliberately set these to a unit of measurement of your choice; 128 MB is a good candidate. You can also get a more human-readable display of a particular setting by running a statement such as SHOW effective_cache_size; or SHOW maintenance_work_mem;, both of which display settings in MBs. If you want to see all settings in friendly units, use SHOW ALL.

❸ setting is the current setting; boot_val is the default setting; reset_val is the new setting if you were to restart or reload the server. Make sure that after any change you make to *postgresql.conf*, setting and reset_val are the same. If they are not, the server is still in need of a restart or reload.

Pay special attention to the following network settings in *postgresql.conf*; changing their values requires a service restart.

If you are running version 9.4 or later, the same-named settings in *postgresql.auto.conf* take precedence over the ones in *postgresql.conf*.

listen_addresses
> Informs PostgreSQL which IP addresses to listen on. This usually defaults to lo calhost or local, but many people change it to *, meaning all available IP addresses.

port
> Defaults to 5432. If you happen to be on Red Hat or CentOS, make changes to the PGPORT value */etc/sysconfig/pgsql/your_service_name_here* to change the listening port.

max_connections
> The maximum number of concurrent connections allowed.

In our experience, we found the following three settings to affect performance across the board and might be worthy of experimentation for your particular setup:

shared_buffers

Defines the amount of memory shared among all connections to store recently accessed pages. This setting profoundly affects the speed of your queries. You want this setting to be fairly high, probably as much as 25% of your onboard memory. However, you'll generally see diminishing returns after more than 8 GB. Changes require a restart.

effective_cache_size

An estimate of how much memory you expect to be available in the OS and Post-greSQL buffer caches. This setting has no effect on actual allocation, but query planner figures in this setting to guess whether intermediate steps and query output would fit in RAM. If you set this much lower than available RAM, the planner may forgo using indexes. With a dedicated server, setting effective_cache_size to half or more of your onboard memory would be a good start. Changes require at least a reload.

work_mem

Controls the maximum amount of memory allocated for operations such as sorting, hash join, and table scans. The optimal setting depends on how you're using the database, how much memory you have to spare, and whether your server is dedicated to PostgreSQL or not. If you have many users running simple queries, you want this setting to be relatively low. How high you set this also depends on how much RAM you have to begin with. A good article to read on work_mem is Understanding work_mem (*http://bit.ly/15SWsHh*). Changes require at least a reload.

maintenance_work_mem

The total memory allocated for housekeeping activities such as vacuuming (pruning records marked for delete). You shouldn't set it higher than about 1 GB. Reload after changes.

These settings can also be set at the database, users, and function levels. For example, you might want to set work_mem higher for an SQL whiz running sophisticated queries. Similarly, if you have one function that is sort-intensive, you could raise the work_mem setting just for it.

New in PostgreSQL 9.4 is ability to change settings using the new ALTER SYSTEM SQL command. For example, to set the work_mem globally, enter the following:

```
ALTER SYSTEM set work_mem = 8192;
```

Depending on the particular setting changed, you may need to restart the service. If just need to reload it, here's a convenient command:

```
SELECT pg_reload_conf();
```

PostgreSQL records changes made through ALTER SYSTEM in an override file called *postgresql.auto.conf*, not directly into *postgresql.conf*.

"I edited my postgresql.conf and now my server is broken."

The easiest way to figure out what you screwed up is to look at the log file, located at the root of the data folder, or in the *pg_log* subfolder. Open the latest file and read what the last line says. The raised error is usually self-explanatory.

A common culprit is setting `shared_buffers` too high. Another suspect is an old *postmaster.pid* left over from a failed shutdown. You can safely delete this file, which is located in the data cluster folder, and try restarting again.

pg_hba.conf

The *pg_hba.conf* file controls which and how users can connect to PostgreSQL databases. Changes to the file require a reload or a server restart to take effect. A typical *pg_hba.conf* looks like Example 2-3.

Example 2-3. Sample pg_hba.conf

```
# TYPE DATABASE USER ADDRESS METHOD
# IPv4 local connections:
host all  all  127.0.0.1/32 ident ❶
# IPv6 local connections:
host all  all ::1/128 ❷trust
host all  all 192.168.54.0/24 ❸md5
hostssl ❹ all all 0.0.0.0/0 md5
# Allow replication connections from localhost, by a user with the ❺
# replication privilege.
#host replication postgres 127.0.0.1/32 trust
#host replication postgres ::1/128 trust
```

❶ Authentication method. The usual choices are `ident`, `trust`, `md5`, and `pass word`. Version 9.1 introduced the peer authentication (*http://bit.ly/1rWZm7V*) method. The `ident` and `peer` options are available only on Linux, Unix, and the Mac, not on Windows. More esoteric options, such as `gss`, `radius`, `ldap`, and `pam`, may not always be installed.

❸ IPv4 syntax for defining network range. The first part—in this case, `192.168.54.0`—is the network address, followed by `/24` as the bit mask. In our *pg_hba.conf*, we allow anyone in our subnet of 192.168.54.0 to connect as long as they provide a valid md5 hashed password.

❷ IPv6 syntax for defining network range. This applies only to servers with IPv6 support and may prevent *pg_hba.conf* from loading if you add this section without actually having IPv6 networking.

❹ SSL connection rule. In our example, we allow anyone to connect to our server as long as they connect using SSL and have a valid md5 password.

❺ Definition of a range of IP addresses allowed to replicate with this server. This is new in version 9.0. These lines are remarked out in this example.

For each connection request, the `postgres` service checks the *pg_hba.conf* file from the top down. As soon as a rule granting access is encountered, processing stops and the connection is allowed. As soon as a rule rejecting access is encountered, processing stops and the connection is denied. If the end of the file is reached without any matching rules, the connection is denied. A common mistake people make is to not put the rules in the proper order. For example, if you put +0.0.0.0/0 `reject`+ before +127.0.0.1/32 `trust`+, local users won't be able to connect, even though a rule is in place allowing them to do so.

"I edited my pg_hba.conf and now my server is broken."

Don't worry. This happens quite often, but it's easily recoverable. This error is generally caused by typos or by adding an unavailable authentication scheme. When the `post gres` service can't parse *pg_hba.conf* file, it blocks all access for safety or won't even start up. The easiest way to figure out what you did wrong is to read the log file. This is located in the root of the data folder or in the *pg_log* subfolder. Open the latest file and read the last line. The error message is usually self-explanatory. If you're prone to slippery fingers, back up the file prior to editing.

Authentication methods

PostgreSQL gives you many choices for authenticating users—probably more than any other database product. Most people stick with the most popular ones: `trust`, `peer`, `ident`, `md5`, and `password`. There is also `reject`, which applies an immediate denial. Authentication methods stipulated in *pg_hba.conf* serve as gatekeepers to the entire PostgreSQL server. Users or devices must still meet role and database access restrictions after connecting.

For more information on the various authentication methods, refer to PostgreSQL Client Authentication (*http://bit.ly/1w5GpkS*). The most commonly used authentication methods are:

`trust`
> The least secure of the authentication schemes. It allows people to self-identify and doesn't ask for a password. As long as the request meets the IP address, user, and database criteria, the user can connect. You should limit `trust` to local connections or private network connections. Even then it's possible for someone to spoof IP addresses, so the more security-minded among us discourage its use entirely. Nevertheless, it's the most common for PostgreSQL installed on a desktop for single-user local access where security is not as much of a concern. The username defaults to the logged-in OS user if not specified.

`md5`
> Very common, requiring an md5-encrypted password to connect.

password
> Uses clear-text password authentication.

ident
> Uses *pg_ident.conf* to see whether the OS account of the user trying to connect has a mapping to a PostgreSQL account. No password is checked.

peer
> Uses the client's OS name from the kernel. It is available only for Linux, BSD, Mac OS X, and Solaris, and can be used only for local connections.

You can elect more than one authentication method, even for the same database. Just keep in mind that *pg_hba.conf* is read from top to bottom.

Reloading the Configuration Files

Many, but not all, changes to configuration files require a restart of the postgres service. Other changes take effect when you perform a reload, which won't kick out active connections. Open a console window and run this command to reload:

```
pg_ctl reload -D your_data_directory_here
```

Or, if you have PostgreSQL installed as a service in RedHat Enterprise Linux, CentOS, or Ubuntu, enter instead:

```
service postgresql-9.3 reload
```

postgresql-9.3 is the name of your service. The service, particularly for older versions, is sometimes just called postgresql sans the version number.

You can also log in as a superuser to any database and execute the following SQL:

```
SELECT pg_reload_conf();
```

You can also reload from pgAdmin; see "Editing postgresql.conf and pg_hba.conf from pgAdmin" on page 63.

Managing Connections

Every once in a while, someone else (never you, of course) will execute a query that he didn't intend to and end up hogging resources. You could also run into a query that's taking much longer than what you have patience for. If one of these things happens, you'll want to cancel the query on the connection or kill the connection altogether. Furthermore, before you can perform a full backup or restore of a database or restore a particular table that's in use, you'll need to kill all affected connections.

Keep in mind that killing is not a graceful end and should be used sparingly. Your client application should catch queries that have gone haywire to begin with. Out of politeness, you probably should inform the connected role that you're about to terminate its connection or do your dirty deed after hours when no one is around.

More often than we'd like, we find ourselves resorting to three SQL commands to cancel running queries and terminate connections. Here is a typical sequence to follow:

1. Retrieve a listing of recent connections and process IDs:

   ```
   SELECT * FROM pg_stat_activity;
   ```

   Additionally, the command provides details of the last query running on each connection, the connected user (`usename`), the database (`datname`) in use, and the start times of the query. You need this view to grab the process IDs of connections that you want to terminate.

2. Now cancel all active queries on a connection:

   ```
   SELECT pg_cancel_backend(procid)
   ```

   This does not terminate the connection itself, though.

3. Kill the connection:

   ```
   SELECT pg_terminate_backend(procid)
   ```

   If you have not canceled the queries on the connection, they are all rudely terminated now. This will be your weapon of choice prior to a restore to prevent an eager user from immediately restarting a canceled query.

PostgreSQL lets you embed functions that perform actions within a regular `SELECT` query. So, although `pg_terminate_backend` and `pg_cancel_backend` can act on only one connection at a time, you can kill multiple connections by wrapping them in a `SELECT`. For example, let's suppose you want to kill all connections belonging to a role with a single blow. Run this SQL command on version 9.2 and later:

```
SELECT pg_terminate_backend(pid) FROM pg_stat_activity WHERE usename =
'some_role';
```

or before version 9.2:

```
SELECT pg_terminate_backend(procpid) FROM pg_stat_activity WHERE usename =
'some_role';
```

The `pg_stat_activity` view has changed considerably since version 9.1 with the renaming and addition of new columns. `procpid` is now `pid`.

Roles

PostgreSQL represents accounts as *roles*. Roles that can log in are called *login roles*. Roles can be members of other roles; roles that contain other roles are called *group roles*. (And yes, group roles can be members of other group roles and so on ad infinitum, but don't go there unless you have a knack for hierarchical thinking.) Roles that are group and can log in are called *group login roles*. However, for easier maintainability and security, DBAs generally don't grant login rights to group roles. A role can be designated as *superuser*. Superuser roles have unfettered access to the PostgreSQL service.

 Recent versions of PostgreSQL no longer use the terms *users* and *groups*. You will still see these terms bandied about on discussion boards; just know that they mean login roles and group roles respectively. For backward compatibility, `CREATE USER` and `CREATE GROUP` still work in current version, but shun them and use `CREATE ROLE` instead.

Creating Login Roles

When you initialize the data cluster during setup, PostgreSQL creates a single role for you with the name `postgres`. (PostgreSQL also creates a namesake database called `postgres`.) You can bypass the password setting by mapping an OS root user to the new role. After you've installed PostgreSQL, before you do anything else, you should log in as `postgres` using psql or pgAdmin and create other roles. pgAdmin has a graphical section for creating user roles, but if you want to create one using SQL, execute an SQL command like the one shown in Example 2-4.

Example 2-4. Creating login roles

```
CREATE ROLE leo LOGIN PASSWORD 'king' CREATEDB VALID UNTIL 'infinity';
```

The `VALID` line is optional and specifies when the role should expire and lose its privileges; the default is `infinity`, which means the role never expires. The `CREATEDB` modifier grants database creation rights to the new role.

To create a user with superuser rights, do so as shown in Example 2-5. Naturally, you can create a superuser only if you are a superuser yourself.

Example 2-5. Creating superuser roles

```
CREATE ROLE regina LOGIN PASSWORD 'queen' SUPERUSER VALID UNTIL '2020-1-1 00:00';
```

We don't really want our queen to reign forever, so we added an abdication date.

Creating Group Roles

Group roles generally have no login rights but serve as containers for other roles. This is merely a best-practice suggestion. Nothing stops you from creating a role that can both log in and contain other roles.

Create a group role through the following SQL:

```
CREATE ROLE royalty INHERIT;
```

Note the use of term INHERIT. This means that any member of `royalty` will automatically have rights granted to the `royalty` role, except for superuser rights. For security, PostgreSQL never passes on superuser rights.

Add roles to the group role with an SQL statement like:

```
GRANT royalty TO leo;
GRANT royalty TO regina;
```

Inheriting rights from group roles

One quirk (or convenience) in PostgreSQL is the ability to specify that a group role not pass its rights to member roles. To avoid having to remember the default value, you should always append the INHERIT keyword if you want members to inherit the rights of the parent role, and NOINHERIT if you don't want them to inherit the rights of the parent role.

Some rights can't be inherited. For example, although you can create a group role that you mark as superuser, this doesn't make its member roles superusers; however, those users can "impersonate" their parent role through the use of SET ROLE, thereby gaining superuser rights for the duration of the session. For instance, a member of the `royalty` group can take on that role through:

```
SET ROLE royalty;
```

Keep in mind that this is per-connection session and not a permanent delegation of rights. To assign noninheritable rights to member roles, you have to do it on a member-by-member basis. This is to guard against inadvertently granting superuser rights to a bunch of roles.

A more powerful impersonation than SET ROLE *some_role* is SET SESSION AUTHORIZATION *some_role*. The main differences between SET ROLE and SET SESSION AUTHORIZATION are:

- Only superusers can execute SET SESSION AUTHORIZATION, and it allows them to impersonate any user regardless of role membership.

- SET SESSION AUTHORIZATION changes the values of the `current_user` and `session_user` variables to those of the user being impersonated. SET ROLE changes only the `current_user` variable.

- Because both the `current_user` and `session_user` are changed by SET SESSION AUTHORIZATION, subsequent SET role commands are limited to those allowed by the user being impersonated. After SET ROLE, roles can be set to any role that the original user has rights to impersonate.

Database Creation

The bare-bones SQL to create a database is:

```
CREATE DATABASE mydb;
```

This creates a copy, owned by the login role that issued the command, of the `tem` `plate1` default. Any role with `CREATEDB` rights can create new databases.

Template Databases

A template database is, as the name suggests, a database that serves as a model for other databases. When you create a new database, PostgreSQL copies all the database settings and data from the template database into yours.

The default PostgreSQL installation comes with two template databases: `template0` and `template1`. If you don't specify a template database to follow when you create a database, the `template1` database is used as the template for the new database.

> You should never alter `template0` because it is the immaculate model that you'll need to copy from if you screw up your templates. Make your customizations to `template1` or a new template database you create. You can't change the encoding and collation of a database you create from `template1` or any other template database you create. So if you need a different encoding or collation from those in `tem` `plate1`, create the database from `template0`.

The basic syntax to create a database modeled after a template is:

```
CREATE DATABASE my_db TEMPLATE my_template_db;
```

You can pick any database to serve as the template. Additionally, you can mark a database as a template database. When you do, PostgreSQL restricts the database from being edited or deleted. Any role with `CREATEDB` rights can use the database. To make any database a template, run the following SQL as a superuser:

```
UPDATE pg_database SET datistemplate = TRUE WHERE datname = 'mydb';
```

If ever you need to make edits to a template database or drop it entirely, first set `datis` `template` to `FALSE` to enable changes. Don't forget to change the value back.

Using Schemas

Schemas organize your database into logical groups. If you have more than two dozen databases on your server, consider cubbyholing them into schemas in a single database. Objects must have unique names within a schema but need not be unique across the database. If you cram all your tables into the default `public` schema, you'll run into name clashes sooner or later. It's up to you how to organize your schemas. For example, if you are an airline, you can place all tables of planes you own and their maintenance records into a plane schema. Place all your crew and their personnel information into another. And create another schema to house passenger-related information.

Another common way to organize schemas is by roles. We found this to be particularly handy with applications that serve multiple clients whose data must be kept separate.

Suppose that you started a business to build and lease a dog-management system to dog spas. Through creative advertising, you now have a dozen clients, but your database still has a single table to store all the dogs. Whimsical government regulation passes, and now you have to put in iron-clad assurances that one spa cannot see dog information from another. To comply, you set up one schema per spa and create the same dogs table in each. You then move the dog records into the schema for the spa where those dogs are pampered. The final touch is to create different login roles for each schema with the same name as the schema, so that the doggy_day_care schema would be owned by the doggy_day_care role, hot_dogs schema would be owned by the hot_dogs role, etc. Dogs are now completely isolated in their respective schemas. When spas log into your database to make edits, they will be able to access only data in their own schemas.

Wait, it gets better. Because we named our roles to match their respective schemas, we're blessed with another useful technique. But we must first introduce the search_path database variable.

As we mentioned earlier, object names must be unique within a schema, but you can have same-named objects in different schemas. For example, you have the same table called dogs in all 12 schemas. When you execute something like SELECT * FROM dogs, how does PostgreSQL know which schema you're referring to? The simple answer is to always prepend the schema name separated from the table name by a dot, such as in SELECT * FROM doggy_day_care.dogs. Another method is to set the search_path variable to be something like public, doggy_day_care, hot_dogs. When the query executes, the planner searches for the dogs table first in the public schema, then dog gy_day_care, then hot_dogs.

PostgreSQL has a little-known variable called user that lists the name of the currently logged-in user. SELECT user returns this name.

Recall how we named our spa schemas to be same as their login roles. We did this so that we can take advantage of the default search path set in *postgresql.conf*:

```
search_path = "$user", public;
```

Now, if role doggy_day_care logs in, all queries will first look in the doggy_day_care schema for the tables before moving to public. And most important, the SQL remains the same for all spas. Even if the spa-management business grows to have thousands or hundreds of thousands of clients, none of the SQL scripts needs to change. To make things easier, create a template database with no dogs. Adding a new spa requires just a few lines to create a schema, database, role, and skeleton tables.

Another practice that we strongly advocate is to create schemas to house extensions ("Step 2: Installing into a database (version 9.1 and later)" on page 35). When you install an extension, new tables, functions, data types, and plenty of other relics enter your server. If they all swarm into the public schema, it gets cluttered. For example, the entire PostGIS suite of extensions will together add more than a thousand functions. If you've already created a few tables and functions of your own in the public schema, imagine how frustrating it would be to scan a list of tables and functions trying to find your own among the thousands.

To create some useful structure, before you install any extensions, create a new schema:

```
CREATE SCHEMA my_extensions;
```

Then add your new schema to the search path:

```
ALTER DATABASE mydb SET search_path='"$user", public, my_extensions';
```

When you install extensions, be sure to indicate your new schema as their new home.

 The SET search_path change will not take effect for existing connections. You'll need to reconnect to experience the change.

Privileges

Privileges (often called permissions) can be tricky to administer in PostgreSQL because of the fine granular control at your disposal. Security can bore down to the object level. You could assign different privileges to each column of your table, if that ever becomes necessary. Teaching you all there's to know about privileges could take a few chapters. What we'll aim for in this section instead is to give you enough information to get up and running and to guide you around some of the more nonintuitive land mines that could either lock you out completely or expose your server inappropriately.

See Privileges (*http://bit.ly/1u01dD4*) for an overview of privileges.

Privilege management in PostgreSQL is no cakewalk. The pgAdmin graphical administration tool can ease some of the tasks or, at the very least, paint you a picture of your privilege settings. You can accomplish most, if not all, of your privilege assignment tasks in pgAdmin. If you're saddled with the task of administering privileges and are new to PostgreSQL, start with pgAdmin. Jump to "Creating Database Assets and Setting Privileges" on page 64 if you can't wait.

Types of Privileges

Some of the object-level privileges you find in PostgreSQL are SELECT, INSERT, UP DATE, ALTER, EXECUTE, TRUNCATE, and a qualifier to those called WITH GRANT. You can infer the privilege from the name alone with the exception of GRANT, which we cover in "GRANT" on page 30. Note that privileges are relevant only with respect to a particular database asset. For example, TRUNCATE for functions and EXECUTE for tables make no sense.

Getting Started

So, you successfully installed PostgreSQL; you should have one superuser, whose password you know by heart. Now you should take the following additional steps to set up additional roles and assign privileges:

1. PostgreSQL creates one superuser and one database for you at installation, both named postgres. Log into your server as postgres.

2. Before creating your first database, create a role that will own the database and can log in, such as:

       CREATE ROLE mydb_admin LOGIN PASSWORD 'something';

3. Create the database and set the owner:

       CREATE DATABASE mydb WITH owner = mydb_admin;

4. Now log in as the mydb_admin user and start setting up additional schemas and tables.

GRANT

The GRANT command assigns privileges to others. The basic usage is:

    GRANT some_privilege TO some_role;

A few things to keep in mind when it comes to GRANT:

- You need to be the holder of the privilege that you're granting and you must have grant privilege yourself. You can't give away what you don't have.

- Some privileges always remain with the owner of an object and can never be granted away. These include DROP and ALTER.

- The owner of an object already has all privileges. Granting an owner privilege in what it already owns is unnecessary.

- When granting privileges, you can add WITH GRANT OPTION. This means that the grantee can grant onwards:

```
GRANT ALL ON ALL TABLES IN SCHEMA public TO mydb_admin WITH GRANT OPTION;
```

- To grant all relevant privileges on an object use ALL instead of the specific privilege:

```
GRANT SELECT, REFERENCES, TRIGGER ON ALL TABLES IN SCHEMA my_schema TO PUB
LIC;
```

- The ALL alias can also be used to grant for all objects within a database or schema:

```
GRANT SELECT, UPDATE ON ALL SEQUENCES IN SCHEMA my_schema TO PUBLIC;
```

- To grant privileges to all roles, you can use the alias PUBLIC:

```
GRANT USAGE ON SCHEMA my_schema TO PUBLIC;
```

The GRANT command is covered in gorgeous detail in GRANT (*http://www.post gresql.org/docs/current/interactive/sql-grant.html*). We strongly recommend that you take the time to study the few pages before you inadvertently knock a big hole in your security wall.

Some privileges are by default granted to PUBLIC. These are CONNECT and CREATE TEMP TABLE for databases, EXECUTE for functions, and USAGE for languages. In many cases you might consider revoking some of defaults for your own safety. Use the REVOKE command:

```
REVOKE EXECUTE ON ALL FUNCTIONS IN SCHEMA my_schema FROM PUBLIC;
```

Default Privileges

PostgreSQL 9.0 introduced *default privileges*, which allow users to set privileges on all database assets within a particular schema or database, as well as in advance of their creation. This will ease your management of privileges, provided you keep default privileges up to date.

Let's suppose we want all users of our database to have EXECUTE and SELECT access to all future tables and functions in a schema. We can define privileges as shown in Example 2-6.

Example 2-6. Defining default privileges on a schema

```
GRANT USAGE ON SCHEMA my_schema TO PUBLIC;
ALTER DEFAULT PRIVILEGES IN SCHEMA my_schema
GRANT SELECT, REFERENCES ON TABLES TO PUBLIC;

ALTER DEFAULT PRIVILEGES IN SCHEMA my_schema
GRANT ALL ON TABLES TO mydb_admin WITH GRANT OPTION;

ALTER DEFAULT PRIVILEGES IN SCHEMA my_schema
GRANT SELECT, UPDATE ON SEQUENCES TO public;

ALTER DEFAULT PRIVILEGES IN SCHEMA my_schema
GRANT ALL ON FUNCTIONS TO mydb_admin WITH GRANT OPTION;
```

```
ALTER DEFAULT PRIVILEGES IN SCHEMA my_schema
GRANT USAGE ON TYPES TO PUBLIC;
```

 Adding or changing default privileges won't affect current privilege settings.

To read more about default privileges, see ALTER DEFAULT PRIVILEGES (*http://bit.ly/1vwCs6L*).

Privilege Idiosyncrasies

Before we unleash you to explore privileges on your own, we do want to point out a few quirks that may not be apparent.

Unlike in other database products, being the owner of a PostgreSQL database does not give you access to all objects in the database, but it does grant you privileges to whatever objects you create and allows you to drop the database. Another role can create objects that you can't access in your owned database. Interestingly, though, you can still drop the whole database.

People often forget to set GRANT USAGE ON SCHEMA or GRANT ALL ON SCHEMA. Even if your tables and functions have rights assigned to a role, these tables and functions will still not be accessible if the role has no USAGE rights to the schema.

Extensions

Extensions, formerly called contribs, are add-ons that you can install in a PostgreSQL database to extend functionality beyond the base offerings. They exemplify the best of open source software: people collaborating, building, and freely sharing new features. Since version 9.1, the new PostgreSQL extension model has made adding extensions a cinch.

 As a note on terminology, older add-ons outside the extension model should still be called *contribs*, but with an eye toward the future, we'll call them all *extensions*.

Not all extensions need to be in all databases. You should install extensions to your individual database on an as-needed basis. If you want all your databases to have a certain set of extensions, you can develop a template database, as discussed in "Template Databases" on page 27, with all the the extensions installed, and then beget future databases from that template.

Occasionally prune extensions that you no longer need, to avoid bloat. Some extensions take up quite a bit of space.

To see which extensions you have already installed on your server, run the query in Example 2-7. Your list could vary significantly from ours.

Example 2-7. Extensions installed on server

```
SELECT name, default_version, installed_version, left(comment,30) As comment
FROM pg_available_extensions
WHERE installed_version IS NOT NULL
ORDER BY name;
```

```
     name       | def   | installed |                     com
----------------+-------+-----------+---------------------------------------------
 btree_gist     | 1.0   | 1.0       | support for indexing common datatypes in..
 fuzzystrmatch  | 1.0   | 1.0       | determine similarities and distance betw..
 hstore         | 1.2   | 1.2       | data type for storing sets of (key, valu..
 plpgsql        | 1.0   | 1.0       | PL/pgSQL procedural language..
 plv8           | 1.3.0 | 1.3.0     | PL/JavaScript (v8) trusted procedural la..
 postgis        | 2.1.3 | 2.1.3     | PostGIS geometry, geography, and raster ..
 www_fdw        | 0.1.8 | 0.1.8     | WWW FDW - extension for handling differe..
```

To get more details about a particular extension already installed on your server, enter the following command from psql:

```
\dx+ fuzzystrmatch
```

Alternatively, execute the following query:

```
SELECT pg_catalog.pg_describe_object(d.classid, d.objid, 0) AS description
FROM pg_catalog.pg_depend AS D INNER JOIN pg_catalog.pg_extension AS E
ON D.refobjid = E.oid
WHERE D.refclassid = 'pg_catalog.pg_extension'::pg_catalog.regclass AND deptype
= 'e' AND E.extname = 'fuzzystrmatch';
```

This shows what's packaged in the extension:

```
description
-------------------------------------------------------------------------------
function dmetaphone_alt(text)
function dmetaphone(text)
function difference(text,text)
function text_soundex(text)
function soundex(text)
function metaphone(text,integer)
function levenshtein_less_equal(text,text,integer,integer,integer,integer)
function levenshtein_less_equal(text,text,integer)
function levenshtein(text,text,integer,integer,integer)
function levenshtein(text,text)
```

Extensions can include database assets of all types: functions, tables, data types, casts, languages, operators classes, etc., but functions usually constitute the bulk of the payload.

Installing Extensions

Getting an extension into your database takes two installation steps. First, download the extension and install it onto your server. Second, install the extension into your database.

 We'll be using the same term—*install*—to refer to both procedures but distinguish between the installation on the server and the installation into the database when the context is unclear.

We cover both steps in this section as well as how to install contribs on PostgreSQL versions prior to extension support.

Step 1: Installing on the server

The installation of extensions on your server varies by OS. The overall idea is to download binary files and requisite libraries, then copy the respective binaries to the *bin* and *lib* folders and the script files to *share/extension* (versions 9.1 and above) or *share/ contrib* (pre-9.1). This makes the extension available for the second step.

For smaller extensions, many of the requisite libraries come prepackaged with your PostgreSQL installation or can be easily retrieved using yum or apt get postgresql-contrib. For others, you'll need to compile your own, find installers that someone has already created, or copy the files from another equivalent server setup. Larger extensions, such as PostGIS, can usually be found at the same location where you downloaded PostgreSQL. To view all extension binaries already available on your server, enter:

```
SELECT * FROM pg_available_extensions;
```

Step 2: Installing into a database (pre-9.1)

Before version 9.1, you had to install extensions manually by running one or more SQL scripts in your database. By convention, if you download an extension with an installer, it automatically dumps the additional scripts into the *contrib* folder of your PostgreSQL installation. The location of this folder varies depending on your particular OS and PostgreSQL distribution.

As an example, on a CentOS running version 9.0, to run the SQL script for the pgAdmin pack extension, type the following from the OS command line:

```
psql -p 5432 -d postgres -f /usr/pgsql-9.0/share/contrib/adminpack.sql
```
This command calls psql noninteractively, passing in the SQL file.

Because scripts weren't packaged into extensions, there was no table of extensions to interrogate on pre-9.1 systems.

Step 2: Installing into a database (version 9.1 and later)

The new extension support makes installation much simpler and more consistent. Use the CREATE EXTENSION command to install extensions into each database. The three big benefits are that you don't have to figure out where the extension files are kept (*share/extension*), you can uninstall them just as easily with DROP EXTENSION, and you have a readily available listing of what is installed and what is available. PostgreSQL installation packages include the most popular extensions, so you really don't need to do more than run the command. To retrieve extensions not packaged with PostgreSQL, visit the PostgreSQL Extension Network (*http://pgxn.org/*).

Here is how we would install the fuzzystrmatch extension using a query:

```
CREATE EXTENSION fuzzystrmatch;
```

You can still install an extension noninteractively using psql. Make sure you're connected to the database where you need the extension, then run a command such as:

```
psql -p 5432 -d mydb -c "CREATE EXTENSION fuzzystrmatch;"
```

 C-based extensions must be installed by a superuser. Most extensions fall into this genre.

We suggest you create one or more schemas to house extensions to keep them separate from production data. After you create the schema, install extensions into it through a command like:

```
CREATE EXTENSION fuzzystrmatch SCHEMA my_extensions;
```

Upgrading to the new extension model

If you've been using a version of PostgreSQL older than 9.1 and restored your old database into version 9.1 or later during a version upgrade, all extensions should continue to function without intervention. For maintainability, you should upgrade your old extensions in the *contrib* folder to use the new approach to extensions. You can upgrade extensions, especially the ones that come packaged with PostgreSQL, from the old contrib model to the new one. Remember that we're referring only to the upgrade in the installation model, not to the extension itself.

For example, suppose you had installed the tablefunc extension (for cross-tab queries) to your PostgreSQL 9.0 in a schema called contrib, and you've just restored your database to a 9.1 server. Run the following command to upgrade:

```
CREATE EXTENSION tablefunc SCHEMA contrib FROM unpackaged;
```

This command searches through contrib, finds all components for the extension, and packages them into a new extension object so it appears in the pg_available_exten sions list as being installed.

You can still install an extension in a database with psql without first connecting to the database:

```
psql -p 5432 -d mydb -c "CREATE EXTENSION fuzzystrmatch;"
```

This command leaves the old functions in the contrib schema intact but removes them from being a part of a database backup.

Common Extensions

Many extensions come packaged with PostgreSQL but are not installed by default. Some past extensions have gained enough traction to become part of the PostgreSQL core database installation, so if you're upgrading from an ancient version, you may get their functionality without needing any extensions.

Popular extensions

Since version 9.1, PostgreSQL prefers the extension model to deliver all add-ons. These include basic extensions consisting only of functions and types, as well as procedural languages (PLs), index types, and foreign data wrappers. In this section we list the most popular extensions (some say, "must-have" extensions) that PostgreSQL doesn't install into your database by default. Depending on your PostgreSQL distribution, you'll find many of these already available on your server:

btree_gist (http://www.postgresql.org/docs/current/interactive/btree-gist.html)
> Provides GiST index-operator classes that implement B-Tree equivalent behavior for common B-Tree services data types. See "PostgreSQL Stock Indexes" on page 115 for more detail.

btree_gin (http://www.postgresql.org/docs/current/interactive/btree-gin.html)
> Provides GIN index-operator classes that implement B-Tree equivalent behavior for common B-Tree serviced data types. See "PostgreSQL Stock Indexes" on page 115 for more detail.

postgis (http://postgis.net)
> Elevates PostgreSQL to a PostGIS in Action (*http://www.postgis.us*) state-of-the-art spatial database outrivaling all commercial options. If you deal with standard OGC GIS data, demographic statistics data, or geocoding, you don't want to be without

this one. You can learn more about PostGIS in our book *PostGIS in Action* (*http://www.postgis.us*). PostGIS is a whopper of an extension, weighing in at more than 800 functions, types, and spatial indexes.

fuzzystrmatch (http://www.postgresql.org/docs/current/interactive/fuzzystrmatch.html)
A lightweight extension with functions such as soundex, levenshtein, and meta phone for fuzzy string matching. We discuss its use in Where is Soundex and Other Warm and Fuzzy Things (*http://www.postgresonline.com/journal/archives/158-Where-is-soundex-and-other-warm-and-fuzzy-string-things.html*).

hstore (http://www.postgresql.org/docs/current/interactive/hstore.html)
An extension that adds key-value pair storage and index support, well-suited for storing pseudonormalized data. If you are looking for a comfortable medium between a relational database and NoSQL, check out hstore.

pg_trgm (trigram) (http://www.postgresql.org/docs/current/interactive/pgtrgm.html)
Another fuzzy string search library, used in conjunction with fuzzystrmatch. In version 9.1, it adds a new operator class, making searches using the ILIKE operator indexable. trigram can also index wildcard searches in the form of LIKE '%some thing%'. See *Teaching ILIKE and LIKE New Tricks* (*http://www.postgreson line.com/journal/archives/212-PostgreSQL-9.1-Trigrams-teaching-LIKE-and-ILIKE-new-tricks.html*) for further discussion.

dblink (http://www.postgresql.org/docs/current/interactive/dblink.html)
Allows you to query a PostgreSQL database on another server. Prior to the introduction of foreign data wrappers in version 9.3, this was the only supported mechanism for cross-database interactions. It remains useful for one-time connections or ad hoc queries. When we have to restore an old database backup to cull accidentally deleted data, we use dblink to connect from the current database to its restored backup.

pgcrypto (http://www.postgresql.org/docs/current/interactive/pgcrypto.html)
Provides encryption tools, including the popular PGP. It's handy for encrypting credit card numbers and other top secret information stored in the database. We placed a quick primer on it at Encrypting Data with pgcrypto (*http://bit.ly/12scJQW*).

Classic extensions

Here we mention a couple extensions that have gained enough of a following to make it into official PostgreSQL releases. We call them out them here because you could still run into them as separate extensions on older servers:

tsearch (http://www.postgresql.org/docs/current/interactive/textsearch-intro.html)
A suite of indexes, operators, custom dictionaries, and functions that enhance full-text searches. It is now part of PostgreSQL proper. If you're still relying on behavior

in from the old extension, you can install tsearch2 (*http://bit.ly/12scNQD*). A better tactic would be just to update servers where you're using the old functions, because compatibility could end at any time.

xml (http://www.postgresql.org/docs/current/interactive/functions-xml.html)
An extension that added an XML data type, related functions, and operators. The XML data type is now an integral part of PostgreSQL, in part to meet the ANSI SQL XML standard. The old extension, now dubbed xml2 (*http://bit.ly/12scKV7*), can still be installed and contains functions that didn't make it into the core. In particular, you need this extension if you relied on the xlst_process function for processing XSL templates. There are also a couple of old XPath functions only found in xml2.

Backup and Restore

PostgreSQL ships with two utilities for backup: pg_dump and pg_dumpall. You'll find both in the *bin* folder. Use pg_dump to back up specific databases and pg_dumpall to back up all databases and server globals. pg_dumpall needs to run under a superuser account so that it has access to back up all databases. Most of the command-line options for these tools exist both in GNU style (two hyphens plus word) and the traditional single-letter style (one hyphen plus alphabetic character). You can use them interchangeably, even in the same command. We'll be covering just the basics here; for a more in-depth discussion, see the PostgreSQL documentation Backup and Restore (*http://bit.ly/12scOUX*).

As you wade through this section, you'll find that we often specify the port and host in our examples. This is because we often run them via scheduled jobs (pg_agent) on a different machine or we have several instances of PostgreSQL running on the same machine, each running on a different port. Sometimes specifying the -h (--host) option can cause problems if your service is set to listen only on local. You can safely leave out the host if you are running the examples directly on the server.

You may also want to create a ~/.pgpass (*http://bit.ly/12scPrZ*) file to store all passwords. pg_dump and pg_dumpall don't have password options. Alternatively, you can set a password in the PGPASSWORD environment variable.

Selective Backup Using pg_dump

For day-to-day backup, pg_dump is more expeditious than pg_dumpall because it can selectively back up tables, schemas, and databases. pg_dump backs up to plain SQL, but also compressed and TAR formats. Compressed and TAR backups can take advantage of the parallel restore feature introduced in version 8.4. Because we believe you'll be using pg_dump as part of your daily regimen, we have included a full dump of the help in "Database Backup Using pg_dump" on page 197 so you can see the myriad of switches in a single glance.

The next example shows a few common backup scenarios and corresponding pg_dump options. They should work for any version of PostgreSQL.

To create a compressed, single database backup:

```
pg_dump -h localhost -p 5432 -U someuser -F c -b -v -f mydb.backup mydb
```

To create a plain-text single database backup, including a CREATE DATABASE statement:

```
pg_dump -h localhost -p 5432 -U someuser -C -F p -b -v -f mydb.backup mydb
```

To create a compressed backup of tables whose names start with "pay" in any schema:

```
pg_dump -h localhost -p 5432 -U someuser -F c -b -v -t *.pay* -f pay.backup mydb
```

To create a compressed backup of all objects in the hr and payroll schemas:

```
pg_dump -h localhost -p 5432 -U someuser -F c -b -v -n hr -n payroll -f hr.back-
up mydb
```

To create a compressed backup of all objects in all schemas, excluding the public schema:

```
pg_dump -h localhost -p 5432 -U someuser -F c -b -v -N public -f all_sch_ex
cept_pub.backup mydb
```

To create a plain-text SQL backup of select tables, useful for porting structure and data to lower versions of PostgreSQL or non-PostgreSQL databases (plain text generates a SQL script that you can run on any system that speaks SQL):

```
pg_dump -h localhost -p 5432 -U someuser -F p --column-inserts -f se
lect_tables.backup mydb
```

 If your file paths contain spaces or other characters that could confuse the command-line shell, wrap the file path in double quotes: "/
path with spaces/mydb.backup". As a general rule, you can always use double quotes if you aren't sure.

The directory format option was introduced in version 9.1. This option backs up each table as a separate file in a folder and gets around potential limitations of file size in your filesystem. This option is the only pg_dump backup format option that generates multiple files, as shown in Example 2-8. It creates a new directory and populates it with a gzipped file for each table, together with a file that lists all the included structures. The command will exit with an error if the directory already exists.

Example 2-8. Directory format backup

```
pg_dump -h localhost -p 5432 -U someuser -F d -f /somepath/a_directory mydb
```

A parallel backup option was introduced in version 9.3 with the `--jobs` (`-j`) option. Setting this to `--jobs=3` runs three backups in parallel. The parallel backup option makes sense only with the directory format option, because each parallel write must write to a separate file. Example 2-9 demonstrates its use.

Example 2-9. Directory format parallel backup

```
pg_dump -h localhost -p 5432 -U someuser -j 3 -Fd -f /somepath/a_directory mydb
```

Systemwide Backup Using pg_dumpall

Use the `pg_dumpall` utility to back up all databases into a single plain-text file, along with server globals such as tablespace definitions and roles. See "Server Backup: pg_dumpall" on page 199 for a listing of available `pg_dumpall` command options.

It's a good idea to back up globals such as roles and tablespace definitions on a daily basis. Although you can use `pg_dumpall` to back up databases as well, we generally don't bother or do it—or use it at most once a month—because waiting for a huge plain-text backup to restore tries our patience.

To back up roles and tablespaces:

```
pg_dumpall -h localhost -U postgres --port=5432 -f myglobals.sql --globals-only
```

If you care only about backing up roles and not tables spaces, use the `--roles-only` option:

```
pg_dumpall -h localhost -U postgres --port=5432 -f myroles.sql --roles-only
```

Restore

There are two ways to restore data in PostgreSQL:

- Using `psql` to restore plain-text backups generated with `pg_dumpall` or `pg_dump`
- Using the `pg_restore` utility to restore compressed, TAR, and directory backups created with `pg_dump`

Using psql to restore plain-text SQL backups

A plain SQL backup is nothing more than a text file containing a chunky SQL script. It's the least convenient of backups to have, but it's the most versatile. With SQL backup, you must execute the entire script. You can't cherry-pick objects unless you're willing to manually edit the file. Run all of the following examples from the OS console or the interactive psql prompt.

To restore a full backup and ignore errors:

```
psql -U postgres -f myglobals.sql
```

To restore, stopping if any error is found:

```
psql -U postgres --set ON_ERROR_STOP=on -f myglobals.sql
```

To restore to a specific database:

```
psql -U postgres -d mydb -f select_objects.sql
```

Using pg_restore

If you backed up using `pg_dump` and chose a format such as `tar`, `custom`, or `directory`, you can use the versatile `pg_restore` utility to restore. `pg_restore` provides you with a dizzying array of options and far surpasses any restore utility found in other database products we've used. Some of its outstanding features are:

- You can perform parallel restores using the `-j` option to control the number of threads to use. This allows each thread to be restoring a separate table simultaneously, thereby significantly picking up the pace of what could otherwise be a lengthy process.

- You can use it to generate a table of contents file from your backup file to confirm what has been backed up. You can also edit this table of contents and use the revised file to control which objects to restore.

- Just as `pg_dump` allows you to do selective backups of objects to save time, `pg_restore` allows you to do selective restores, even from within a backup of a full database.

- `pg_restore` is backward-compatible, for the most part. You can back up a database on an older version of PostgreSQL and restore to a newer version.

See "Database Restore: pg_restore" on page 200 for a listing of `pg_restore` command options.

To perform a restore using `pg_restore`, first create the database using SQL:

```
CREATE DATABASE mydb;
```

Then restore:

```
pg_restore --dbname=mydb --jobs=4 --verbose mydb.backup
```

If the database is the same as the one you backed up, you can create and restore the database in one step:

```
pg_restore --dbname=postgres --create --jobs=4 --verbose mydb.backup
```

When you use the --create option, the database name is always the name of the one you backed up. You can't rename it. If you're also using the --dbname option, that database name must be different from the name of the database being restored. We usually just specify the postgres database.

If you are running version 9.2 or later, you can take advantage of the --section option to restore just the structure without the data. This is useful if you want to use an existing database as a template for a new one. To do so, first create the target database:

```
CREATE DATABASE mydb2;
```

Then use pg_restore:

```
pg_restore --dbname=mydb2 --section=pre-data --jobs=4 mydb.backup
```

Managing Disk Storage with Tablespaces

PostgreSQL uses tablespaces to ascribe logical names to physical locations on disk. Initializing a PostgreSQL cluster automatically begets two tablespaces: pg_default, which stores all user data, and pg_global, which stores all system data. These are located in the same folder as your default data cluster. You're free to create tablespaces at will and house them on any server disks. You can explicitly assign default tablespaces for new objects by database. You can also move existing database objects to new ones.

Creating Tablespaces

To create a new tablespace, specify a logical name and a physical folder and make sure that the postgres service account has full access to the physical folder. If you are on a Windows server, use the following command (note the use of Unix-style forward slashes):

```
CREATE TABLESPACE secondary LOCATION 'C:/pgdata94_secondary';
```

For Unix-based systems, you first must create the folder or define an fstab location, then use this command:

```
CREATE TABLESPACE secondary LOCATION '/usr/data/pgdata94_secondary';
```

Moving Objects Between Tablespaces

You can shuffle database objects among different tablespaces. To move all objects in the database to our secondary tablespace, we issue the following SQL command:

```
ALTER DATABASE mydb SET TABLESPACE secondary;
```

To move just one table:

```
ALTER TABLE mytable SET TABLESPACE secondary;
```

New in PostgreSQL 9.4 is the ability move a group of objects from one tablespace to another. If the person running the command is a superuser, all objects will be moved. If a nonsuperuser is running the statement, only the objects that she owns will be moved.

To move all objects from default tablespace to secondary:

```
ALTER TABLESPACE pg_default MOVE ALL TO secondary;
```

During the move, your database or table will be locked.

Verboten Practices

We have been witness to many ways that people have managed to break their PostgreSQL server, so we thought it best to end this chapter by itemizing the most common mistakes. For starters, if you don't know what you did wrong, the log file could provide clues. Look for the *pg_log* folder in your PostgreSQL data folder or the root of the PostgreSQL data folder for the log files. It's also possible that your server shut down before a log entry could be written, in which case the log won't help you. If your server fails to restart, try the following from the OS command line:

```
path/to/your/bin/pg_ctl -D your_postgresql_data_folder
```

Don't Delete PostgreSQL Core System Files and Binaries

Perhaps this is stating the obvious, but when people run out of disk space, the first thing they do is panic and start deleting files from the PostgreSQL data cluster folder because it's so darn big. Part of the reason this mistake happens so frequently is that some folders names such as *pg_log*, *pg_xlog*, and *pg_clog* sound like folders for logs that you expect to build up and be safe to delete. There are some files you can safely delete and some that will destroy your data if you do.

The *pg_log* folder, often found in your data folder, is a folder that builds up quickly, especially if you have logging enabled. You can always purge files from this folder without harm. In fact, many people schedule jobs to remove log files on a regular basis.

Files in the other folders, except for *pg_xlog*, should never be deleted, even if they have log-sounding names. Don't even think of touching pg_clog, the active commit log.

pg_xlog stores transaction logs. Some systems we've seen are configured to move processed transaction logs into a subfolder called *archive*. You'll often have an archive folder somewhere (not necessarily as a subfolder of *pg_xlog*) if you are running synchronous replication, doing continuous archiving, or just keeping logs around in case you need to revert to a different point in time. Deleting files in the root of *pg_xlog* will destroy data. Deleting files in the archived folder will just prevent you from performing point-in-time recovery, or if a slave server hasn't played back the logs, will prevent the slave from fetching them. If these scenarios don't apply to you, it's safe to delete or move files in the archive folder.

Be leery of overzealous antivirus programs, especially on Windows. We've seen cases in which antivirus software removed important binaries in the PostgreSQL *bin* folder. If PostgreSQL fails to start on a Windows system, the event viewer is the first place to look for clues as to why.

Don't Give Full OS Administrative Rights to the Postgres System Account (postgres)

Many people are under the misconception that the `postgres` account needs to have full administrative rights to the server. In fact, depending on your PostgreSQL version, if you give the `postgres` account full administrative rights to the server, your database server might not even start.

The `postgres` account should always be created as a regular system user in the OS with rights just to the data cluster and additional tablespace folders. Most installers will set up the correct permissions without you needing to worry. Don't try to do `postgres` any favors by giving it more rights than it needs. Granting unnecessary rights leaves your system vulnerable if you fall under an SQL injection attack.

There are cases where you'll need to give the `postgres` account write/delete/read rights to folders or executables outside of the data cluster. With scheduled jobs that execute batch files, this need often arises. We advise you to practice restraint and bestow only the minimum rights necessary to get the job done.

Don't Set shared_buffers Too High

Loading up your server with RAM doesn't mean you can set the `shared_buffers` as high as your physical RAM. Try it and your server may crash or refuse to start. If you are running PostgreSQL on 32-bit Windows, setting it higher than 512 MB often results in instability. With 64-bit Windows, you can push the envelop a bit higher and can even exceed 1 GB without any issues. On some Linux systems, `shared_buffers` can't be set higher than the compiled SHMMAX variable, which is usually quite low. PostgreSQL 9.3 changed how kernel memory is used, so that many of the issues people ran into with kernel limitations in prior versions are nonissues in version 9.3. You can find more details in Kernel Resources (*http://bit.ly/12scSDW*).

Don't Try to Start PostgreSQL on a Port Already in Use

If you try to start PostgreSQL on a port that's already in use, you'll see errors in your *pg_log* files of the form: `make sure PostgreSQL is not already running`. Here are the common reasons why this happens:

- You've already started the `postgres` service.
- You are trying to run PostgreSQL on a port already in use by another service.
- Your `postgres` service had a sudden shutdown and you have an orphan *post gresql.pid* file in the data folder. Just delete the file and try again.
- You have an orphaned PostgreSQL process. When all else fails, kill all running PostgreSQL processes and then try starting again.

psql

psql is the de rigueur command-line utility packaged with PostgreSQL. Aside from its most common use of running queries, you can use psql as an automated scripting tool; as a tool for importing or exporting data, restoring tables, and database administration; and even as a minimalistic reporting tool. As with other command-line tools, you have to be familiar with a myriad of options. If you have access only to a server's command line with no GUI, psql is pretty much your only choice for querying and managing PostgreSQL. If you fall into this category, we suggest that you print out the dump of psql help from the "psql Interactive Commands" on page 201 and frame it right above your workstation.

Environment Variables

As in the other command-line tools packaged with PostgreSQL, you can forgo explicitly specifying your host, port, and user by setting the PGHOST, PGPORT, and PGUSER environment variables as described in Environment Variables (*http://bit.ly/12scTrH*). You can also set your password in PGPASSWORD or use a password file as described in The Password File (*http://bit.ly/12scPrZ*). psql since version 9.2 accepts two new environment variables:

PSQL_HISTORY
: Sets the name of the psql history file that lists all commands executed in the recent past. The default is *~/.psql_history*.

PSQLRC
: Sets the location and name of the configuration file.

If you omit the parameters without having set the environment variables, psql will use the standard defaults. In the examples in this chapter, we'll assume you are using default values or have these variables set. If you're using pgAdmin as well, you can jump right to psql using the plug-in interface (see "Accessing psql from pgAdmin" on page 63). A console window will open from pgAdmin with psql and already connected to the database.

Interactive versus Noninteractive psql

You can run psql interactively by simply typing `psql` from your OS command line. Your prompt will switch to the psql prompt, signaling that you are now in the interactive psql console. Begin typing in commands. Don't forget to terminate SQL statements with a semicolon. If you press Enter without a semicolon, psql will assume that your statement continues.

Typing \? while in the psql console brings up a list of all available commands. For convenience, we reprinted this list in the appendix, highlighting new additions in the latest versions; see "psql Interactive Commands" on page 201. Typing \h followed by the command will bring up the relevant sections of the PostgreSQL documentation pertaining to the command.

To use psql noninteractively, execute `psql` from your OS prompt and pass it a script file. Within this script you can mix an unlimited number of SQL and psql commands. Alternatively you can pass in one or more SQL statements surrounded by double quotes. Noninteractive psql is well-suited for automated tasks. Batch your commands into a file, and then schedule it to run at regular intervals using a job-scheduling agent like pgAgent (covered in "Job Scheduling with pgAgent" on page 75), Linux/Unix `crontab`, or Windows scheduler. For situations in which many commands must be run in sequence or repeatedly, you're better off creating a script first and then running it using psql. Syntax-wise, noninteractively offers just a few options because the script file does most of the work. To execute a file, use the `-f` option:

```
psql -f some_script_file
```

To execute SQL statements on the fly, use the `-c` option. Join multiple statements with a semicolon:

```
psql -d postgresql_book -c "DROP TABLE IF EXISTS dross; CREATE SCHEMA staging;"
```

For the listing of all options, see "psql Noninteractive Commands" on page 203.

You can embed interactive commands inside script files. Suppose you created the script in Example 3-1 and named it *build_stage.psql*:

Example 3-1. Script with interactive psql commands

```
\a \t ❶
SELECT 'CREATE TABLE
 staging.count_to_50 (array_to_string(array_agg('x' || i::text ' varchar(10)));' As
create_sql ❷
FROM generate_series(1,9) As i;
```

```
\g create_script.sql ❸
\i create_script.sql ❹
```

❶   Because we want the output of our query to be saved as an executable statement, we need to remove the headers by using \t. We use \a to remove extra line breaks that psql normally puts in.

❷   Create a table with nine varchar columns.

❸   We use the \g option to force our query to output to a file.

❹   The \i followed by the script name executes the script. \i is the interactive equivalent of the noninteractive -f.

To run Example 3-1, we enter the following at an OS prompt:

```
psql -f build_stage.psql -d postgresql_book
```

Example 3-1 is an adaptation of an approach we describe in How to Create an N-column Table (*http://bit.ly/12scVQi*). As noted in the article, you can perform this without an intermediary file by using the DO command introduced in PostgreSQL 9.0.

psql Customizations

If you spend most of your day in psql, consider tailoring the psql environment to your needs. psql reads settings from a configuration file called *psqlrc*, if present. When psql launches, it searches for this file and runs all commands therein.

On Linux/Unix, the file is generally named *.psqlrc* and should be placed in your home directory. On Windows, the file is called *psqlrc.conf* and is located in the *%APPDATA %\postgresql* folder, which usually resolves to *C:\Users\username\AppData\Roaming \postgresql*. Don't worry if you can't find the file right after installation; you usually need to create it. Any settings in the file will override psql defaults. To find more details about the file, see the psql documentaion (*http://bit.ly/12scWne*).

The contents of a *psqlrc* file looks like Example 3-2. You can add any psql command to it for execution at start-up.

Example 3-2. Example psqlrc file

```
\pset null 'NULL'
\encoding latin1
\set PROMPT1 '%n@%M:%>%x %/# '
\pset pager always
\timing on
\set qstats92 'SELECT usename, datname, left(query,100) || ''...'' As query
FROM pg_stat_activity WHERE state != ''idle'' ;'
```

Each set command should be on a single line. For example, the qstats92 statements in Example 3-2 should be all on the same line. We had to break it into multiple lines to fit the printed page.

When you launch psql now, you'll see the results of executing the startup file:

```
Null display is "NULL".
Timing is on.
Pager is always used.
psql (9.3.2)
Type "help" for help.
postgres@localhost:5442 postgresql_book#
```

Some commands work only on Linux/Unix systems, not on Windows, and vice versa. In either OS, you should use the Linux/Unix slash (solidus) for path to distinguish it from the forward slash used for options. If you want to start psql bypassing *psqlrc*, use the -X option.

To remove a configuration variable or set it back to the default, issue the \unset command followed by the variable name, as in: \unset qstat92.

We'll cover popular psql configuration settings. Even if you don't add them to your *psqlrc* file, you can still set them during your session on an as-needed basis. You can find more examples at psqlrc File for DBAs (*http://bit.ly/12scZzv*) and Silencing Commands in .psqlrc (*http://bit.ly/1z39RH3*).

Custom Prompts

If you spend your waking hours playing with psql and you connect to multiple servers and databases, chances are you'll be switching among them using \connect. Customizing your prompt to show which server and database you're connected to will enhance your situational awareness and avoid disaster. In our example *psqlrc* file, we set our prompt as follows:

```
\set PROMPT1 '%n@%M:%>%x %/# '
```

This includes who we are logged in as (%n), the host server (%M), the port (%>), the transaction status (%x), and the database (%/). This is probably overkill, so economize as you see fit. The complete listing of prompt symbols is documented in the psql Reference Guide (*http://www.postgresql.org/docs/current/interactive/app-psql.html*).

When we connect with psql to our database, our prompt looks like:

```
postgres@localhost:5442 postgresql_book#
```

If we change to another database with \connect postgis_book, our prompt changes to:

```
postgres@localhost:5442 postgis_book#
```

Timing Executions

You may find it instructive to have psql output the time it took for each query to execute. Use the \timing command to toggle it on and off.

When that is enabled, each query you run will report the duration at the end. For example, with \timing on, executing SELECT COUNT(*) FROM pg_tables; outputs:

```
count
--------
73
(1 row)
Time: 18.650 ms
```

Autocommit Commands

By default, AUTOCOMMIT is on, meaning any SQL command you issue that changes data will immediately commit. Each command is its own transaction and is irreversible. If you are running a large batch of precarious updates, you may want a safety net. Start by turning off autocommit: \set AUTOCOMMIT off. Now, you have the option to roll back your statements:

```
UPDATE census.facts SET short_name = 'This is a mistake.';
```

To undo the update, run:

```
ROLLBACK;
```

To make the update permanent, run

```
COMMIT;
```

 Don't forget to commit your changes; otherwise, they'll automatically roll back if you exit psql.

Shortcuts

You can use the \set command to create useful typing shortcuts. Store universally applicable shortcuts in your *psqlrc* file. For example, if you use EXPLAIN ANALYZE VERBOSE once every 10 minutes and you're tired of typing it all out each time, set a variable:

```
\set eav 'EXPLAIN ANALYZE VERBOSE'
```

Now, whenever you want to enter EXPLAIN ANALYZE VERBOSE, simply type :eav (the colon resolves the variable):

```
:eav SELECT COUNT(*) FROM pg_tables;
```

You can even save commonly used queries as strings in your *psqlrc* file, as we did for `qstats91` and `qstats92`. We recommend using lowercase for your shortcuts to avoid conflict with psql environment variables, which are uppercase.

Retrieving Prior Commands

As with many command-line tools, you can use the up arrows in psql to recall commands. The `HISTSIZE` variable determines the number of previous commands that you can recall. For example, `\set HISTSIZE 10` lets you recover the past 10 commands and no more.

If you spent time building and testing a difficult query or performing a series of important updates, you may want to have the history of commands piped into separate files for perusal later:

```
\set HISTFILE ~/.psql_history- :HOST - :DBNAME
```

 Windows does not store command history unless you're running a Unix environment like Cygwin.

psql Gems

In this section, we cover helpful featurettes buried inside the psql documentation.

Executing Shell Commands

In psql, you can call out to the OS shell with the `\!` command. Let's say you're on Windows and need a directory listing. Instead of exiting psql, you can just directly type `\! dir` at the prompt.

Watching Statements

The `\watch` command is a new feature in psql since PostgreSQL 9.3. Use it to repeatedly run an SQL statement at fixed intervals so you can watch the output. For example, suppose you want to monitor the queries that have not completed. You can run a query such as the one shown in Example 3-3.

Example 3-3. Watching other connection traffic every 10 seconds

```
SELECT datname, waiting, query
FROM pg_stat_activity
WHERE state = 'active' AND pid != pg_backend_pid(); \watch 10
```

Although \watch is primarily designed for monitoring query output, you can also use it to run statements at fixed intervals. In Example 3-4, we log activity every five seconds.

Example 3-4. Log traffic every five seconds

```
SELECT * INTO log_activity FROM pg_stat_activity; ❶
         INSERT INTO log_activity SELECT * FROM pg_stat_activity; \watch 5 ❷
```

❶   Create table and perform first insert.

❷   Insert every five seconds.

If you want to kill a watch, use CTRL-X CTRL-C. Needless to say, watches are meant for interactive psql only.

You can find more examples of using watch at Michael Paquier: Watch in psql (*http:// bit.ly/1FUf6sW*).

Lists

Various psql commands can give you lists of objects along with details. Example 3-5 demonstrates how to list all tables in the pg_catalog schema that start with pg_t, along with their sizes.

Example 3-5. List tables with \dt+

```
\dt+ pg_catalog.pg_t*

 Schema     |       Name       | Type  |  Owner   | Size   | Description
------------+------------------+-------+----------+--------+-------------
 pg_catalog | pg_tablespace    | table | postgres | 40 kB  |
 pg_catalog | pg_trigger       | table | postgres | 16 kB  |
 pg_catalog | pg_ts_config     | table | postgres | 40 kB  |
 pg_catalog | pg_ts_config_map | table | postgres | 48 kB  |
 pg_catalog | pg_ts_dict       | table | postgres | 40 kB  |
 pg_catalog | pg_ts_parser     | table | postgres | 40 kB  |
 pg_catalog | pg_ts_template   | table | postgres | 40 kB  |
 pg_catalog | pg_type          | table | postgres | 112 kB |
```

If we wanted details about a particular object, such as the pg_ts_config table, we would use the \d+ command, as shown in Example 3-6.

Example 3-6. Describe object with \d+

```
\d+ pg_ts_dict

Table "pg_catalog.pg_ts_dict"
 Column        | Type | Modifiers | Storage | Stats target | Description
---------------+------+-----------+---------+--------------+-------------
 dictname      | name | not null  | plain   |              |
 dictnamespace | oid  | not null  | plain   |              |
 dictowner     | oid  | not null  | plain   |              |
```

```
dicttemplate   | oid  | not null | plain    |            |
dictinitoption | text |          | extended |            |
Indexes:
    "pg_ts_dict_dictname_index" UNIQUE, btree (dictname, dictnamespace)
    "pg_ts_dict_oid_index" UNIQUE, btree (oid)
Has OIDs: yes
```

Importing and Exporting Data

psql has a \copy command that lets you import data from and export data to a text file. Tab is the default delimiter, but you can specify others. New line breaks must separate the rows. For our first example, we downloaded data from US Census Fact Finder (*http://factfinder2.census.gov*) covering racial demographics of housing in Massachusetts. You can download the file we use in this example, *DEC_10_SF1_QTH1_with_ann.csv*, from the PostgreSQL Book Data (*http://bit.ly/1tZXANx*).

psql Import

Our usual practice in loading denormalized or unfamiliar data is to create a separate staging schema to accept the incoming data. We then write a series of explorative queries to get a good sense of what we have on our hands. Finally, we distribute the data into various normalized production tables and delete the staging schema.

Before bringing the data into PostgreSQL, you must first create a table to hold the incoming data. The data must match the file both in the number of columns and data types. This could be an annoying extra step for a well-formed file, but it does obviate the need for psql to guess at data types. psql processes the entire import as a single transaction; if it encounters any errors in the data, the entire import will fail. If you're unsure about the data contained in the file, we recommend setting up the table with the most accommodating data types and then recasting them later if necessary. For example, if you can't be sure that a column will just have numeric values, make it character varying to get the data in for inspection and then recast it later.

Launch psql from the command line and run the commands in Example 3-7 in the psql console.

Example 3-7. Importing data with psql

```
\connect postgresql_book
\cd /postgresql_book/ch03
\copy staging.factfinder_import FROM DEC_10_SF1_QTH1_with_ann.csv CSV
```

In Example 3-7, we launch interactive psql, connect to our database, use \cd to change the current directory to the folder containing our file, and import our data using the \copy command. Because the default delimiter is a tab, we augment our statement with CSV to tell psql that our data is comma-separated instead.

If your file has nonstandard delimiters such as pipes, indicate the delimiter:

```
\copy sometable FROM somefile.txt DELIMITER '|';
```

If you want to replace null values with something else, add a NULL AS:

```
\copy sometable FROM somefile.txt NULL As '';
```

 Don't confuse the \copy command in psql with the COPY statement provided by the SQL language. Because psql is a client utility, all paths are interpreted relative to the connected client. The SQL copy is server-based and runs under the context of the postgres service OS account. The input file must reside in a path accessible by the post-gres service account. We detail the differences between the two in Import Fixed-width Data in PostgreSQL with psql (*http://bit.ly/ 1vwDijW*).

psql Export

Exporting data is even easier than importing data. You can even export selected rows from a table. Use the psql \copy command to export. In Example 3-8, we demonstrate how to export the data we just loaded back to a tab-delimited file.

Example 3-8. Exporting data with psql

```
\connect postgresql_book
\copy (SELECT * FROM staging.factfinder_import  WHERE s01 ~ E'^[0-9]+' ) TO '/
test.tab'
WITH DELIMITER E'\t' CSV HEADER
```

The default behavior of exporting data without qualifications is to export to a tab-delimited file. However, the tab-delimited format does not export header columns. You can use the HEADER option only with the CSV format (see Example 3-9).

Example 3-9. Exporting data with psql

```
\connect postgresql_book
\copy staging.factfinder_import TO '/test.csv' WITH CSV HEADER QUOTE '"' FORCE
QUOTE *
```

FORCE QUOTE * ensures that all columns are double quoted. For clarity, we also indicate the quoting character even though psql assumes double quotes if quotes are omitted.

Copy from/to Program

Since PostgreSQL 9.3, psql can fetch data from the output of command-line programs —such as curl, ls, and wget—and dump the data into a table. Example 3-10 imports a directory listing from a dir command.

Example 3-10. Import dir listing with psql

```
\connect postgresql_book
CREATE TABLE dir_list (filename text);
\copy dir_list FROM PROGRAM 'dir C:\projects /b'
```

Hubert Lubaczewski has more examples of using \copy. Visit Depesz: Piping copy to from an external program (*http://bit.ly/1BlpKLt*).

Basic Reporting

Believe it or not, psql is capable of producing basic HTML reports. Try the following and check out the HTML output, shown in Figure 3-1.

```
psql -d postgresql_book -H -c
"SELECT category, count(*) As num_per_cat
FROM pg_settings
WHERE category LIKE '%Query%'
GROUP BY category
ORDER BY category;" -o test.html
```

category	num_per_cat
Query Tuning / Genetic Query Optimizer	7
Query Tuning / Other Planner Options	5
Query Tuning / Planner Cost Constants	6
Query Tuning / Planner Method Configuration	11
Statistics / Query and Index Statistics Collector	6

(5 rows)

Figure 3-1. Minimalist HTML report

Not too shabby. But the command outputs only an HTML table, not a fully qualified HTML document. To create a meatier report, compose a script, as shown in Example 3-11.

Example 3-11. Settings report content of settings_report.psql

```
\o settings_report.html ❶
\T 'cellspacing=0 cellpadding=0' ❷
\qecho '<html><head><style>H2{color:maroon}</style>' ❸
\qecho '<title>PostgreSQL Settings</title></head><body>'
\qecho '<table><tr valign=''top''><td><h2>Planner Settings</h2>'
\x on ❹
\t on ❺
\pset format html ❻
SELECT category, string_agg(name || '=' || setting, E'\n' ORDER BY name) As set-
tings ❼
```

```
FROM pg_settings
WHERE category LIKE '%Planner%'
GROUP BY category
ORDER BY category;
\H
\qecho '</td><td><h2>File Locations</h2>'
\x off ❽
\t on
\pset format html
SELECT name, setting FROM pg_settings WHERE category = 'File Locations' ORDER BY
name;
\qecho '<h2>Memory Settings</h2>'
SELECT name, setting, unit FROM pg_settings WHERE category ILIKE '%memory%' ORDER
BY name;
\qecho '</td></tr></table>'
\qecho '</body></html>'
\o
```

❶ Redirects query output to a file.

❷ HTML table settings for query output.

❸ Appends additional HTML.

❹ Expand mode. Repeats the column headers for each row and outputs each column of each row as a separate row.

❻ Forces the queries to output as HTML tables.

❼ string_agg( ), introduced in PostgreSQL 9.0 to concatenate all properties in the same category into a single column.

❽ Turns off expand mode. The second and third queries should output one row per table row.

❺ Toggles tuples mode. When on, column headers and row counts are omitted.

Example 3-11 demonstrates that by interspersing SQL and psql commands, you can create a fairly comprehensive tabular report replete with subreports. Run Example 3-11 by connecting interactively with psql and executing \i settings_report.psql, or run psql -f settings_report.psql from your OS command line. The output generated by *settings_report.html* is shown in Figure 3-2.

Planner Settings

category	Query Tuning / Other Planner Options
settings	constraint_exclusion=partition cursor_tuple_fraction=0.1 default_statistics_target=100 from_collapse_limit=8 join_collapse_limit=8
category	Query Tuning / Planner Cost Constants
settings	cpu_index_tuple_cost=0.005 cpu_operator_cost=0.0025 cpu_tuple_cost=0.01 effective_cache_size=16384 random_page_cost=4 seq_page_cost=1
category	Query Tuning / Planner Method Configuration
settings	enable_bitmapscan=on enable_hashagg=on enable_hashjoin=on enable_indexonlyscan=on enable_indexscan=on enable_material=on

File Locations

config_file	C:/projects/pg/pg92edb/data/postgresql.conf
data_directory	C:/projects/pg/pg92edb/data
external_pid_file	
hba_file	C:/projects/pg/pg92edb/data/pg_hba.conf
ident_file	C:/projects/pg/pg92edb/data/pg_ident.conf

Memory Settings

maintenance_work_mem	16384	kB
max_prepared_transactions	0	
max_stack_depth	2048	kB
shared_buffers	4096	8kB
temp_buffers	1024	8kB
track_activity_query_size	1024	
work_mem	1024	kB

Figure 3-2. Advanced HTML report

Scripts allow you to show the output from many queries in a single report and to schedule it as a job using pgAgent or `crontab`.

## CHAPTER 4

Using pgAdmin

pgAdmin III is the current rendition of the tried-and-true graphical administration tool for PostgreSQL. Although it has its shortcomings, we are always encouraged by not only how quickly bugs are fixed, but also how quickly new features are added. Since it's positioned as the official graphical-administration tool for PostgreSQL and packaged with many binary distributions of PostgreSQL, pgAdmin has the responsibility to always be kept in sync with the latest PostgreSQL releases. If a new release of PostgreSQL introduce new features, you can count on the latest pgAdmin to let you manage it. If you're new to PostgreSQL, you should definitely start with pgAdmin before exploring other tools.

Getting Started

Download pgAdmin from pgadmin.org. While on the site, you can opt to peruse one of the guides introducing pgAdmin. The tool is well-organized and, for the most part, guides itself quite well. For the adventurous, you can always try beta and alpha releases of pgAdmin. Your help in testing would be greatly appreciated by the PostgreSQL community.

Overview of Features

To whet your appetite, here's a list of our favorite goodies in pgAdmin. More are listed in pgAdmin Features (*http://pgadmin.org/features.php*):

Graphical explain for your queries
> This awesome feature offers pictorial insight into what the query planner is thinking. Gone are the days of trying to wade through the verbosity of text-based planner output.

SQL pane
> pgAdmin ultimately interacts with PostgreSQL via SQL, and it's not shy about letting you see the generated SQL. When you use the graphical interface to make changes to your database, pgAdmin automatically displays the underlying SQL in the SQL pane that will perform the tasks. For novices, studying the generated SQL is a superb learning opportunity. For pros, taking advantage of the generated SQL is a great time-saver.

GUI editor for configuration files such as postgresql.conf and pg_hba.conf
> You no longer need to dig around for the files and use another editor.

Data export and import
> pgAdmin can easily export query results as a CSV file or other delimited format and import such files as well. It can even export as HTML, providing you with a turn-key reporting engine, albeit a bit crude.

Backup and restore wizard
> Can't remember the myriad of commands and switches to perform a backup or restore using *pg_restore* and *pg_dump*? pgAdmin has a nice interface that lets you selectively back up and restore databases, schemas, single tables, and globals. You can view and copy the underlying *pg_dump* or *pg_restore* command that pgAdmin used in the Message tab.

Grant wizard
> This time-saver allows you to change privileges on many database objects in one fell swoop.

pgScript engine
> This is a quick-and-dirty way to run scripts that don't have to complete as a transaction. With this you can execute loops that commit on each iteration, unlike functions that require all steps to be completed before the work is committed. Unfortunately, you cannot use this engine outside of pgAdmin.

Plug-in architecture
> Access newly developed add-ons with a single mouse click. You can even install your own. We describe this feature in Change in pgAdmin Plug-Ins (*http://bit.ly/ 1A0UAVD*).

pgAgent
> We'll devote an entire section to this cross-platform job scheduling agent. pgAdmin provides a cool interface to it.

Connecting to a PostgreSQL Server

Connecting to a PostgreSQL server with pgAdmin is straightforward. The Properties and Advanced tabs are shown in Figure 4-1.

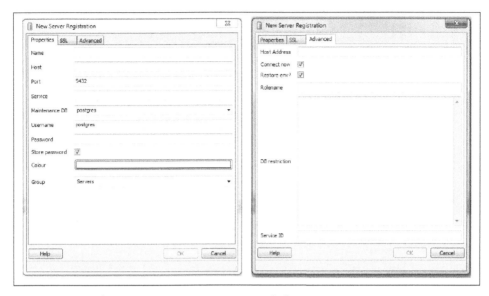

Figure 4-1. pgAdmin register server connection dialog

Navigating pgAdmin

The tree layout of pgAdmin is intuitive to follow but does start off showing you every esoteric object found in the database. You can pare down the tree display by going into the Options tab and deselecting objects that you would rather not have to stare at every time you use pgAdmin. To declutter the browse tree sections, go to Tools→Options→Browser. You will see the screen shown in Figure 4-2.

Figure 4-2. Hide or unhide database objects in pgAdmin browse tree

If you select Show System Objects in the tree view check box, you'll see the guts of your server: internal functions, system tables, hidden columns in tables, and so forth. You will also see the metadata stored in the PostgreSQL system catalogs: `information_sche ma` catalog and the `pg_catalog`. `information_schema` is an ANSI SQL standard catalog found in other databases such as MySQL and SQL Server. You may recognize some of the tables and columns from working with other database products.

 pgAdmin does not always keep the tree in sync with the current state of the database. For example, if one person alters a table, the tree viewed by a second person will not automatically refresh. There is a setting in recent versions that forces an automatic refresh if you select it, but you'll have to contend with a slight wait time as pgAdmin repaints.

pgAdmin Features

pgAdmin is chock full of goodies. We don't have the space to bring them all to light, so we'll just highlight the features that we use on a regular basis.

Accessing psql from pgAdmin

Although pgAdmin is a great tool, psql does a better job in a few cases. One of them is the execution of very large SQL files, such as those created by *pg_dump* and other dump tools. You can easily jump to psql from pgAdmin. Click the plug-in menu, as shown in Figure 4-3, and then click PSQL Console. This opens a psql session connected to the database you are currently connected to in pgAdmin. You can then use \cd and \i commands to change directory and run the SQL file.

Figure 4-3. psql plug-in

Because this feature relies on a database connection, you'll see it disabled until you're connected to a database.

Editing postgresql.conf and pg_hba.conf from pgAdmin

You can edit configuration files directly from pgAdmin provided that you installed the adminpack extension on your server. PostgreSQL one-click installers generally create the adminpack extension. You should see the menu enabled, as shown in Figure 4-4.

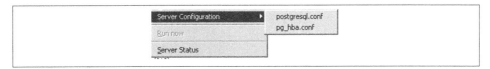

Figure 4-4. PgAdmin configuration file editor

If the menu is grayed out and you are connected to a PostgreSQL server, either you don't have the adminpack installed on that server or you are not logged in as a superuser. To install the adminpack on a server running PostgreSQL 9.0 or earlier, connect to the database named postgres as a superuser and run the file *share/contrib/adminpack.sql*. For PostgreSQL 9.1 or later, connect to the database named postgres and run the SQL statement CREATE EXTENSION adminpack; or use the graphical interface for installing extensions, as shown in Figure 4-5. Disconnect from the server and reconnect; you should see the menu enabled.

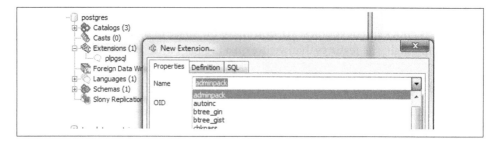

Figure 4-5. Installing extensions using pgAdmin

Creating Database Assets and Setting Privileges

pgAdmin lets you create all kinds of database assets and assign privileges.

Creating databases and other database assets

Creating a new database in pgAdmin is easy. Just right-click the database section of the tree and choose New Database, as shown in Figure 4-6. The definition tab provides a drop-down menu for you to select a template database, similar to what we did in "Template Databases" on page 27.

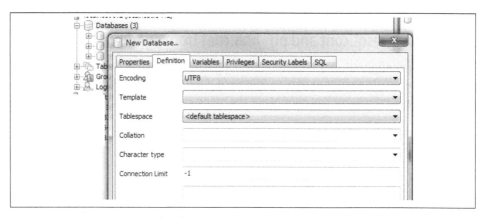

Figure 4-6. Creating a new database

Follow the same steps to create roles, schemas, and other objects. Each will have its own relevant set of tabs for you to specify additional attributes.

Privilege management

To manage privileges of database assets, nothing beats the pgAdmin Grant Wizard, which you access from the Tools→Grant Wizard menu of pgAdmin. As with many other features, this option is grayed out unless you are connected to a database. It's also sensitive to the location in the tree you are on. For example, to set privileges for items in the census schema, select the schema and then choose the Grant Wizard. The Grant Wizard screen is shown in Figure 4-7. You can then select all or some of the items and switch to the Privileges tab to set the roles and privileges you want to grant.

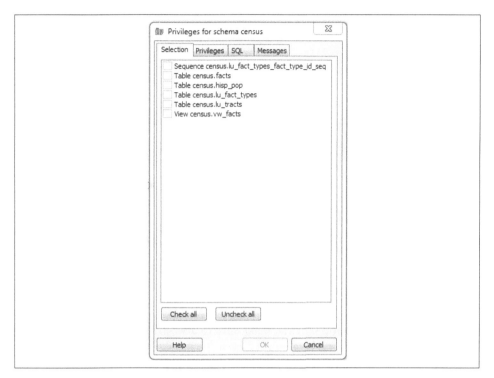

Figure 4-7. Grant Wizard

More often than setting privileges on existing objects, you may want to set default privileges for new objects in a schema or database. To do so, right-click the schema or database, select Properties, and then go to the Default Privileges tab, as shown in Figure 4-8. Default privileges are available only for PostgreSQL 9.0 and later.

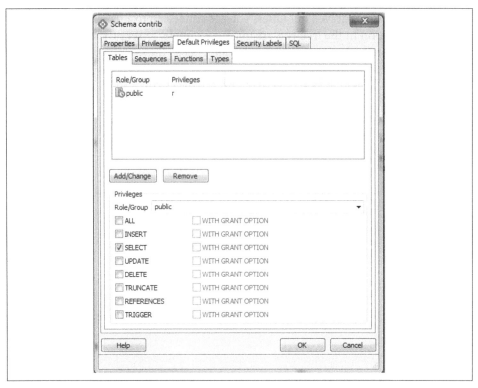

Figure 4-8. Granting default privileges

When setting privileges for a schema, make sure to also set the usage privilege on the schema to the groups you will be giving access to.

Import and Export

Like psql, pgAdmin allows you to import and export text files.

Importing files

The import feature is really a wrapper around the psql \copy command and requires the table that will receive the data to exist already. In order to import data, right-click the table you want to import data to, as shown in Figure 4-9.

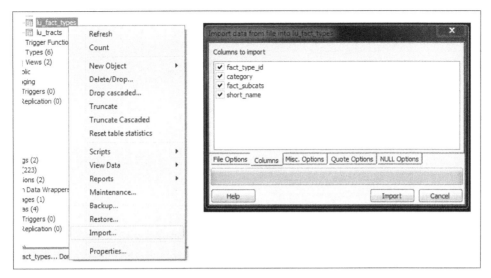

Figure 4-9. Import menu

Exporting queries as a structured file or report

In addition to importing data, you can export your queries to delimited, HTML, or XML formats. To export with delimiters, perform the following:

1. Open the query window ( ).
2. Write the query.
3. Run the query.
4. Choose File→Export.
5. Fill out the settings as shown in Figure 4-10.

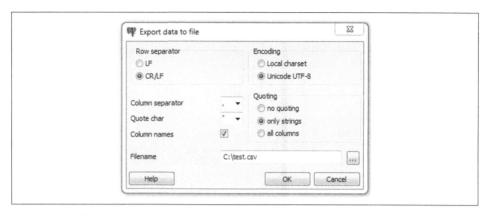

Figure 4-10. Export menu

Exporting as HTML or XML is much the same, except you use the File→Quick Report option (see Figure 4-11).

Figure 4-11. Export report options

Backup and Restore

pgAdmin offers a graphical interface to `pg_dump` and `pg_restore`, covered in "Backup and Restore" on page 38. In this section, we'll repeat some of the same examples using pgAdmin instead of the command line.

If several versions of PostgreSQL or pgAdmin are installed on your computer, it's a good idea to make sure that the pgAdmin version is using the versions of the utilities that you expect. Check what the *bin* setting in pgAdmin is pointing to in order to ensure it's the latest available, as shown in Figure 4-12.

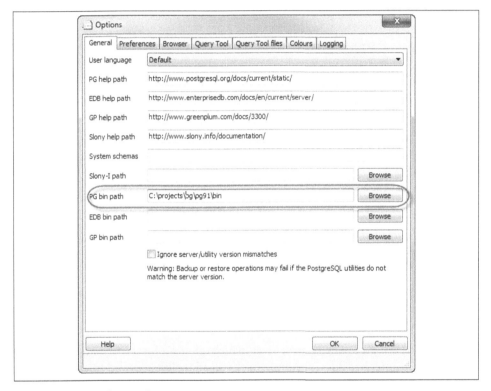

Figure 4-12. pgAdmin File→Options

 If your server is remote or your databases are huge, we recommend using the command-line tools for backup and restore instead of pgAdmin to avoid adding another layer of complexity to what could already be a pretty lengthy process. Also keep in mind that if you do a compressed/TAR/directory backup with a newer version of `pg_dump`, you need to use the same or later version of `pg_restore`.

Backing Up an Entire Database

In "Selective Backup Using pg_dump" on page 38, we demonstrated how to back up a database. To repeat the same steps using the pgAdmin interface, right-click the database you want to back up and choose Custom for format, as shown in Figure 4-13.

Figure 4-13. Backup database

Backing up system-wide objects

pgAdmin provides a graphical interface to `pg_dumpall` for backing up system objects. To use the interface, first connect to the server you want to back up. Then, from the top menu, choose Tools→Backup Globals.

pgAdmin doesn't give you control over which global objects to back up, as the command-line interface does. pgAdmin backs up all tablespaces and roles.

If you ever want to back up the entire server, perform a `pg_dumpall` by going to the top menu and choosing Tools→Backup Server.

Selective backup of database assets

pgAdmin provides a graphical interface to `pg_dump` for selective backup. Right-click the asset you want to back up and select Backup (see Figure 4-14). You can back up an entire database, a particular schema, a table, or anything else.

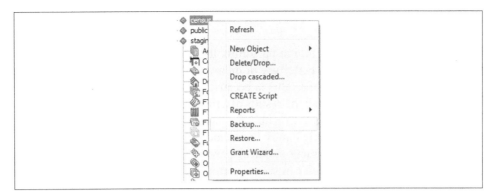

Figure 4-14. pgAdmin schema backup

To back up the selected asset, you can forgo the other tabs (seeFigure 4-13). However, you can selectively drill down to more items by clicking the Objects tab, as shown in Figure 4-15.

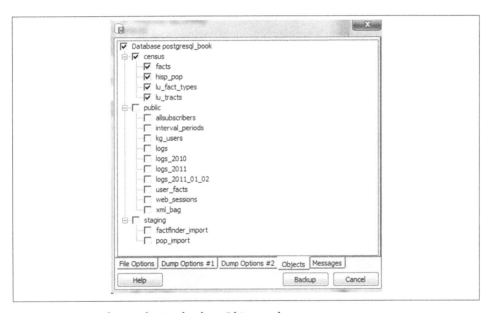

Figure 4-15. pgAdmin selective backup Objects tab

Behind the scenes, pgAdmin simply runs `pg_dump` to perform back-ups. If you ever want to know the actual commands pgAdmin is using, say for scripting, look at the Messages tab after you click the Backup button. You'll see the exact call with arguments to `pg_dump`.

pgScript

pgScript is a built-in scripting tool in pgAdmin. It's most useful for running repetitive SQL tasks. pgScript can make better use of memory, and thus be more efficient, than equivalent PostgreSQL functions. This is because stored functions maintain all their work in memory and commit all the results of a function in a single batch. In contrast, pgScript commits each SQL insert or update statement as it runs through the script. This makes pgScript particularly handy for memory-hungry processes that you don't need completed as a single transaction. Once a particular transaction commits, memory is available for the next one. You can see an example of where we use it for batch geocoding at a Using pgScript for Geocoding (*http://bit.ly/126mRPB*).

The pgScript language is lazily typed and supports conditionals, loops, data generators, basic print statements, and record variables. The general syntax is similar to that of Transact SQL, the stored procedure language of Microsoft SQL Server. Variables, prepended with @, can hold scalars or arrays, including the results of SQL commands. Commands such as DECLARE and SET, and control constructs such as IF-ELSE and WHILE loops, are part of the pgScript language.

Launch pgScript by opening a regular SQL query window. After typing in your script, execute it by clicking the pgScript icon (📖).

We'll now show you some examples of pgScripts. Example 4-1 demonstrates how to use pgScript record variables and loops to build a cross-tab table, using the lu_fact_types table we create in Example 7-18. The pgScript creates an empty table called census.hisp_pop with numeric columns: hispanic_or_latino, white_alone, black_or_african_american_alone, and so on.

Example 4-1. Create table using record variables in pgScript

```
DECLARE @I, @labels, @tdef;
SET @I = 0;
```

Labels will hold records.
```
SET @labels =
    SELECT
        quote_ident(
            replace(
                replace(lower(COALESCE(fact_subcats[4], fact_subcats[3])), ' ',
'_'),':','')
            )
        ) As col_name,
    fact_type_id
    FROM census.lu_fact_types
    WHERE category = 'Population' AND fact_subcats[3] ILIKE 'Hispanic or Latino%'
    ORDER BY short_name;

SET @tdef = 'census.hisp_pop(tract_id varchar(11) PRIMARY KEY ';
```

Loop through records using LINES function.
```
WHILE @I < LINES(@labels)
BEGIN
    SET @tdef = @tdef + ', ' + @labels[@I][0] + ' numeric(12,3) ';
    SET @I = @I + 1;
END

SET @tdef = @tdef + ')';
```

Print out table def.
```
PRINT @tdef;
```

create the table.
```
CREATE TABLE @tdef;
```

Although pgScript does not have an execute command that allows you to run dynamically generated SQL, we accomplished the same in Example 4-1 by assigning a SQL string to a variable. Example 4-2 pushes the envelope a bit further by populating the census.hisp_pop table we just created.

Example 4-2. Populating tables with pgScript loop
```
DECLARE @I, @labels, @tload, @tcols, @fact_types;
SET @I = 0;
SET @labels =
    SELECT
        quote_ident(
            replace(
                replace(
                    lower(COALESCE(fact_subcats[4], fact_subcats[3]))), ' ',
'_'),':',''
                )
        ) As col_name,
    fact_type_id
    FROM census.lu_fact_types
    WHERE category = 'Population' AND fact_subcats[3] ILIKE 'Hispanic or Latino%'
    ORDER BY short_name;

SET @tload = 'tract_id';
SET @tcols = 'tract_id';
SET @fact_types = '-1';

WHILE @I < LINES(@labels)
BEGIN
    SET @tcols = @tcols + ', ' + @labels[@I][0] ;
    SET @tload = @tload +
        ', MAX(CASE WHEN fact_type_id = ' +
        CAST(@labels[@I][1] AS STRING) +
        ' THEN val ELSE NULL END)';
    SET @fact_types = @fact_types + ', ' + CAST(@labels[@I][1] As STRING);
    SET @I = @I + 1;
END
```

```
INSERT INTO census.hisp_pop(@tcols)
SELECT @tload FROM census.facts
WHERE fact_type_id IN(@fact_types) AND yr=2010
GROUP BY tract_id;
```

The lesson to take away from Example 4-2 is that you can dynamically append SQL fragments into a variable.

Graphical Explain

One of the great gems in pgAdmin is its at-a-glance graphical explain of the query plan. You can access the graphical explain plan by opening up an SQL query window, writing a query, and clicking the explain icon ( ).

If we run the query:

```
SELECT left(tract_id, 5) As county_code, SUM(hispanic_or_latino) As tot,
    SUM(white_alone) As tot_white,
    SUM(COALESCE(hispanic_or_latino,0) - COALESCE(white_alone,0)) AS non_white
FROM census.hisp_pop
GROUP BY county_code
ORDER BY county_code;
```

we will get the graphical explain shown in Figure 4-16. Here's a quick tip for reading the graphical explain: trim the fat! The fatter the arrow, the longer a step takes to complete.

Figure 4-16. Graphical explain example

Graphical explain is disabled if Query→Explain→Buffers is enabled. So make sure to uncheck buffers before trying a graphical explain. In addition to the graphical explain, the Data Output tab shows the textual explain plan, which for this example looks like:

```
GroupAggregate  (cost=111.29..151.93 rows=1478 width=20)
      Output:   ("left"((tract_id)::text,   5)),   sum(hispanic_or_latino),
sum(white_alone), ...
  -> Sort  (cost=111.29..114.98 rows=1478 width=20)
     Output: tract_id, hispanic_or_latino, white_alone,
     ("left"((tract_id)::text, 5)) Sort Key: ("left"((tract_id)::text, 5)) ->
Seq Scan on census.hisp_pop  (cost=0.00..33.48 rows=1478 width=20)    Output:
tract_id, hispanic_or_latino    , white_alone, "left"((tract_id)::text, 5)
```

Job Scheduling with pgAgent

pgAgent is a handy utility for scheduling PostgreSQL jobs. But it can also execute batch scripts in the OS, replacing `crontab` on Linux/Unix and the task scheduler on Windows. pgAgent goes even further: you can schedule jobs to run on any other host regardless of OS. All you have to do is install the pgAgent service on the host and point it to use a specific PostgreSQL database with pgAgent tables and functions installed. The PostgreSQL server itself is not required, but the client connection libraries are. Because pgAgent is built atop PostgreSQL, you are blessed with the added advantage of having access to all the tables controlling the agent. If you ever need to replicate a complicated job multiple times, you can go straight into the database tables directly and insert the records for new jobs, skipping the pgAdmin interface.

We'll get you started with pgAgent in this section. Visit Setting Up pgAgent and Doing Scheduled Backups (*http://bit.ly/1AvqVVs*) to see more working examples and details of how to set it up.

Installing pgAgent

You can download pgAgent from pgAgent Download (*http://www.pgadmin.org/down load/pgagent.php*). It is also available via the EDB Application Stackbuilder commonly used to install PostgreSQL on Windows. The packaged SQL installation script creates a new schema named pgAgent in the `postgres` database. When you connect to your server via pgAdmin, you will see a new section called Jobs, as shown in Figure 4-17.

Figure 4-17. pgAdmin with pgAgent installed

If you want pgAgent to run batch jobs on additional servers, follow the same steps, except you don't have to reinstall the SQL script packaged with pgAgent. Pay particular attention to the OS permission settings of the pgAgent service/daemon account. Make sure each agent has sufficient privileges to execute the batch jobs that you will be scheduling.

> Batch jobs often fail in pgAgent even when they might run fine from the command line. This is often due to permission issues. pgAgent always runs under the same account as the pgAgent service/daemon. If this account doesn't have sufficient privileges or the necessary network path mappings, jobs fail.

Scheduling Jobs

Each scheduled job has two parts: the execution steps and the schedule. When creating a new job, start by adding one or more job steps. Figure 4-18 shows what the step add/edit screen looks like.

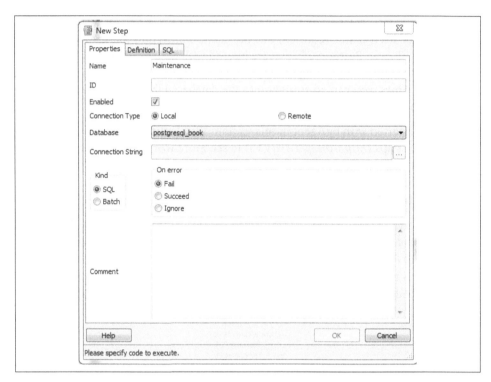

Figure 4-18. pgAdmin step edit screen

For each step, you can enter an SQL statement to run, point to a shell script on the OS, or even cut and paste in a full shell script as we commonly do.

If you choose SQL, the connection type option becomes enabled and defaults to local. With a local connection, the job step runs on the same server as the pgAgent and uses the same authentication username and password. You need to additionally specify the database that pgAgent should connect to to run the jobs. The screen offers you a drop-down list of databases to choose from. If you choose a remote connection type, the text box for entering a connection string becomes enabled. Type in the full connection string, including credentials, and database. When you connect to a remote PostgreSQL server with an earlier version of PostgreSQL, make sure that you don't use SQL constructs that are not supported.

If you choose to run batch jobs, the syntax must be specific to the OS running the job. For example, if your pgAgent is running on Windows, your batch jobs should have valid DOS commands. If you are on Linux, your batch jobs should have valid shell or Bash commands.

Steps run in alphabetical order, and you can decide what kinds of actions you want to take upon success or failure of each. You have the option of disabling steps that should remain dormant but that you don't want to delete because you might reactivate them later.

Once you have the steps ready, go ahead and set up a schedule to run them. You can set up intricate schedules with the scheduling screen. You can even set up multiple schedules.

If you installed pgAgent on multiple servers and have them all pointing to the same pgAgent database, all these agents by default will execute all jobs.

If you want to run the job on just one specific machine, fill in the host agent field when creating the job. Agents running on other servers will skip the job if it doesn't match their host name.

 pgAgent consists of two parts: the data defining the jobs and the logging of the job. Log information resides in the pgAgent schema, usually in postgres database; the job agents query the jobs for the next job to run and then insert relevant logging information in the database. Generally, both the PostgreSQL server holding the data and the job agent executing the jobs reside on the same server, but they are not required to. Additionally, a single PostgreSQL server can service many job agents residing on different servers.

A fully formed job is shown in Figure 4-19.

Figure 4-19. pgAgent jobs in pgAdmin

Helpful pgAgent Queries

With your finely honed SQL skills, you can easily replicate jobs, delete jobs, and edit jobs directly by messing with pgAgent metatables. Just be careful! For example, to get a glimpse inside the tables controlling all of your agents and jobs, connect to the post gres database and execute the query in Example 4-3.

Example 4-3. Description of pgAgent tables

```
SELECT c.relname As table_name, d.description
FROM
    pg_class As c INNER JOIN
    pg_namespace n ON n.oid = c.relnamespace INNER JOIN
    pg_description As d ON d.objoid = c.oid AND d.objsubid = 0
WHERE n.nspname = 'pgagent'
ORDER BY c.relname;

table_name     |      description
---------------+-------------------------
pga_job        | Job main entry
pga_jobagent   | Active job agents
pga_jobclass   | Job classification
pga_joblog     | Job run logs.
pga_jobstep    | Job step to be executed
pga_jobsteplog | Job step run logs.
pga_schedule   | Job schedule exceptions
```

Although pgAdmin already provides an intuitive interface to pgAgent scheduling and logging, you may find the need to generate your own jobs reports. This is especially true if you have many jobs or you want to compile stats from your job results. Example 4-4 demonstrates the one query we use often.

Example 4-4. List log step results from today

```
SELECT j.jobname, s.jstname, l.jslstart,l.jslduration, l.jsloutput
FROM
    pgagent.pga_jobsteplog As l INNER JOIN
    pgagent.pga_jobstep As s ON s.jstid = l.jsljstid INNER JOIN
    pgagent.pga_job As j ON j.jobid = s.jstjobid
WHERE jslstart > CURRENT_DATE
ORDER BY j.jobname, s.jstname, l.jslstart DESC;
```

We find this query essential for monitoring batch jobs because sometimes a job will report success even though it failed. pgAgent can't always discern the success or failure of a shell script on the OS. The jsloutput field in the logs provides the shell output, which usually details what went wrong.

In some versions of pgAgent running on Windows, shell scripts often default to failed when they succeeded. If this happens, you should set the step status to ignore. This is a known bug that we hope will be fixed in a future release.

## CHAPTER 5

Data Types

PostgreSQL supports the workhorse data types of any database: numerics, strings, dates and times, and Booleans. But PostgreSQL sprints ahead by adding support for arrays, datetimes with time zones, time intervals, ranges, JSON, XML, and many more types. If that's not enough, you can invent custom types. In this chapter, we don't intend to cover every data type. For that, there's always the manual. We'll focus on showing you some of the data types that are unique to PostgreSQL and nuances of common data types.

No data type would be useful without the functions and operators used to navigate and work with it. PostgreSQL has an army of functions and operators that cater to each data type, and many extensions add their own. We'll cover some of the more popular ones in this chapter.

 When we use the term *function*, we're talking about something that's of the form f(x). When we use the term *operator*, we're talking about something that's symbolic and or unary (having only one argument) or binary (having two arguments) such as +, -, *, /. The simplest operator is a symbol alias for a function that takes one or more arguments. When using operators, keep in mind that the same symbol can take on a different meaning when applied to different data types. For example, the plus sign means adding for numerics but unioning for ranges.

Numerics

You will find your everyday integers, decimals, and floating point numbers in PostgreSQL. Of the numeric types, we want to discuss serial data types and a nifty function to quickly generate arithmetic series of integers.

Serials

serial and its bigger sibling, bigserial, are autoincrementing integers often used as primary keys of tables in which a natural key is not apparent. This data type goes by different names in different database products, with autonumber being the most common alternative moniker. When you create a table and specify a column as serial, PostgreSQL first creates an integer column and then creates a sequence object named *table_name_column_name_*seq located in the same schema as the table. It then sets the default of the new integer column to read its value from the sequence. If you delete the column, PostgreSQL also deletes the companion sequence object.

In PostgreSQL, the sequence type is a database asset in its own right. You can inspect and edit the sequence using pgAdmin or SQL with the ALTER SEQUENCE command. You can set its current value, boundary values (the upper and lower bounds), and even how many numbers to increment each time. Though it is rare to increment downward, you can set the increment value to a negative number to achieve that. Because sequences are independent database assets, you can create them separately from a table using the CREATE SEQUENCE (*http://bit.ly/1w5Hvgn*) command, and you can use the same sequence object for more than one table. The cross-table sharing of the same sequence comes in handy when you're assigning a "universal" key in your database.

In order to use the same sequence for multiple tables, define the column as integer or bigint, then set the default value of the column to the next sequence number using nextval(*sequence_name*) (*http://bit.ly/1yx5TXd*) function.

 If you rename a table that has a serial based on a sequence, PostgreSQL will not automatically rename the sequence object. If maintaining naming symmetry is important, you should rename the sequence object.

Generate Series Function

PostgreSQL has a nifty function called generate_series (*http://bit.ly/1yUbohy*) that we have yet to find in other database products. What makes generate_series so convenient is that it allows you to effectively mimic a for loop in SQL. Suppose we want a list of the last day of each month for a particular date range. Doing this without generate_series would involve either a procedural loop or creating a massive Cartesian product of dates and then filtering them. With generate_series, your code is a one-liner, as shown later in Example 5-11.

Example 5-1 uses integers with an optional step parameter.

Example 5-1. generate_series() with stepping of 13

```
SELECT x FROM generate_series(1,51,13) As x;
```

```
x
----
1
14
27
40
```

As shown in Example 5-1, you can pass in an optional step argument that defines how many steps to skip for each successive element. Leaving out the step will default it to 1. Also note that the end value will never exceed our prescribed range, so although our range ends at 51, our last number is 40 because adding another 13 to our 40 exceeds the upper bound.

Characters and Strings

There are three primitive character types in PostgreSQL: character (aka char), character varying (aka varchar), and text. varchar and text are useful for fields that can have very different sizes in different rows. The actual storage assigned to the field for each row reflects just what the field needs for that row. The two fields are stored the same way and have equivalent performance.

Use char only where the values stored are a fixed length, such as zip codes, phone numbers, and Social Security numbers. char (*http://bit.ly/1w5HDwq*) is right-padded with spaces out to the specified size for both storage and display; this is more costly in terms of storage. You'll find no other performance difference between varchar and char in PostgreSQL.

The difference between varchar with no size modifier and text is subtle. You can sort on a text column regardless of how many characters it contains. Database drivers such as ODBC might treat the two types differently. Both varchar and text have a cap of around 1 GB. Behind the scenes, any data larger than what can fit in a record page gets pushed to TOAST (*http://bit.ly/12sdEAM*).

 In versions prior to 9.2, if you try to expand the size of an existing varchar field for a table with many rows, PostgreSQL will recreate the table. The process could take a while and locks the table. As a result, people often used text with a length constraint instead.

People have different opinions as to whether you should abandon varchar and always use text. Rather than waste space arguing about it here, read the debate at In Defense of VarcharX (*http://bit.ly/1vwE68w*).

Often, for cross-system compatibility, you want to remove case sensitivity from your character types. To do this, you need to override comparison operators that take case into consideration. Overriding operators is easier for varchar than it is for text. We demonstrate an example in Using MS Access with PostgreSQL (*http://bit.ly/1w5HIQF*), where we show how to make varchar behave without case sensitivity and still be able to use an index.

String Functions

Common string manipulations are padding (lpad, rpad), trimming whitespace (rtrim, ltrim, trim, btrim), extracting substrings (substring), and concatenating (||). Example 5-2 demonstrates padding, and Example 5-3 demonstrates trimming.

Example 5-2. Using lpad and rpad

```
SELECT lpad('ab', 4, '0') As ab_lpad, rpad('ab', 4, '0') As ab_rpad, lpad('abcde',
4, '0') As ab_lpad_trunc; ❶

ab_lpad | ab_rpad | ab_lpad_trunc
--------+---------+--------------
00ab    | ab00    | abcd
```

❶   lpad truncates instead of padding if string is too long.

By default, trim functions remove spaces, but you can pass in an optional argument indicating other characters to trim.

Example 5-3. Trimming spaces and characters

```
SELECT
a As a_before, trim(a) As a_trim, rtrim(a) As a_rt,
i As i_before, ltrim(i, '0') As i_lt_0,
rtrim(i, '0') As i_rt_0, trim(i, '0') As i_t_0
FROM ( SELECT repeat(' ', 4) || i || repeat(' ', 4) As a, '0' || i As i FROM gener
ate_series(0, 200, 50) As i
) As x;
```

a_before	a_trim	a_rt	i_before	i_lt_0	i_rt_0	i_t_0
0	0	0	00			
50	50	50	050	50	05	5
100	100	100	0100	100	01	1
150	150	150	0150	150	015	15
200	200	200	0200	200	02	2

Version 9.0 introduced a helpful string aggregate function called string_agg, which we demonstrate in Example 3-11 and Example 5-21. string_agg is equivalent in concept to the group_concat function in MySQL.

Splitting Strings into Arrays, Tables, or Substrings

There are a couple of useful functions in PostgreSQL for tearing strings apart.

The `split_part` function is useful for getting an element of a delimited string, as shown in Example 5-4.

Example 5-4. Getting the nth element of a delimited string

```
SELECT split_part('abc.123.z45', '.', 2) As x;

x
--------
123
```

The `string_to_array` is useful for creating an array of elements from a delimited string. By combining `string_to_array` with the `unnest` function, you can expand the returned array into a set of rows, as shown in Example 5-5.

Example 5-5. Converting delimited string to array to rows

```
SELECT unnest(string_to_array('abc.123.z45', '.')) As x;

x
--------
abc
123
z45
```

Regular Expressions and Pattern Matching

PostgreSQL's regular expression support is downright fantastic. You can return matches as tables or arrays and do fairly sophisticated replaces and updates. Back-referencing and other fairly advanced search patterns are also supported. In this section, we'll provide a small sampling of these. For more information, see Pattern Matching (*http://bit.ly/1s2nQXB*) and String Functions (*http://bit.ly/1Iaix2K*).

Example 5-6 shows you how to format phone numbers stored simply as contiguous digits:

Example 5-6. Reformat a phone number using back-referencing

```
SELECT regexp_replace(
'6197306254',
'([0-9]{3})([0-9]{3})([0-9]{4})',
 E'\(\\1\) \\2-\\3'
 ) As x;

x
--------------
(619) 730-6254
```

The \\1, \\2, etc. refer to the elements in our pattern expression. We use the reverse solidus (\) to escape the parentheses. The E ' construct is PostgreSQL syntax for denoting that a string is an expression so that special characters like \ are treated literally.

Suppose some field contains text with embedded phone numbers; Example 5-7 shows how to extract the phone numbers and turn them into rows all in one step.

Example 5-7. Return phone numbers in piece of text as separate rows

```
SELECT unnest(regexp_matches( 'Cell (619)852-5083. Casa 619-730-6254. Bésame mucho.
        E'[(]{0,1}[0-9]{3}[)-.]{0,1}[0-9]{3}[-.]{0,1}[0-9]{4}', 'g')
) As x;

x
-------------
(619)852-5083
619-730-6254
```

The matching rules for Example 5-7 are:

- `[(]{0,1}`: starts with 0 or 1 (.
- `[0-9]{3}`: followed by 3 digits.
- `[)-.]{0,1}`: followed by 0 or 1 of),-, or.
- `[0-9]{4}`: followed by 4 digits.
- `regexp_matches` returns a string array consisting of matches of a regular expression. If you don't pass in the g parameter, your array will return just the first match of the regular expression. The g stands for global and returns all matches of a regular expression as separate elements.
- `unnest` explodes an array into a row set.

 There are many ways to compose the same regular expression. For instance, \\d is shorthand for [0-9]. But given the few characters you'd save, we prefer the more descriptive longhand.

In addition to the wealth of regular-expression functions, you can use regular expressions with the SIMILAR TO (~) operators. This sequence returns all description fields with embedded phone numbers:

```
SELECT description
FROM mytable
WHERE description ~ E'[(]{0,1}[0-9]{3}[)-.]{0,1}[0-9]{3}[-.]{0,1}[0-9]{4}';
```

Temporals

PostgreSQL support for temporal data is second to none. In addition to the usual dates and times types, PostgreSQL has support for time zones, enabling the automatic handling of daylight saving time (DST) conversions by region. Specialized data types such as `interval` offer datetime arithmetic. PostgreSQL also understands infinity and negative infinity, relieving us from having to create conventions that we'll surely forget. Finally, version 9.2 unveiled range types (*http://bit.ly/126nQPP*) that provide support for temporal ranges with a whole slew of companion operators, functions, and indexes. We cover range types in "Range Types" on page 95.

At last count, PostgreSQL has nine temporal data types. Understanding their distinctions is important to ensuring that you choose the right data type for the job. All of the types except `range` abide by ANSI SQL standards. Other leading database products support some, but not all, of these data types. Oracle has the most varieties of temporal types; SQL Server ranks second; and MySQL comes in last, with no support for time zones in any version.

Because PostgreSQL temporal types could be unique, we'll describe each in finer detail:

date
> Just stores the month, day, and year, with no time zone awareness and no concept of hours, minutes, or seconds.

time *(aka* time without time zone*)*
> Records hours, minutes, and seconds with no awareness of time zone or calendar dates.

timestamp *(aka* timestamp without time zone*)*
> Records both calendar dates and time (hours, minutes, seconds) but does not care about the time zone. As such, the displayed value of this data won't change when you change your server's time zone.

timestamptz *(aka* timestamp with time zone*)*
> A time zone–aware date and time data type. Internally, `timestamptz` is stored in Coordinated Universal Time (UTC), but its display defaults to the time zone of the server (or database/user/session if you observe differing time zones at those levels). If you input a timestamp with no time zone and cast it to one with the time zone, PostgreSQL assumes the server's time zone. If you change your server's time zone, you'll see all the displayed times change.

timetz *(aka* time with time zone*)*
> The lesser-used sister of `timestamptz`. It is time zone–aware but does not store the date. It always assumes DST of the current time. For some programming languages with no concept of time without date, it might map `timetz` to a timestamp with a time zone at the beginning of time (for example, Unix Epoch 1970, thus resulting in DST of year 1970 being used).

interval
> A duration of time in hours, days, months, minutes, and others. It comes in handy for doing date-time arithmetic. For example, if the world is supposed to end in

exactly 666 days from now, all you have to do is add an interval of 666 days to the current time to get the exact moment when it will happen (and plan accordingly).

tsrange

New in version 9.2; allows you to define opened and closed ranges of timestamp with no timezone. The type consists of two timestamps and opened/closed range qualifiers. For example, '[2012-01-01 14:00, 2012-01-01 15:00)'::tsrange defines a period starting at 14:00 but ending before 15:00. Refer to Range Types (*http://bit.ly/1vXxIXI*) for details.

tstzrange

New in version 9.2; allows you to define opened and closed ranges of timestamp with timezone.

daterange

New in version 9.2; allows you to define opened and closed ranges of dates.

Time Zones: What They Are and Are Not

A common misconception with PostgreSQL time zone–aware data types is that PostgreSQL records an extra time marker with the datetime value itself. This is incorrect. If you save 2012-2-14 18:08:00-8 (-8 being the Pacific offset from UTC), PostgreSQL internally works like this:

1. Get the UTC time for 2012-02-14 18:08:00-8. This is 2012-02-15 04:08:00-0.
2. Store the value 2012-02-15 04:08:00.

When you call the data back for display, PostgreSQL internally works like this:

1. Find the time zone observed by the server or the requested time zone (for instance, America/New_York).
2. Compute the offset for time zone for this UTC time. (-5 for America/New_York).
3. Determine the datetime with the offset (2012-02-15 16:08:00 with a -5 offset becomes 2012-02-15 21:08:00).
4. Display the result (2012-02-15 21:08:00-5).

As you can see, PostgreSQL doesn't store the time zone but only uses it to convert the datetime to UTC before storage. After that, the time zone information is gone. When PostgreSQL displays the datetime, it always does so in the default time zone dictated by the session, user, database, or server, in that order. If you use time-zone-aware data types, we implore you to consider the consequence of a server move from one time zone to another. Suppose you based a server in New York City and subsequently restored the database in Los Angeles. All timestamps with time zone fields would suddenly display in Pacific time. This is fine as long as you anticipate this behavior.

Here's an example of how something can go wrong. Suppose that McDonald's had its server on the East Coast and the opening time for stores is `timetz`. A new McDonald's opens up in San Francisco. The new franchisee phones McDonald's headquarters to add its store to the master directory with an opening time of 7 a.m. The data entry dude entered the information as he is told: 7 a.m. The East Coast PostgreSQL server interprets this to mean 7 a.m. Eastern, and now early risers in San Francisco are lining up at the door wondering why they can't get their McBreakfasts at 4 a.m. Being hungry is one thing, but we can imagine many situations in which confusion over a difference of three hours could mean life or death.

Given the pitfalls, why would anyone want to use time-zone-aware data types? First, it does spare you from having to do time zone conversions manually. For example, if a flight leaves Boston at 8 a.m. and arrives in Los Angeles at 11 a.m., and your server is in Europe, you don't want to have to figure out the offset for each manually. You could just enter the data with the Boston and Los Angeles local times. There's another convincing reason to use time-zone-aware data types: the automatic handling of DST. With countries deviating more and more from one another in DST schedules, manually keeping track of DST changes for a globally used database would require a dedicated programmer who does nothing but keep up to date with the latest DST schedules and map them to geographic enclaves.

Here's an interesting example: a traveling salesperson catches a flight home from San Francisco to nearby Oakland. When she boards the plane, the clock at the terminal reads 2012-03-11 1:50 a.m. When she lands, the clock in the terminal reads 2012-03-11 3:10 a.m. How long was the flight? The key to the solution is that the change to DST occurred during the flight—the clocks sprang forward. With time-zone-aware timestamps, you get 20 minutes, which the plausible answer for a short flight across the Bay. We get the wrong answer if we don't use time-zone-aware timestamps:

```
SELECT '2012-03-11 3:10 AM America/Los_Angeles'::timestamptz
  - '2012-03-11 1:50 AM America/Los_Angeles'::timestamptz;
```

gives you 20 minutes, whereas:

```
SELECT '2012-03-11 3:10 AM'::timestamp - '2012-03-11 1:50 AM'::timestamp;
```

gives you 1 hour and 20 minutes.

Let's drive the point home with more examples, using a Boston server. For Example 5-8, I input my time in Los Angeles local time, but because my server is in Boston, I get a time returned in Boston local time. Note that it does give me the offset, but that is merely display information. The timestamp is internally stored in UTC.

Example 5-8. Inputting time in one time zone and output in another

```
SELECT '2012-02-28 10:00 PM America/Los_Angeles'::timestamptz;

2012-02-29 01:00:00-05
```

In Example 5-9, we are getting back a timestamp without time zone. So the answer you get when you run this same query will be the same as mine, regardless of where in the world you are.

Example 5-9. Timestamp with time zone to timestamp at location

```
SELECT '2012-02-28 10:00 PM America/Los_Angeles'::timestamptz AT TIME ZONE 'Europe/
Paris';
```

```
2012-02-29 07:00:00
```

The query is asking: what time is it in Paris if it's 2012-02-28 10:00 p.m. in Los Angeles? Note the absence of UTC offset in the result. Also, notice how you can specify a time zone with its official name rather than just an offset. Visit Wikipedia for a list of official time zone names (*http://en.wikipedia.org/wiki/Zoneinfo*).

Datetime Operators and Functions

The inclusion of a temporal interval data type greatly eases date and time arithmetic in PostgreSQL. Without it, we'd have to create another family of functions or use a nesting of functions as many other databases do. With intervals, we can add and subtract timestamp data simply by using the arithmetic operators we're intimately familiar with. The following examples demonstrate operators and functions used with date and time data types.

The + adds an interval to a temporal type:

```
SELECT '2012-02-10 11:00 PM'::timestamp + interval '1 hour';

2012-02-11 00:00:00
```

You can also add intervals:

```
SELECT '23 hours 20 minutes'::interval + '1 hour'::interval;

24:20:00
```

The - operator subtracts an interval from a temporal type:

```
SELECT '2012-02-10 11:00 PM'::timestamptz - interval '1 hour';

2012-02-10 22:00:00-05
```

OVERLAPS, demonstrated in Example 5-10, returns true if two temporal ranges overlap. This is an ANSI SQL operator equivalent to the overlaps function. OVERLAPS takes four parameters, the first pair constituting one range and the last pair constituting the other range. An overlap considers the time periods to be half open, meaning that the start time is included but the end time is outside the range. This is slightly different behavior from the common BETWEEN operator, which considers both start and end to be included. This quirk won't make a difference unless one of your ranges is a fixed point in time (a period for which start and end are identical). Watch out for this if you're a avid user of the OVERLAPS function.

Example 5-10. OVERLAPS for timestamp and date

```
SELECT ('2012-10-25 10:00 AM'::timestamp, '2012-10-25 2:00 PM'::timestamp) OVERLAPS
('2012-10-25 11:00 AM'::timestamp,'2012-10-26 2:00 PM'::timestamp) AS x,
('2012-10-25'::date,'2012-10-26'::date) OVERLAPS
('2012-10-26'::date,'2012-10-27'::date) As y;

x  |y
---+---
t  |f
```

In addition to the operators, PostgreSQL comes with functions supporting temporal types. A full listing can be found at Datetime Functions and Operators (*http://bit.ly/1A0Wju9*). We'll demonstrate a sampling here.

Once again, we start with the versatile `generate_series` function. You can use this function with temporal types and interval steps.

As you can see in Example 5-11, we can express dates in our local datetime format or the more global ISO Y-M-D format. PostgreSQL automatically interprets differing input formats. To be safe, we tend to stick with entering dates in ISO, because date formats vary from culture to culture, server to server, or even database to database.

Example 5-11. Generate time series using generate_series()

```
SELECT (dt - interval '1 day')::date As eom
FROM generate_series('2/1/2012', '6/30/2012', interval '1 month') As dt;

eom
-----------
2012-01-31
2012-02-29
2012-03-31
2012-04-30
2012-05-31
```

Another popular activity is to extract or format parts of a datetime value. Here, the functions date_part and to_char (*http://bit.ly/15SXGCd*) fit the bill. Example 5-12 also drives home the behavior of DST for a time-zone-aware data type. We intentionally chose a period that crosses a daylight saving switchover in US/East. Because the clock springs forward at 2 a.m., the final row of the table reflects the new time.

Example 5-12. Extracting elements of a datetime

```
SELECT dt, date_part('hour',dt) As mh, to_char(dt, 'HH12:MI AM') As tm
FROM
generate_series( '2012-03-11 12:30 AM', '2012-03-11 3:00 AM', interval '15 minutes'
) As dt;
```

```
dt                      | mh | tm
------------------------+----+----------
2012-03-11 00:30:00-05  |  0 | 12:30 AM
2012-03-11 00:45:00-05  |  0 | 12:45 AM
2012-03-11 01:00:00-05  |  1 | 01:00 AM
2012-03-11 01:15:00-05  |  1 | 01:15 AM
2012-03-11 01:30:00-05  |  1 | 01:30 AM
2012-03-11 01:45:00-05  |  1 | 01:45 AM
2012-03-11 03:00:00-04  |  3 | 03:00 AM
```

By default, `generate_series` assumes `timestamptz` if you don't explicitly cast values to `timestamp`.

Arrays

Arrays play an important role in PostgreSQL. They are particularly useful in building aggregate functions, forming IN and ANY clauses, and holding intermediary values for morphing to other data types. In PostgreSQL, every data type has a companion array type. If you define your own data type, PostgreSQL creates a corresponding array type in the background for you. For example, `integer` has an integer array type `integer[]`, `character` has a character array type `character[]`, and so forth. We'll show you some useful functions to construct arrays short of typing them in manually. We will then point out some handy functions for array manipulations. You can get the complete listing of array functions and operators in the Official Manual: Array Functions and Operators (*http://www.postgresql.org/docs/current/interactive/functions-array.html*).

Array Constructors

The most rudimentary way to create an array is to type the elements:

```
SELECT ARRAY[2001, 2002, 2003] As yrs;
```

If the elements of your array can be extracted from a query, you can use the more sophisticated constructor function: `array()`:

```
SELECT array(
SELECT DISTINCT date_part('year', log_ts) FROM logs ORDER BY date_part('year',
log_ts)
);
```

Although the `array` function has to be used with a query returning a single column, you can specify a composite type as the output, thereby achieving multicolumn results. We demonstrate this in "Custom and Composite Data Types" on page 105.

You can cast a string representation of an array to an array with syntax of the form:

```
SELECT '{Alex,Sonia}'::text[] As name, '{43,40}'::smallint[] As age;
```

```
name        | age
------------+--------
{Alex,Sonia} | {43,40}
```

You can convert delimited strings to an array with the `string_to_array` function, as demonstrated in Example 5-13.

Example 5-13. Converting a delimited string to an array

```
SELECT string_to_array('ca.ma.tx', '.') As estados;

estados
----------
{ca,ma,tx}
```

`array_agg` is a variant aggregate function that can take a set of any data type and convert it to an array, as demonstrated in Example 5-14.

Example 5-14. Using array_agg

```
SELECT array_agg(log_ts ORDER BY log_ts) As x
FROM logs
WHERE log_ts BETWEEN '2011-01-01'::timestamptz AND '2011-01-15'::timestamptz;

x
-----------------------------------------
{'2011-01-01', '2011-01-13', '2011-01-14'}
```

Referencing Elements in an Array

Elements in arrays are most commonly referenced using the index of the element. PostgreSQL array indexes start at 1. If you try to access an element above the upper bound, you won't get an error—only NULL will be returned. The next example grabs the first and last element of our array column:

```
SELECT fact_subcats[1] AS primero,
  fact_subcats[array_upper(fact_subcats, 1)] As segundo
FROM census.lu_fact_types;
```

We used the `array_upper` function to get the upper bound of the array. The second, required parameter of the function indicates the dimension. In our case, our array is one-dimensional, but PostgreSQL does support multidimensional arrays.

Array Slicing and Splicing

PostgreSQL also supports array slicing using the *start:end* syntax. It returns another array that is a subarray of the original. For example, to return new arrays that just contain elements 2 through 4 of each original array, type:

```
SELECT fact_subcats[2:4] FROM census.lu_fact_types;
```

To glue two arrays together end to end, use the concatenation operator ||:

```
SELECT fact_subcats[1:2] || fact_subcats[3:4] FROM census.lu_fact_types;
```

Unnesting Arrays to Rows

A common function used with arrays is unnest, which allows you to expand the elements of an array into a set of rows, as demonstrated in Example 5-15.

Example 5-15. Expanding array with unnest

```
SELECT unnest('{XOX,OXO,XOX}'::char(3)[]) As tic_tac_toe;
```

```
tic_tac_toe
---
XOX
OXO
XOX
```

Although you can add multiple unnests to a single SELECT, if the number of resultant rows from each array is not balanced, you get some head-scratching results.

A balanced unnest, as shown in Example 5-16, gives you three rows, as you would often want.

Example 5-16. Unnesting balanced arrays

```
SELECT
unnest('{three,blind,mice}'::text[]) As t,
unnest('{1,2,3}'::smallint[]) As i;
```

```
t     |i
------+-
three |1
blind |2
mice  |3
```

If you remove an element of one array so that you don't have an equal number of elements in both, you get the result shown in Example 5-17.

Example 5-17. Unnesting unbalanced arrays

```
SELECT
unnest( '{blind,mouse}'::varchar[]) As v,
unnest('{1,2,3}'::smallint[]) As i;
```

```
v     |i
------+-
blind |1
mouse |2
blind |3
mouse |1
blind |2
mouse |3
```

Version 9.4 introduces a multiargument unnest function that puts in null placeholders where the arrays are not balanced. The main drawback with the new unnest is that it can appear only in the FROM clause. Example 5-18 revisits our unbalanced arrays using the version 9.4 construct.

Example 5-18. Unnesting unbalanced arrays with multiargument unnest

```
SELECT * FROM unnest('{blind,mouse}'::text[], '{1,2,3}'::int[]) As f(t,i);
```

```
t      | i
-------+---
blind  | 1
mouse  | 2
<NULL> | 3
```

Range Types

Range data types (http://www.postgresql.org/docs/current/interactive/rangetypes.html) are data types introduced in version 9.2 that define a range of values. Besides adding the convenience of having to deal with one fewer field, PostgreSQL also rolled out many operators and functions to identify overlapping ranges, check to see if a value falls inside the range, and combine adjacent smaller ranges into larger ranges. Prior to range types, we had to kludge our own functions. These often were clumsy and slow, and didn't always produce the expected results. We've been so happy with ranges that we've converted all of our temporal tables to use them where possible. We hope you share our joy.

Range types replace the need to use two separate fields to represent ranges. Suppose we want all integers between -2 and 2, but not including 2. The range representation would be [-2,2). The square bracket indicates a range that is closed on that end, whereas a parenthesis indicates a range that is open on that end. Thus, [-2,2) includes exactly four integers: -2, -1, 0, 1. Similarly:

- The range (-2,2] would have four integers: -1, 0, 1, 2.
- The range (-2,2) would have three integers: -1, 0, 1.
- The range [-2,2] would have five integers: -2, -1, 0, 1, 2.

Discrete Versus Continuous Ranges

PostgreSQL makes a distinction between discrete and continuous ranges. A range of integers or dates is discrete because you can enumerate each value within the range. Think of dots on a number line. A range of numerics or timestamps is continuous, because an infinite number of values lie between the end points.

A discrete range has multiple representations. Our earlier example of [-2,2) can be represented in the following ways and still include the same number of values in the range: `[-2,1]`, `(-3,1]`, `(-3,2)`, `[-2,2)`. Of these four representations, the one with `()` is considered the *canonical form*. There's nothing magical about closed-open ranges except that if everyone agrees to using that representation for discrete ranges, we can easily compare among many ranges without having to worry first about converting open to close or vice versa. PostgreSQL canonicalizes all discrete ranges, for both storage and display. So if you enter a date range as `(2014-1-5,2014-2-1]`, PostgreSQL rewrites it as `[2014-01-06,2014-02-02)`.

Built-in Range Types

PostgreSQL comes with six built-in range types for numbers and datetimes:

`int4range, int8range`
> A range of integers. Integer ranges are discrete and subject to canonicalization.

`numrange`
> A continuous range of decimals, floating-point numbers, or double-precision numbers.

`daterange`
> A discrete date range of calendar dates without time zone awareness.

`tsrange, tstzrange`
> A continuous date and time (timestamp) range allowing for fractional seconds. `tstrange` is not time-zone-aware. `tstzrange` is time-zone-aware.

For number-like ranges, if either the start point or the end point is left blank, PostgreSQL replaces it with a `null`. For practicality, you can interpret the null to represent either `-infinity` on the left or `infinity` on the right. In actuality, you're bound by the smallest and largest values for the particular data type. So a `int4range` of `(,)` would be `[-2147483648,2147483647)`.

For temporal ranges, `-infinity` and `infinity` are valid upper and lower bounds.

In addition to the built-in range types, you can create your own range types. When you do, you can set the range to be either discrete or continuous.

Defining Ranges

A range, regardless of type, is always composed of two elements of the same type with bounding condition denoted by [,], (, or), as shown in Example 5-19.

Example 5-19. Defining ranges with casts

```
SELECT '[2013-01-05,2013-08-13]'::daterange; ❶
SELECT '(2013-01-05,2013-08-13]'::daterange; ❷
SELECT '(0,)'::int8range; ❸
SELECT '(2013-01-05 10:00,2013-08-13 14:00]'::tsrange; ❹
```

```
[2013-01-05,2013-08-14)
[2013-01-06,2013-08-14)
[1,)
("2013-01-05 10:00:00","2013-08-13 14:00:00"]
```

❶ A date range between 2013-01-05 and 2013-08-13 inclusive. Note the
    canonicalization on the upper bound.

❷ A date range greater than 2013-01-05 and less than or equal to 2013-08-13.
    Notice the canonicalization.

❸ An integer greater than 0 and less than or equal to infinity. Note the
    canonicalization.

❹ A timestamp greater than 2013-01-05 10:00 and less than or equal to 2013-08-13
    14:00:00.

 Datetimes in PostgreSQL can take on the values of -infinity and
infinity. For uniformity and in keeping with convention, we suggest that you always use [for the former and) for the latter where you
have a choice: tsrange and tstzrange.

Ranges can also be defined using *constructor range* functions, which go by the same
name as the range and can take two or three arguments. Here's an example:

```
SELECT daterange('2013-01-05','infinity','[]');
```

The third argument denotes the bound. If omitted, [) is the default. We suggest that
you always include the third element for clarity, because the default is not obvious.

Defining Tables with Ranges

Temporal ranges are popular. Suppose you have an employment table that stores employment history. Instead of creating start and end dates, you can design a table as shown
in Example 5-20. In the example, we add an index to the period column to speed up
queries using our range column.

Example 5-20. Table with date range

```
CREATE TABLE employment (id serial PRIMARY KEY, employee varchar(20), period dater
ange);
CREATE INDEX idx_employment_period ON employment USING gist (period); ❶
INSERT INTO employment (employee, period)
VALUES ('Alex', '[2012-04-24, infinity)'::daterange), ('Sonia', '[2011-04-24,
2012-06-01)'::daterange), ('Leo', '[2012-06-20, 2013-04-20)'::daterange), ('Regi
na', '[2012-06-20, 2013-04-20)'::daterange);
```

❶ Add a GiST index on the range field.

Range Operators

Two range operators tend to be used more often than all others: overlap (&&) and contains (@>). To see the full catalog of range operators, go to Range Operators (*http://bit.ly/1s2o6WE*).

Overlap operator

As the name suggests, the overlap operator && returns `true` if two ranges have any values in common. Example 5-21 demonstrates this operator as well as putting to use the `string_agg` function for aggregating the list of employees into a single text field.

Example 5-21. Who worked with whom?

```
SELECT e1.employee, string_agg(DISTINCT e2.employee, ', ' ORDER BY e2.employee) As
colleagues
FROM employment As e1 INNER JOIN employment As e2
ON e1.period && e2.period
WHERE e1.employee <> e2.employee
GROUP BY e1.employee;

 employee | colleagues
----------+------------------
 Alex     | Leo, Regina, Sonia
 Leo      | Alex, Regina
 Regina   | Alex, Leo
 Sonia    | Alex
```

Contains and contained in operators

In the contains operator (@>), the first argument is a range and the second is a value. If the second is within the first, the contains operator returns true. Example 5-22 demonstrates its use.

Example 5-22. Who is currently working?

```
SELECT employee FROM employment WHERE period @> CURRENT_DATE GROUP BY employee;

employee
----
Alex
```

The reverse of the contains operator is the contained operator (<@), whose first argument is the value and the second the range.

JSON

JSON (*http://json.org*) data type and support functions came on the scene with version 9.2. JSON is a popular data type for web applications, as it serves as the lingua franca for data in JavaScript. Version 9.3 significantly beefed up JSON support with new functions for extracting, editing, and casting to other data types. Version 9.4 introduced the jsonb data type, which is a binary form of JSON that can also take advantage of indexes. We'll cover mostly JSON functions and operators introduced in version 9.3. We'll also show you how to use jsonb, functions it shares with its json brethren, and new operators it supports. Refer to JSON Functions and Operators (*http://www.postgresql.org/docs/current/interactive/functions-json.html*) for a full listing.

Inserting JSON Data

To create a table to hold json objects, define a column as a json type:

```
CREATE TABLE families_j (id serial PRIMARY KEY, profile json);
```

Example 5-23 inserts JSON data. PostgreSQL will validate the input to make sure what you are adding is valid JSON.

Example 5-23. Populating JSON field

```
INSERT INTO families_j (profile) VALUES (
'{"name":"Gomez", "members":[
{"member":{"relation":"padre", "name":"Alex"}},
{"member":{"relation":"madre", "name":"Sonia"}},
{"member":{"relation":"hijo", "name":"Brandon"}},
{"member":{"relation":"hija", "name":"Azaleah"}}
]}');
```

 You can't cast invalid JSON strings to the json type, nor can you store invalid JSON strings in a json column. PostgreSQL conducts background checks to ensure that the JSON string is well-behaved before letting it take up residency in the database.

Querying JSON

New in version 9.3 are various functions for inspecting JSON data. Example 5-24 uses json_extract_path, json_array_elements, and json_extract_path_text to obtain family members.

Example 5-24. Query subelements

```
SELECT json_extract_path_text(profile, 'name') As family, ❶ json_ex
tract_path_text( ❷ json_array_elements( ❸    json_extract_path(profile,'mem
bers') ❹ ), 'member','name' ) As member
FROM families_j;

family |member
-------+------
Gomez  |Alex
Gomez  |Sonia
Gomez  |Brandon
Gomez  |Azaleah
```

❶ Return name of family as text.

❷ Return the member/name path element as text.

❸ Expand the array of members into individual JSON objects.

❹ Get list of members as a new JSON object.

The ->> and #>> operators are shorthand for `json_extract_path_text`. The #>> takes a path array. Example 5-25 rewrites Example 5-24 using these symbolic operators.

Example 5-25. Extract path equivalent operators

```
SELECT profile->>'name' As family, json_array_elements((profile->'members')) #>>
'{member,name}'::text[] As member
FROM families_j;
```

A companion function, `json_extract_path`, which can be represented as -> and #>, returns a JSON object representing the subelement. This function is particularly useful for passing complex elements such as `members` into another function for further manipulation.

Although there weren't any functions for easily querying JSON data in version 9.2, you can accomplish much of what is native in version 9.3 by writing PL/V8 functions. We demonstrate how to create a jQuery-like selector function in Using PLV8 to Build JSON Selectors (*http://bit.ly/1Blrkgm*).

Several functions are available for working with arrays in a JSON structure. You already saw the use of `json_array_elements` in Example 5-25. In addition to `json_array_el ements`, you can use `json_array_length` to get a count of elements and -> with an index position to return specific index element. You can chain operators together to burrow into the JSON object, as shown in Example 5-26.

Example 5-26. Query subelements of members

```
SELECT id, json_array_length(profile->'members') As numero, profile->'members'-
>0#>>'{member,name}'::text[] As primero
FROM families_j;

id | numero | primero
---+--------+--------
 1 |   4    | Alex
```

Example 5-26 uses two versions of the -> operator. The -> operator always returns a json or jsonb object, but it takes as a second argument either a text field (shorthand for `json_object_field`) or an integer (shorthand for `json_array_element`). So `profile->'members'` returns the JSON object's members field, which happens to be a JSON array. ->0 works against a JSON array field and returns the first element. In our example, it returns the first member of our family. #>>'{member,name}'::text[] is shorthand for `json_extract_path_text`, so it returns the text value corresponding to the JSON member/name node of our first member. Note how we can seamlessly chain operators together. `jsonb`, which we will cover shortly, has the same operators, but they are aliases for `jsonb_object_field`, `jsonb_array_element`, and so on.

 Arrays in JSON start at zero. PostgreSQL arrays start at one.

Outputting JSON

In addition to being able to query JSON data, you can convert other data to JSON. In these next examples, we'll demonstrate the use of JSON built-in functions to create JSON objects.

Example 5-27 demonstrates the use of `row_to_json` to convert a subset of columns in each record from the table we created and loaded in Example 5-23.

Example 5-27. Converting rows to individual JSON objects (requires version 9.3 or later)

```
SELECT row_to_json(f) As x
FROM (SELECT id, profile->>'name' As name FROM families_j) As f;

          x
------------------------
 {"id":1,"name":"Gomez"}
```

To output each row in our `families` table as JSON, the following works in version 9.2 and later:

```
SELECT row_to_json(f) FROM families_j As f;
```

The use of a row as an output field in a query is a feature unique to PostgreSQL. It's handy for creating complex JSON objects. We describe it further in "Composite Types in Queries" on page 130, and Example 7-16 demonstrates the use of `array_agg` and `array_to_json` to output a set of rows as a single JSON object. In version 9.3 we have at our disposal the `json_agg` function. We demonstrate its use in Example 7-17.

Binary JSON: jsonb

New in PostgreSQL 9.4 is the `jsonb` data type. It has same-named operators as the `json` type and similarly named functions, plus several additional ones. There are a couple of key differences between the `jsonb` and `json` data types:

- `jsonb` is internally stored as a binary object and does not maintain the formatting of the original JSON text as the `json` data type does. Spaces aren't preserved, numbers can appear slightly different, and attributes become sorted. For example, a number input as e‑5 would be converted to its decimal representation.

- jsonb does not allow duplicate keys and silently picks one, whereas the json type preserves duplicates. This is demonstrated in Michael Paquier: Manipulating jsonb data by abusing of key uniqueness (*http://bit.ly/1zvz3V4*).

- jsonb performance is much better than json performance because jsonb doesn't need to be reparsed during operations.

- jsonb columns can be directly indexed using the GIN index method (covered in "Indexes" on page 114, whereas json requires a functional index to extract key elements.

To demonstrate these concepts, we'll create another families table, replacing the json column with a jsonb:

```
CREATE TABLE families_b (id serial PRIMARY KEY, profile jsonb);
```

To insert data into our new table, we would repeat Example 5-23.

So far, working with JSON and binary JSON has been the same. Differences appear when you query. To make the binary JSON readable, PostgreSQL converts it to a canonical text representation, as shown in Example 5-28.

Example 5-28. jsonb vs. json output

```
SELECT profile As b FROM families_b WHERE id = 1; ❶
SELECT profile As j FROM families_j WHERE id = 1;❷
```

```
b
-------------------------------------------------------------------------------
 {"name": "Gomez", "members": [{"member": {"name": "Alex", "relation": "padre"}}
, {"member": {"name": "Sonia", "relation": "madre"}}, {"member": {"name": "Brand
on", "relation": "hijo"}}, {"member": {"name": "Azaleah", "relation": "hija"}}]]
```

```
j
-------------------------------------------------------------------------
{"name":"Gomez","members":[{"member":{"relation":"padre", "name":"Alex"}},
{"member":{"relation":"madre", "name":"Sonia"}},
{"member":{"relation":"hijo", "name":"Brandon"}},
{"member":{"relation":"hija", "name":"Azaleah"}}]]
```

❶ jsonb reformats input and removes whitespace. Also, the order of relation and name attributes is flipped from their original order.

❷ json maintains input whitespace and the order of attributes.

jsonb has similarly named functions and the same-named operators as json, plus some additional ones. So, for example, the json family of functions such as json_ex tract_path_text and json_each are matched in jsonb by jsonb_ex tract_path_text, jsonb_each, etc. However, the equivalent operators are the same, so you will find that Example 5-25 and Example 5-26 work largely without change for the jsonb type—just replace the table name and change the `json_array_length` function to the equivalent `jsonb_array_length` function.

In addition to the operators supported by `json`, `jsonb` has additional comparator operators for equality (=), contains (@>), contained (<@), key exists (?), any of array of keys exists (?|), and all of array of keys exists (?&).

So, for example, to list all families that have a member named Alex, use the contains operator as demonstrated in Example 5-29.

Example 5-29. jsonb contains operator

```
SELECT profile->>'name' As family
FROM families_b
WHERE profile @> '{"members":[{"member":{"name":"Alex"} }]}';

family
-----
Gomez
```

These additional operators provide very fast checks when you complement them with a GIN index on the `jsonb` column:

```
CREATE INDEX idx_familes_jb_profile_gin ON families_b USING gin (profile);
```

We don't have enough records in our puny table for the index to kick in, but for more rows, you'd see that Example 5-29 utilizes the index.

XML

The XML data type, similar to JSON, is "controversial" in a relational database because it violates principles of normalization. Nonetheless, all of the high-end relational databases products (IBM DB2, Oracle, SQL Server) support XML. PostgreSQL also jumped on the bandwagon and offers plenty of functions to boot. We've authored many articles on working with XML in PostgreSQL. (You can find these articles at PostgreSQL XML Examples (*http://bit.ly/1yx7ixc*).) PostgreSQL comes packaged with functions for generating, manipulating, and parsing XML data. These are outlined in XML Functions (*http://bit.ly/1BlrAvL*). Unlike the `jsonb` type, there is currently no direct index support for it. So you need to use functional indexes to index subparts, similarly to what you can do with the plain `json` type.

Inserting XML Data

When you create a column of the xml data type, PostgreSQL automatically ensures that only valid XML values populate the rows. This is what distinguishes an XML column from just any text column. However, the XML is not validated against any Document Type Definition (DTD) or XML Schema Definition (XSD), even if it is specified in the

XML document. To freshen up on what constitutes valid XML, Example 5-30 shows you how to append XML data to a table, by declaring a column as xml and inserting into it as usual.

Example 5-30. Populate XML field

```
CREATE TABLE families (id serial PRIMARY KEY, profile xml);
INSERT INTO families(profile)
VALUES (
    '<family name="Gomez">
        <member><relation>padre</relation><name>Alex</name></member>
        <member><relation>madre</relation><name>Sonia</name></member>
        <member><relation>hijo</relation><name>Brandon</name></member>
        <member><relation>hija</relation><name>Azaleah</name></member>
        </family>');
```

Each XML value could have a different XML structure. To enforce uniformity, you can add a check constraint, covered in "Check Constraints" on page 113, to the XML column. Example 5-31 ensures that all family has at least one relation element. The '/family/ member/relation' is XPath syntax, a basic way to refer to elements and other parts of XML.

Example 5-31. Ensure that all records have at least one member relation

```
ALTER TABLE families ADD CONSTRAINT chk_has_relation
CHECK (xpath_exists('/family/member/relation', profile));
```

If we then try to insert something like:

```
INSERT INTO families (profile) VALUES ('<family name="HsuObe"></family>');
```

we will get this error: ERROR: new row for relation "families" violates check constraint "chk_has_relation".

For more involved checks that require checking against DTD or XSD, you'll need to resort to writing functions and using those in the check constraint, because PostgreSQL doesn't have built-in functions to handle those kinds of checks.

Querying XML Data

To query XML, the xpath function is really useful. The first argument is an XPath query, and the second is an xml object. The output is an array of XML elements that satisfy the XPath query. Example 5-32 combines xpath with unnest to return all the family members. unnest unravels the array into a row set. We then cast the XML fragment to text.

Example 5-32. Query XML field

```
SELECT family,
    (xpath('/member/relation/text()', f))[1]::text As relation,
    (xpath('/member/name/text()', f))[1]::text As mem_name ❶
FROM (SELECT (xpath('/family/@name', profile))[1]::text As family, ❷
```

```
  unnest(xpath('/family/member', profile)
  ) As f FROM families) x; ❸
```

```
family | relation | mem_name
-------+-----------+----------
Gomez  | padre     | Alex
Gomez  | madre     | Sonia
Gomez  | hijo      | Brandon
Gomez  | hija      | Azaleah
```

❶ Get the text element in the relation and name tags of each member element. We need to use array subscripting because xpath always returns an array, even if only one element is returned.

❷ Get the name attribute from family root. For this we use *@attribute_name*.

❸ Break into subelements <member>, <relation>, </relation>, <name>, </name>, and </member> tags. The slash is a way of getting at subtag elements. For example, xpath('/family/member', 'profile') will return an array of all members in each family that is defined in a profile. The @ sign is used to select attributes of a an element. So, for example, family/@name returns the name attribute of a family. By default, xpath always returns an element, including the tag part. The text() forces a return of just the text body of an element.

Custom and Composite Data Types

This section demonstrates how to define and use a custom type. The composite (aka record, row) object type is often used to build an object that is then cast to a custom type, or as a return type for functions needing to return multiple columns.

All Tables Are Custom Data Types

PostgreSQL automatically creates custom types for all tables. For all intents and purposes, you can use custom types just as you would any other built-in type. So we could conceivably create a table that has a column type that is another table's custom type, and we can go even further and make an array of that type. We demonstrate this "turducken" in Example 5-33.

Example 5-33. Turducken

```
CREATE TABLE chickens (id integer PRIMARY KEY);
CREATE TABLE ducks (id integer PRIMARY KEY, chickens chickens[]);
CREATE TABLE turkeys (id integer PRIMARY KEY, ducks ducks[]);

INSERT INTO ducks VALUES (1, ARRAY[ROW(1)::chickens, ROW(1)::chickens]);
INSERT INTO turkeys VALUES (1, array(SELECT d FROM ducks d));
```

We create an instance of a chicken without adding it to the chicken table itself; hence we're able to repeat id with impunity. We take our array of two chickens, stuff them into one duck, and add it to the ducks table. We take the duck we added and stuff it into the turkeys table.

Finally, let's see what we have in our turkey:

```
SELECT * FROM turkeys;

output
-----------------------
id |        ducks
---+-----------------------
 1 | {"(1,\"{(1),(1)}\")"}
```

We can also replace subelements of our turducken. This next example replaces our second chicken in our first turkey with a different chicken:

```
UPDATE turkeys SET ducks[1].chickens[2] = ROW(3)::chickens
WHERE id = 1 RETURNING *;

output
--------------
id |        ducks
---+-----------------------
 1 | {"(1,\"{(1),(3)}\")"}
```

We used the RETURNING clause as discussed in "Returning Affected Records to the User" on page 130 to output the changed record.

PostgreSQL internally keeps track of object dependencies. The ducks.chickens column is dependent on the chickens table. The turkeys.ducks column is dependent on the ducks table. You won't be able to drop the chickens table without specifying CASCADE or first dropping the ducks.chickens column. If you do a CASCADE, the ducks.chickens column will be gone, and without warning, your turkeys will have no chickens in their ducks.

Building Custom Data Types

Although you can easily create composite types just by creating a table, at some point, you'll probably want to build your own from scratch. For example, let's build a complex number data type with the following statement:

```
CREATE TYPE complex_number AS (r double precision, i double precision);
```

We can then use this complex number as a column type:

```
CREATE TABLE circuits (circuit_id serial PRIMARY KEY, ac_volt complex_number);
```

We can then query our table with statements such as:

```
SELECT circuit_id, (ac_volt).* FROM circuits;
```

or an equivalent:

```
SELECT circuit_id, (ac_volt).r, (ac_volt).i FROM circuits;
```

 Puzzled by the parentheses surrounding ac_volt? If you leave them out, PostgreSQL will raise the error missing FROM-clause entry for table "ac_volt", because it assumes ac_volt without parentheses refers to a table.

Building Operators and Functions for Custom Types

After you build a custom type such as a complex number, naturally you'll want to create functions and operators for it. We'll demonstrate building a + operator for the com plex_number we created. For more details about building functions, see Chapter 8. As stated earlier, an operator is a symbol alias for a function that takes one or two arguments. You can find more details about what symbols and set of symbols are allowed in CREATE OPERATOR (*http://www.postgresql.org/docs/current/interactive/sql-createoperator.html*).

In addition to being an alias, an operator contains optimization information that can be used by the query optimizer to decide how indexes should be used, how best to navigate the data, and which operator expressions are equivalent. More details about these optimizations and how each can help the optimizer are in Operator Optimization (*http://bit.ly/1vXzPek*).

The first step to creating an operator is to create a function, as shown in Example 5-34.

Example 5-34. Add function for complex number

```
CREATE OR REPLACE FUNCTION add(complex_number, complex_number) RETURNS complex_num
ber AS
$$
 SELECT ( (COALESCE(($1).r,0) + COALESCE(($2).r,0)),
    (COALESCE(($1).i,0) + COALESCE(($2).i,0)) )::complex_number;
$$
language sql;
```

The next step is to create a symbolic operator to wrap the function, as in Example 5-35.

Example 5-35. + operator for complex number

```
CREATE OPERATOR +(
  PROCEDURE = add,
  LEFTARG = complex_number,
  RIGHTARG = complex_number,
  COMMUTATOR = +);
```

We can then test our new + operator:

```
SELECT (1,2)::complex_number + (3,-10)::complex_number;
```

which outputs (4,-8).

Although we didn't demonstrate it here, you can overload functions and operators to take different types as inputs. For example, you can create an add function and companion + operator that takes a complex_number and an integer.

The ability to build custom types and operators pushes PostgreSQL to the boundary of a full-fledged development environment, bringing us ever closer to our utopia where everything is table-driven.

CHAPTER 6
Tables, Constraints, and Indexes

Tables form the building block of relational-database storage. Structuring tables so that they form meaningful relationships is the key to relational-database design. In PostgreSQL, constraints enforce relationships between tables. To distinguish a table from just a heap of data, we establish indexes. Much like the indexes you find at the end of books or the tenant list at the entrances to grand office buildings, indexes point to locations in the table so you don't have to scour the table from top to bottom every time you're looking for something.

In this chapter, we introduce syntax for creating tables and adding rows. We then move on to constraints to ensure that your data doesn't get out of line. Finally, we show you how to add indexes to your tables to expedite search. Indexing a table is as much a programming task as it is an experimental endeavor. A misappropriated index is worse than useless. Not all indexes are created equal. Algorithmists have devised different kinds of indexes for different data types, all in the attempt to scrape that last zest of speed from a query.

Tables

In addition to ordinary data tables, PostgreSQL offers several kinds of tables that are rather uncommon: temporary, unlogged, inherited, typed, and foreign (covered in Chapter 10).

Basic Table Creation

Example 6-1 shows the table creation syntax, which is similar to what you'll find in all SQL databases.

Example 6-1. Basic table creation

```
CREATE TABLE logs ( log_id serial PRIMARY KEY, ❶ user_name varchar(50), ❷ descrip
tion text, ❸ log_ts timestamp with time zone NOT NULL DEFAULT current_timestamp);
❹
CREATE INDEX idx_logs_log_ts ON logs USING btree (log_ts);
```

❶   `serial` is the data type used to represent an incrementing autonumber. Adding a serial column automatically adds an accompanying sequence object to the database schema. A `serial` data type is always an integer with the default value set to the next value of the sequence object. Each table usually has just one serial column, which often serves as the primary key.

❷   `varchar` is shorthand for `character varying`, a variable-length string similar to what you will find in other databases. You don't need to specify a maximum length; if you don't, `varchar` is almost identical to the `text` data type.

❸   `text` is a string of indeterminate length. It's never followed by a length restriction.

❹   `timestamp with time zone` (shorthand `timestamptz`) is a date and time data type, always stored in UTC. It always displays date and time in the server's own time zone unless you tell it to otherwise. See "Time Zones: What They Are and Are Not" on page 88 for a a more thorough discussion.

Inherited Tables

PostgreSQL stands alone as the only database offering inherited tables. When you specify that a table (the child table) inherit from another table (the parent table), PostgreSQL creates the child table with its own columns plus all the columns of the parent table(s). PostgreSQL will remember this parent-child relationship so that any structural changes later made to the parent automatically propagate to its children. Parent-child table design is perfect for partitioning your data. When you query the parent table, PostgreSQL automatically includes all rows in the child tables. Not every trait of the parent passes down to the child. Notably, primary key constraints, uniqueness constraints, and indexes are never inherited. Check constraints are inherited, but children can have their own check constraints in addition to the ones they inherit from their parents (see Example 6-2).

Example 6-2. Inherited table creation

```
CREATE TABLE logs_2011 (PRIMARY KEY(log_id)) INHERITS (logs);
CREATE INDEX idx_logs_2011_log_ts ON logs USING btree(log_ts);
ALTER TABLE logs_2011 ADD CONSTRAINT chk_y2011
 CHECK (log_ts >= '2011-1-1'::timestamptz
   AND log_ts < '2012-1-1'::timestamptz ); ❶
```

❶   We define a check constraint to limit data to the year 2011. Having the check constraint in place tells the query planner to skip over inherited tables that do not satisfy the query condition.

Unlogged Tables

For ephemeral data that could be rebuilt in event of a disk failure or doesn't need to be restored after a crash, you might prefer having more speed than redundancy. In version 9.1, the UNLOGGED modifier allows you to create unlogged tables, as shown in Example 6-3. These tables will not be part of any write-ahead logs. If you accidentally unplug the power cord on the server and then turn the power back on, all data in your unlogged tables will be wiped clean during the rollback process. You can find more examples and caveats at Depesz: Waiting for 9.1 Unlogged Tables (*http://bit.ly/1u06x9p*).

There is also an option in pg_dump that allows you to skip over backing up of unlogged data.

Example 6-3. Unlogged table creation

```
CREATE UNLOGGED TABLE web_sessions ( session_id text PRIMARY KEY, add_ts time
stamptz, upd_ts timestamptz, session_state xml);
```

The big advantage of an unlogged table is that writing data to it is much faster than to a logged table. Our experience suggests on the order of 15 times faster. Keep in mind that you're making sacrifices with unlogged tables:

- If your server crashes, PostgreSQL will truncate all unlogged tables. (Truncate means erase all rows.)
- Unlogged tables don't support GiST indexes (defined in "PostgreSQL Stock Indexes" on page 115). They are therefore unsuitable for exotic data types that rely on GiST for speedy access.

Unlogged tables will accommodate the common B-Tree and GIN, though.

TYPE OF

PostgreSQL automatically creates a corresponding composite data type in the background whenever you create a new table. The reverse is not true. But, as of version 9.0, you can use a composite data type as a template for creating tables. We'll demonstrate this by first creating a type with the definition:

```
CREATE TYPE basic_user AS (user_name varchar(50), pwd varchar(10));
```

We can then create a table with rows that are instances of this type via the OF clause, as shown in Example 6-4.

Example 6-4. Using TYPE to define new table structure

```
CREATE TABLE super_users OF basic_user (CONSTRAINT pk_su PRIMARY KEY (user_name));
```

When creating tables from data types, you can't alter the columns of the table. Instead, add or remove columns to the composite data type, and PostgreSQL will automatically propagate the changes to the table structure. Much like inheritance, the advantage of this approach is that if you have many tables sharing the same underlying structure and you need to make a universal alteration, you can do so by simply changing the underlying composite type.

Let's say we now need to add a phone number to our `super_users` table from Example 6-4. All we have to do is execute the following command to alter the underlying type:

```
ALTER TYPE basic_user ADD ATTRIBUTE phone varchar(10) CASCADE;
```

Normally, you can't change the definition of a type if tables depend on that type. The `CASCADE` modifier overrides this restriction, applying the same change to all the dependent tables.

Constraints

PostgreSQL constraints are the most advanced (and most complex) of any database we've worked with. Not only do you create constraints, but you can also control all facets of how a constraint handles existing data, any cascade options, how to perform the matching, which indexes to incorporate, conditions under which the constraint can be violated, and more. On top of it all, you can pick your own name for each constraint. For the full treatment, we suggest you review the official documentation (*http://bit.ly/ 1q2fBPG*). You'll find comfort in knowing that taking the default settings usually works out fine. We'll start off with something familiar to most relational folks: foreign key, unique, and check constraints. Then we'll move on to exclusion constraints, introduced in version 9.0.

 Names of primary key and unique key constraints must be unique within a given schema. The general practice is to include the name of the table and column as part of the name of the key. For the sake of brevity, our examples might not abide by this general practice.

Foreign Key Constraints

PostgreSQL follows the same convention as most databases that support referential integrity. You can specify cascade update and delete rules to avoid pesky orphaned records. We show you how to add foreign key constraints in Example 6-5.

Example 6-5. Building foreign key constraints and covering indexes

```
set search_path=census, public;
ALTER TABLE facts ADD CONSTRAINT fk_facts_1 FOREIGN KEY (fact_type_id)
REFERENCES lu_fact_types (fact_type_id) ❶
ON UPDATE CASCADE ON DELETE RESTRICT;  ❷
CREATE INDEX fki_facts_1 ON facts (fact_type_id); ❸
```

❶ We define a foreign key relationship between our `facts` and `fact_types` tables. This prevents us from introducing fact types into `facts` unless they are already present in the fact types lookup table.

❷ We add a cascade rule that automatically updates the `fact_type_id` in our `facts` table should we renumber our fact types. We restrict deletes from our lookup table so fact types in use cannot be removed. `RESTRICT` is the default behavior, but we suggest stating it for clarity.

❸ Unlike for primary key and unique constraints, PostgreSQL doesn't automatically create an index for foreign key constraints; you should add this yourself to speed up queries.

Unique Constraints

Each table can have no more than a single primary key. If you need to enforce uniqueness on other columns, you must resort to unique constraints or unique indexes. Adding a unique constraint automatically creates an associated unique index. Similar to primary keys, unique key constraints can participate in `REFERENCES` part of foreign key constraints and cannot have `NULL` values. A unique index without a unique key constraint does allow `NULL` values. The following example shows how to add a unique index:

```
ALTER TABLE logs_2011 ADD CONSTRAINT uq UNIQUE (user_name,log_ts);
```

Often you'll find yourself needing to ensure uniqueness for only a subset of your rows. PostgreSQL does not offer conditional unique constraints, but you can achieve the same effect by using a partial uniqueness index. See "Partial Indexes" on page 118.

Check Constraints

Check constraints are conditions that must be met for a field or a set of fields for each row. The query planner can also take advantage of check constraints and abandon queries that don't meet the check constraint outright. We saw an example of a check constraint in Example 6-2. That particular example prevents the planner from having to scan rows failing to satisfy the date range specified in a query. You can exercise some creativity in your check constraints, because you can use functions and Boolean expressions to build complicated matching conditions. For example, the following constraint requires all user names in the `logs` tables to be lowercase:

```
ALTER TABLE logs ADD CONSTRAINT chk CHECK (user_name = lower(user_name));
```

The other noteworthy aspect of check constraints is that unlike primary key, foreign key, and unique key constraints, they inherit from parent tables.

Exclusion Constraints

Introduced in version 9.0, exclusion constraints allow you to incorporate additional operators to enforce uniqueness that can't be satisfied by the equality operator. Exclusion constraints are especially useful in problems involving scheduling.

PostgreSQL 9.2 introduced the range data types that are perfect candidates for exclusion constraints. You'll find a fine example of using exclusion constraints for range data types at Waiting for 9.2 Range Data Types (*http://bit.ly/1z3emS1*).

Exclusion constraints are generally enforced using GiST indexes, but you can create compound indexes that incorporate B-Tree as well. Before you do this, you need to install the btree_gist extension. A classic use of a compound exclusion constraint is for scheduling resources.

Here's an example using exclusion constraints. Suppose you have a fixed number of conference rooms in your office, and groups must book them in advance. See how we'd prevent double-booking in Example 6-6. Take note of how we are able to use the overlap operator (&&) for our temporal comparison and the usual equality operator for the room number.

Example 6-6. Prevent overlapping bookings for same room

```
CREATE TABLE schedules(id serial primary key, room smallint, time_slot tstzrange);
ALTER TABLE schedules ADD CONSTRAINT ex_schedules
EXCLUDE USING gist (room WITH =, time_slot WITH &&);
```

Just as with uniqueness constraints, PostgreSQL automatically creates a corresponding index of the type specified in the constraint declaration.

Indexes

PostgreSQL ships stocked with a lavish framework for creating and fine-tuning indexes. The art of PostgreSQL indexing could fill a tome all by itself. At the time of writing, PostgreSQL comes with at least four types of indexes, often referred to as *index methods*. If you find these insufficient, you can define new index operators and modifiers to supplement them. If still unsatisfied, you're free to invent your own index type.

PostgreSQL also allows you to mix and match different index types in the same table with the expectation that the planner will consider them all. For instance, one column could use a B-Tree index while an adjacent column uses a GiST index, with both indexes contributing to the speed of the query. To delve more into the mechanics of how the planner takes advantage of indexes, visit bitmap index scan strategy (*http://bit.ly/ 1vUs2fU*).

 Index names must be unique within a given schema.

PostgreSQL Stock Indexes

To take full advantage of all that PostgreSQL has to offer, you'll want to understand the various types of indexes and situations where they will aid or harm. The index methods are:

B-Tree
> B-Tree is a general-purpose index common in relational databases. You can usually get by with B-Tree alone if you don't want to experiment with additional types. If PostgreSQL automatically creates an index for you or you don't bother specifying the index method, B-Tree will be chosen. It is currently the only index method for primary keys and unique keys.

GiST
> Generalized Search Tree (GiST) is an index optimized for full-text search, spatial data, scientific data, unstructured data, and hierarchical data. Although you can't use it to enforce uniqueness, you can create the same effect by using it in an exclusion constraint.

> GiST is a lossy index, in the sense that the index itself will not store the value of what it's indexing, but merely a caricature of the value such as a box for a polygon. This creates the need for an extra look-up step if you need to retrieve the value or do a more fine-tuned check.

GIN
> Generalized Inverted Index (GIN) is geared toward the built-in full text search (*http://bit.ly/1vwG2ht*) and jsonb data type of PostgreSQL. Many other extensions, such as hstore and pg_trgm also utilize it. GIN is a descendent of GiST without lossiness. GIN will make a copy of the values in the columns that are part of the index. If you ever need to pull data limited to covered columns, GIN is faster than GiST. However, the extra copying required by GIN index means updating the index is slower than a comparable GiST index. Also, because each index row is limited to a certain size, you can't use GIN to index large objects such as large hstore documents or text. If there is a possibility you'll be inserting a 600-page manual into a field of a table, don't use GIN to index that column.

You can find a wonderful example of GIN in Waiting for Faster LIKE/ILIKE (*http://bit.ly/1FUiaW9*). In version 9.3, you can index regular expressions that leverage the GIN-based pg_trgm extension (*http://bit.ly/1vnL7DJ*).

SP-GiST

Space-Partitioning Trees Generalized Search Tree (*http://bit.ly/1vXAtIK*) (SP-GiST), introduced in version 9.2, can be used in the same situations as GiST but can be faster for certain kinds of data distribution. PostgreSQL's native geometric data types, such as `point` and `box`, and the `text` data type, were the first to support SP-GiST. In version 9.3, support extended to range types. The PostGIS spatial extension also has plans to take advantage of this specialized index in the near future.

hash

Hash indexes were popular prior to the advent of GiST and GIN. General consensus rates GiST and GIN above hash in terms of both performance and transaction safety. The write-ahead log does not track hash indexes; therefore, you can't use them in streaming replication setups. PostgreSQL has relegated hash to legacy status. You may still encounter this index type in other databases, but it's best to eschew hash in PostgreSQL.

B-Tree-GiST/B-Tree-GIN

If you want to explore stock beyond what PostgreSQL installs by default, either out of need or curiosity, start with the composite B-Tree-GiST or B-Tree-GIN indexes, both available as extensions.

These hybrids support the specialized operators of GiST or GIN, but also offers indexablity of the equality operator in B-Tree indexes. You'll find them indispensable when you want to create a compound index composed of multiple columns with data types like `character varying` or `number`—normally serviced by equality operators—or like a hierarchical `ltree` type or full-text vector with operators supported only by GIN/GiST.

Operator Classes

We would have loved to skip this section on operator classes. Many of you will sail through your index-capades without ever needing to know what they are and why they matter for indexes. But if you falter, you'll need to understand operator classes to troubleshoot the perennial question, "Why is the planner not taking advantage of my index?"

Algorithm experts intend for their indexes to work against certain data types and comparison operators. An expert in indexing ranges could obsess over the overlap operator (&&), whereas an expert inventing indexes for faster text search may find little meaning in an overlap. A computational linguist trying to index Chinese or other logographic languages probably has little use for inequalities, whereas A-to-Z sorting is critical for an alphabetical writing system.

PostgreSQL groups comparison operators that are similar and permissible data types into operator classes (opclass for short). For example, the int4_ops operator class includes the operators = < > > < to be applied against the data type of int4. The pg_op class system table provides a complete listing of available operator classes, both from your original install and from extensions. A particular index method will work only against a given set of opclasses. To see this complete list, you can either open up pgAdmin and look under operators, or execute the query in Example 6-7 against the system catalog to get a comprehensive view.

Example 6-7. Which data types and operator classes does B-Tree support?

```
SELECT am.amname AS index_method, opc.opcname AS opclass_name,
opc.opcintype::regtype AS indexed_type, opc.opcdefault AS is_default
FROM pg_am am INNER JOIN pg_opclass opc ON opc.opcmethod = am.oid
WHERE am.amname = 'btree'
ORDER BY index_method, indexed_type, opclass_name;
```

```
index_method |     opclass_name     |       indexed_type        | is_default
-------------+----------------------+---------------------------+-----------
btree        | bool_ops             | boolean                   | t
:
btree        | text_ops             | text                      | t
btree        | text_pattern_ops     | text                      | f
btree        | varchar_ops          | text                      | f
btree        | varchar_pattern_ops  | text                      | f
:
```

In Example 6-7, we limit our result to B-Tree. Notice that one opclass per indexed data type is marked as the default. When you create an index without specifying the opclass, PostgreSQL chooses the default opclass for the index. Generally, this is good enough, but not always.

For instance, B-Tree against text_ops (aka varchar_ops) doesn't include the ~~ operator (the LIKE operator), so none of your LIKE searches can use an index in the text_ops opclass. If you plan on doing many wildcard searches on varchar or text columns, you'd be better off explicitly choosing the text_pattern_ops/varchar_pattern_ops opclass for your index. To specify the opclass, just append the opclass after the column name, as in:

```
CREATE INDEX idx1 ON census.lu_tracts USING btree (tract_name text_pattern_ops);
```

You will notice there are both varchar_ops and text_ops in the list, but they map only to text. character varying doesn't have B-Tree operators of its own, because it is essentially text with a length constraint. varchar_ops and varchar_pattern_ops are just aliases for text_ops and text_pattern_ops to satisfy the desire of some to maintain this symmetry of opclasses starting with the name of the type they support.

Finally, remember that each index you create works against only a single opclass. If you would like an index on a column to cover multiple opclasses, you must create separate indexes. To add the default index `text_ops` to a table, run:

```
CREATE INDEX idx2 ON census.lu_tracts USING btree (tract_name);
```

Now you have two indexes against the same column. (There's no limit to the number of indexes you can build against a single column.) The planner will choose `idx2` for basic equality queries and `idx1` for comparisons using `like`.

You'll find operator classes detailed in Operator Classes (*http://bit.ly/1yx8sZs*). We also strongly recommend that you read our article for tips on troubleshooting index issues, Why is My Index Not Used? (*http://bit.ly/1FZVSnP*)

Functional Indexes

PostgreSQL lets you add indexes to functions of columns. Functional indexes prove their usefulness in mixed-case textual data. PostgreSQL is a case-sensitive database. To perform a case-insensitive search you could create a functional index:

```
CREATE INDEX fidx ON featnames_short
  USING btree (upper(fullname) varchar_pattern_ops);
```

Creating such an index ensures that queries such as `SELECT fullname FROM feat names_short WHERE upper(fullname) LIKE 'S%';` can utilize an index.

Always use the same function when querying to ensure usage of the index.

Both PostgreSQL and Oracle provide functional indexes. MySQL and SQL Server provide computed columns, which you can index. As of version 9.3, PostgreSQL supports indexes on materialized views as well as tables.

Partial Indexes

Partial indexes (sometimes called filtered indexes) are indexes that cover only rows fitting a predefined `WHERE` condition. For instance, if you have a table of 1,000,000 rows, but you care about a fixed set of 10,000, you're better off creating partial indexes. The resulting indexes can be faster because more of them can fit into RAM, plus you'll save a bit of disk space on the index itself.

Partial indexes let you place uniqueness constraints only on some rows of the data. Pretend that you manage newspaper subscribers who signed up in the past 10 years and want to ensure that nobody is getting more than one paper delivered per day. With dwindling interest in print media, only about 5% of your subscribers have a current subscription. You don't care about subscribers who have stopped getting newspapers being duplicated, because they're not on the carriers' list anyway. Your table looks like this:

```
CREATE TABLE subscribers (
  id serial PRIMARY KEY,
  name varchar(50) NOT NULL, type varchar(50),
  is_active boolean);
```

We add a partial index to guarantee uniqueness only for current subscribers:

```
CREATE UNIQUE INDEX uq ON subscribers USING btree(lower(name)) WHERE is_active;
```

 Functions used in index WHERE condition must be immutable. This means you can't use time functions like CURRENT_DATE or data from other tables (or other rows of indexed table) to determine whether a record should be indexed.

One warning we stress is that when you query the data using a SELECT statement, the conditions used when creating the index must be a subset of your WHERE condition. An easy way to not have to worry about this is to use a view as a proxy. Back to our subscribers example, create a view as follows:

```
CREATE OR REPLACE VIEW vw_subscribers_current AS
SELECT id, lower(name) As name FROM subscribers WHERE is_active = true;
```

Then always query the view instead of the table (many purists advocate never querying tables directly anyway):

```
SELECT * FROM vw_active_subscribers WHERE user_name = 'sandy';
```

You can open up the planner and double-check that the planner indeed used your index.

Multicolumn Indexes

You've already seen many examples of compound (aka multicolumn) indexes in this chapter. On top of that, you can create functional indexes using more than one underlying column. Here is an example of a multicolumn index:

```
CREATE INDEX idx ON subscribers USING btree (type, upper(name) varchar_pat
tern_ops);
```

The PostgreSQL planner uses a strategy called *bitmap index scan* that automatically tries to combine indexes on the fly, often from single-column indexes, to achieve the same goal as a multicolumn index. If you're unable to predict how you'll be querying compound fields in the future, you may be better off creating single-column indexes and let the planner decide how to combine them during search.

If you have a compound B-Tree index on type, upper(name) .., then there is no need for an index on just type, because the planner can happily use the compound index for cases in which you just need to filter by type.

Version 9.2 introduced index-only scans, which made compound indexes even more relevant because the planner can just scan the index and use data from the index without ever needing to check the underlying table. So if you commonly filter by the same set of fields and output those, a compound index should improve speed. Keep in mind that the more columns you have in an index, the fatter your index and the less of it that can easily fit in RAM. Don't go overboard with compound indexes.

## CHAPTER 7

SQL: The PostgreSQL Way

PostgreSQL already outclasses other database products when it comes to ANSI SQL compliance. It cements its lead by adding constructs that range from convenient syntax shorthands to avant-garde features that break the bounds of traditional SQL. In this chapter, we'll cover some SQL tidbits not often found in other databases. For this chapter, you should have a working knowledge of SQL; otherwise, you may not appreciate the labor-saving *amuse-bouche* that PostgreSQL brings to the table.

Views

In a relational database, tables store normalized data. To access these scattered tables of data, you write queries that join underlying tables. When you find yourself writing the same query over and over again, consider creating a view. Simply put, a view is nothing more than a query permanently stored in the database.

Some purists have argued that one should never directly query an underlying table except via views. This means you'd create a view for every table that you intend to query directly. The benefit is the added layer of indirection useful for controlling permissions and abstraction of logic. We find this to be sound advice, but laziness gets the better of us.

Views have evolved over the years. Prior to version 9.1, the only way to update data in a view was to use rules. You can see an example in Database Abstraction with Updatable Views (*http://bit.ly/1A0YJc4*). Although you can still use rules to update view data, the preferred way is to use INSTEAD OF triggers. The trigger approach complies with standards and is what you'll find in other database products.

Version 9.3 unveiled automatically updatable views. If your view draws from a single table and you include the primary key as an output column, you can issue an UPDATE command directly against your view. The underlying table will store the update.

Version 9.3 also introduced *materialized views*. When you mark a view as materialized, it will requery the data only when you issue the REFRESH command. The upside is that you're not wasting resources running complex queries repeatedly; the downside is that you might not have the most up-to-date data when you use the view.

Version 9.4 allows users to access materialized views while it refreshes. It also introduced the WITH CHECK OPTION modifier, which prevents inserts and updates outside the scope of the view.

Single Table Views

The simplest view draws from a single table. Always include the primary key if you intend to write data back to the table, as shown in Example 7-1.

Example 7-1. Single table view

```
CREATE OR REPLACE VIEW census.vw_facts_2011 AS
SELECT fact_type_id, val, yr, tract_id FROM census.facts WHERE yr = 2011;
```

As of version 9.3, you can alter the data in this view by using an INSERT, UPDATE, or DELETE command. Updates and deletes will abide by any WHERE condition you have as part of your view. For example, the following delete will delete only records whose yr is 2011:

```
DELETE FROM census.vw_facts_2011 WHERE val = 0;
```

And the following will not update any records:

```
UPDATE census.vw_facts_2011 SET val = 1 WHERE val = 0 AND yr = 2012;
```

Be aware that you can insert and update data that places it outside of the view's WHERE condition:

```
UPDATE census.vw_facts_2011 SET yr = 2012 WHERE yr = 2011;
```

The update does not violate the WHERE condition. But once it's executed, you would have emptied your view. For the sake of sanity, you may find it desirable to prevent updates or inserts that could put records outside of the scope of the WHERE. Version 9.4 introduced the WITH CHECK OPTION to accomplish this. Include this modifier when creating the view and PostgreSQL will forever balk at any attempts to add records outside the view and to update records that will put them outside the view. In our example view, our goal is to limit the vw_facts_2011 to allow inserts only of 2011 data and disallow updates of the yr to something other than 2011. To add this restriction, we revise our view definition as shown in Example 7-2.

Example 7-2. Single table view WITH CHECK OPTION

```
CREATE OR REPLACE VIEW census.vw_facts_2011 AS
SELECT fact_type_id, val, yr, tract_id
FROM census.facts WHERE yr = 2011 WITH CHECK OPTION;
```

Now try to run an update such as:

```
UPDATE census.vw_facts_2011 SET yr = 2012 WHERE val > 2942;
```

You'll get an error:

```
ERROR:  new row violates WITH CHECK OPTION for view "vw_facts_2011"
DETAIL:  Failing row contains (1, 25001010500, 2012, 2985.000, 100.00).
```

Using Triggers to Update Views

Views encapsulate joins among tables. When a view draws from more than one table, updating the underlying data with a simple command is no longer possible. Having more than one table introduces an inherent ambiguity when you're trying to change the underlying data, and PostgreSQL is not about to make an arbitrary decision for you. For instance, if you have a view that joins a table of countries with a table of provinces, and then decide to delete one of the rows, PostgreSQL won't know whether you intend to delete only a country, a province, or a particular country-province pairing. Nonetheless, you can still modify the underlying data through the view—using triggers.

Let's start by creating a view pulling from the facts table and a lookup table, as shown in Example 7-3.

Example 7-3. Creating view vw_facts

```
CREATE OR REPLACE VIEW census.vw_facts AS
SELECT y.fact_type_id, y.category, y.fact_subcats, y.short_name, x.tract_id, x.yr,
x.val, x.perc
FROM census.facts As x INNER JOIN census.lu_fact_types As y
ON x.fact_type_id = y.fact_type_id;
```

To make this view updatable with a trigger, you can define one or more INSTEAD OF triggers. We first define the trigger function to handle the trifecta: INSERT, UPDATE, DELETE. You can use any language to write the function, and you're free to name it whatever you like. We chose PL/pgSQL (*http://bit.ly/1w5ISeU*) in Example 7-4.

Example 7-4. Trigger function for vw_facts to insert, update, delete

```
CREATE OR REPLACE FUNCTION census.trig_vw_facts_ins_upd_del() RETURNS trigger AS
$$
BEGIN
    IF (TG_OP = 'DELETE') THEN ❶
        DELETE FROM census.facts AS f
        WHERE
            f.tract_id = OLD.tract_id AND f.yr = OLD.yr AND
            f.fact_type_id = OLD.fact_type_id;
        RETURN OLD;
    END IF;
    IF (TG_OP = 'INSERT') THEN ❷
        INSERT INTO census.facts(tract_id, yr, fact_type_id, val, perc)
        SELECT NEW.tract_id, NEW.yr, NEW.fact_type_id, NEW.val, NEW.perc;
```

```
        RETURN NEW;
    END IF;
    IF (TG_OP = 'UPDATE') THEN ❸
        IF
            ROW(OLD.fact_type_id, OLD.tract_id, OLD.yr, OLD.val, OLD.perc) !=
            ROW(NEW.fact_type_id, NEW.tract_id, NEW.yr, NEW.val, NEW.perc)
        THEN ❹
            UPDATE census.facts AS f
            SET
                tract_id = NEW.tract_id,
                yr = NEW.yr,
                fact_type_id = NEW.fact_type_id,
                val = NEW.val,
                perc = NEW.perc
            WHERE
                f.tract_id = OLD.tract_id AND
                f.yr = OLD.yr AND
                f.fact_type_id = OLD.fact_type_id;
            RETURN NEW;
        ELSE
            RETURN NULL;
        END IF;
    END IF;
END;
$$
LANGUAGE plpgsql VOLATILE;
```

❶ Handle deletes. Delete only the record with matching keys in the OLD record.

❷ Handle inserts.

❸ Handle the updates. Use the OLD record to determine which records to update with the NEW record data.

❹ Update rows only if at least one of the columns from facts table has changed.

Next, we bind the trigger function to the view, as shown in Example 7-5.

Example 7-5. Bind trigger function to view

```
CREATE TRIGGER census.trig_01_vw_facts_ins_upd_del
INSTEAD OF INSERT OR UPDATE OR DELETE ON census.vw_facts
FOR EACH ROW EXECUTE PROCEDURE census.trig_vw_facts_ins_upd_del();
```

Now when we update, delete, or insert into our view, it will update the underlying facts table instead:

```
UPDATE census.vw_facts SET yr = 2012 WHERE yr = 2011 AND tract_id =
'25027761200';
```

This will output a note:

```
Query returned successfully: 56 rows affected, 40 ms execution time.
```

If we try to update a field not in our update row comparison, as shown here, the update will not take place:

```
UPDATE census.vw_facts SET short_name = 'test';
```

The output message would be:

```
Query returned successfully: 0 rows affected, 931 ms execution time.
```

Although this example created a single trigger function to handle multiple events, we could have just as easily created a separate trigger and trigger function for each event.

Materialized Views

Materialized views cache the data fetched. This happens when you first create the view as well as when you run the REFRESH MATERIALIZED VIEW command. To use materialized views, you need at least version 9.3.

The most convincing cases for using materialized views are when the underlying query takes a long time and when having timely data is not critical. You encounter these scenarios when building online analytical processing (OLAP) applications.

Unlike with nonmaterialized views, you can add indexes to materialized views to speed up the read.

Example 7-6 demonstrates how to make a materialized view version of Example 7-1.

Example 7-6. Materialized view

```
CREATE MATERIALIZED VIEW census.vw_facts_2011_materialized AS
SELECT fact_type_id, val, yr, tract_id FROM census.facts WHERE yr = 2011;
```

Create an index on a materialized view as you would do on a regular table, as shown in Example 7-7.

Example 7-7. Add index to materialized view

```
CREATE UNIQUE INDEX ix
ON census.vw_facts_2011_materialized (tract_id, fact_type_id, yr);
```

For speedier access to a materialized view with a large number of records, you may want to control the physical sort of the data. The easiest way is to include an ORDER BY when you create the view. Alternatively, you can add a cluster index to the view. First create an index in the physical sort order you want to have. Then run the CLUSTER (*http://bit.ly/1FZWaeg*) command, passing it the index, as shown in Example 7-8.

Example 7-8. Clustering a view on an index

```
CLUSTER census.vw_facts_2011_materialized USING ix; ❶
CLUSTER census.vw_facts_2011_materialized; ❷
```

❶ Name the index to cluster on. Needed only during view creation.

❷ Each time you refresh, you must recluster the data.

The advantage of using ORDER BY in the materialized view over using the CLUSTER approach is that the sort is maintained with each REFRESH MATERIALIZED VIEW call, leaving no need to recluster. The downside is that ORDER BY generally adds more processing time to the REFRESH step of the view. You should test the effect of ORDER BY on performance of REFRESH before using it. One way to test is just to run the underlying query of the view with an ORDER BY clause.

To refresh the view in PostgreSQL 9.3 you must use:

```
REFRESH MATERIALIZED VIEW census.vw_facts_2011_materialized;
```

In PostgreSQL 9.4, to avoid locking tables that the views draw from during the refresh, you can use:

```
REFRESH MATERIALIZED VIEW CONCURRENTLY census.vw_facts_2011_materialized;
```

Limitations of materialized views include:

- You can't use CREATE OR REPLACE to edit an existing materialized view. You must drop and recreate the view even for the most trivial of changes. Use DROP MATERI ALIZED VIEW *name_of_view*. Sadly, you'll lose all your indexes.

- You need to run REFRESH MATERIALIZED VIEW to rebuild the cache. PostgreSQL doesn't perform automatic recaching of any kind. You need to resort to a mechanism such as a crontab, pgAgent job, or trigger to automate any kind of refresh. We have an example using triggers in Caching Data with Materialized Views and Statement-Level Triggers (*http://bit.ly/1yn1ySK*).

- Refreshing materialized views in version 9.3 is a blocking operation, meaning that the view will not be accessible during the refresh process. In version 9.4 you can lift this quarantine by adding the CONCURRENTLY keyword to your REFRESH command, provided that you have established a unique index on your view. The trade-off is that a concurrent refresh will take longer to complete.

Handy Constructions

In our many years of writing SQL, we have come to appreciate the little things that make better use of our typing. Only PostgreSQL offers some of the gems we present in this section. Often this means that the construction is not ANSI-compliant. If thy God demands strict observance to the ANSI SQL standard or if you need to compose SQL that you can port to other database products, abstain from the shortcuts that we'll be showing.

DISTINCT ON

One of our favorites is the DISTINCT ON. It behaves like DISTINCT, but with two enhancements: you can tell it which columns to consider as distinct and to sort the remaining columns. The first row after the sort will be returned. One little word—ON—replaces numerous lines of additional code to achieve the same result.

In Example 7-9, we demonstrate how to get the details of the first tract for each county.

Example 7-9. DISTINCT ON

```
SELECT DISTINCT ON (left(tract_id, 5))
    left(tract_id, 5) As county, tract_id, tract_name
FROM census.lu_tracts
ORDER BY county, tract_id;

county | tract_id    |                    tract_name
-------+-------------+----------------------------------------------------
25001  | 25001010100 | Census Tract 101, Barnstable County, Massachusetts
25003  | 25003900100 | Census Tract 9001, Berkshire County, Massachusetts
25005  | 25005600100 | Census Tract 6001, Bristol County, Massachusetts
25007  | 25007200100 | Census Tract 2001, Dukes County, Massachusetts
25009  | 25009201100 | Census Tract 2011, Essex County, Massachusetts
:
```

The ON modifier can take on multiple columns, all of which will be considered to determine uniqueness. The ORDER BY clause has to start with the set of columns in the DISTINCT ON; then you can follow with your preferred ordering.

LIMIT and OFFSET

LIMIT returns only the number of rows indicated, and OFFSET indicates the number of rows to skip. You can use them in tandem or separately. You almost always use them in conjunction with an ORDER BY. In Example 7-10, we demonstrate use of a positive offset. Leaving out the offset is the same as setting the offset to zero.

These constructs are not unique to PostgreSQL and are in fact copied from MySQL, although implementation differs widely among database products.

Example 7-10. First tract for counties 2 through 5

```
SELECT DISTINCT ON (left(tract_id, 5))
    left(tract_id, 5) As county, tract_id, tract_name
FROM census.lu_tracts
ORDER BY county, tract_id LIMIT 3 OFFSET 2;

county | tract_id    |                 tract_name
-------+-------------+-------------------------------------------------
25005  | 25005600100 | Census Tract 6001, Bristol County, Massachusetts
25007  | 25007200100 | Census Tract 2001, Dukes County, Massachusetts
25009  | 25009201100 | Census Tract 2011, Essex County, Massachusetts
```

Shorthand Casting

ANSI SQL defines a construct called CAST that allows you to morph one data type to another. For example, CAST('2011-1-11' AS date) casts the text 2011-1-1 to a date. PostgreSQL has a shorthand for doing this using a pair of colons, as in '2011-1-1'::date. This syntax is shorter and easier to apply for cases in which you can't directly cast from one type to another and have to intercede with one or more intermediary types, such as someXML::text::integer.

Multirow Insert

PostgreSQL supports the multirow constructor to insert more than one record at a time. Example 7-11 demonstrates how to use a multirow construction to insert data into the table we created in Example 6-2.

Example 7-11. Using multirow constructor to insert data

```
INSERT INTO logs_2011 (user_name, description, log_ts)
VALUES
    ('robe', 'logged in', '2011-01-10 10:15 AM EST'),
    ('lhsu', 'logged out', '2011-01-11 10:20 AM EST');
```

The latter portion of the multirow constructor starting with the VALUES keyword is often referred to as a *values list*. A values list can stand alone and effectively creates a table on the fly, as in Example 7-12.

Example 7-12. Using multirow constructor as a virtual table

```
SELECT *
FROM (
    VALUES
        ('robe', 'logged in', '2011-01-10 10:15 AM EST'::timestamptz),
        ('lhsu', 'logged out', '2011-01-11 10:20 AM EST'::timestamptz)
    ) AS l (user_name, description, log_ts);
```

When you use VALUES as stand-in for a virtual table, you need to specify the names for the columns and explicitly cast the values to the data types in the table, if the parser can't infer the data type from the data.

ILIKE for Case-Insensitive Search

PostgreSQL is case-sensitive. However, it does have mechanisms in place to do a case-insensitive search. You can apply the upper function to both sides of the ANSI LIKE operator, or you can simply use the ILIKE (~) operator found only in PostgreSQL:

```
SELECT tract_name FROM census.lu_tracts WHERE tract_name ILIKE '%duke%';

tract_name
--------------------------------------------------
Census Tract 2001, Dukes County, Massachusetts
```

```
Census Tract 2002, Dukes County, Massachusetts
Census Tract 2003, Dukes County, Massachusetts
Census Tract 2004, Dukes County, Massachusetts
Census Tract 9900, Dukes County, Massachusetts
```

Returning Functions

PostgreSQL allows functions that return sets to appear in the SELECT clause of an SQL statement. This is not true of many other databases, in which only scalar functions can appear in the SELECT.

Interweaving some set-returning functions inside an already complicated query could easily produce results that are beyond what you expect, because these functions usually result in the creation of new rows in the results. You must anticipate this if you'll be using the results as a subquery. In Example 7-13, we demonstrate this with a temporal version of generate_series. The example uses a table that we construct with:

```
CREATE TABLE interval_periods (i_type interval);
INSERT INTO interval_periods (i_type)
VALUES ('5 months'), ('132 days'), ('4862 hours');
```

Example 7-13. Set-returning function in SELECT

```
SELECT i_type,
    generate_series('2012-01-01'::date,'2012-12-31'::date,i_type) As dt
FROM interval_periods;
```

```
i_type      |          dt
------------+------------------------
5 months    | 2012-01-01 00:00:00-05
5 months    | 2012-06-01 00:00:00-04
5 months    | 2012-11-01 00:00:00-04
132 days    | 2012-01-01 00:00:00-05
132 days    | 2012-05-12 00:00:00-04
132 days    | 2012-09-21 00:00:00-04
4862 hours  | 2012-01-01 00:00:00-05
4862 hours  | 2012-07-21 15:00:00-04
```

Restricting DELETE, UPDATE, SELECT from Inherited Tables

When you query from a table that has child tables, the query drills down into the children, creating a union of all the child records satisfying the query condition. DELETE and UPDATE work the same way, drilling down the hierarchy for victims. Sometimes this is not desirable and you want data to come only from the table you specified, without the kids tagging along.

This is where the ONLY keyword comes in handy. We show an example of its use in Example 7-30, where we want to delete only those records from the production table that haven't migrated to the log table. Without the ONLY modifier, we'd end up deleting records from the child table that might have already been moved previously.

DELETE USING

Often, when you delete data from a table, you'll want to delete the data based on its presence in another set of data. You can use the table or queries you added to the USING clause in the WHERE clause of the delete to control what gets deleted. Multiple items can be included, separated by commas. Example 7-14 deletes all records from *census.facts* that correspond to a fact type of short_name = 's01'.

Example 7-14. DELETE USING

```
DELETE FROM census.facts
USING census.lu_fact_types As ft
WHERE facts.fact_type_id = ft.fact_type_id AND ft.short_name = 's01';
```

The standards-compliant way would be to use a clunkier IN expression in the WHERE clause.

Returning Affected Records to the User

The RETURNING clause is supported by ANSI SQL standards but not commonly found in other relational databases. We show an example of it in Example 7-30, where we return the records deleted. RETURNING can also be used for INSERT and UPDATE. For inserts into tables with serial keys, RETURNING is invaluable because it returns the key value of the new rows—something you don't know prior to the query execution. Although RETURNING is often accompanied by * for all fields, you can limit the fields as we do in Example 7-15.

Example 7-15. Returning changed records of an UPDATE with RETURNING

```
UPDATE census.lu_fact_types AS f
SET short_name = replace(replace(lower(f.fact_subcats[4]),' ','_'),':','')
WHERE f.fact_subcats[3] = 'Hispanic or Latino:' AND f.fact_subcats[4] > ''
RETURNING fact_type_id, short_name;
```

```
fact_type_id |                    short_name
-------------+-------------------------------------------------------
96           | white_alone
97           | black_or_african_american_alone
98           | american_indian_and_alaska_native_alone
99           | asian_alone
100          | native_hawaiian_and_other_pacific_islander_alone
101          | some_other_race_alone
102          | two_or_more_races
```

Composite Types in Queries

PostgreSQL automatically creates data types of all tables. Because data types derived from tables contain other data types, they are often called *composite data types*, or just *composites*. The first time you see a query with composites, you might be surprised. In fact, you might come across their versatility by accident when making a typo in an SQL statement. Try the following query:

```
SELECT x FROM census.lu_fact_types As x LIMIT 2;
```

At first glance, you might think that we left out a .* by accident, but check out the result:

```
x
-----------------------------------------------------------------
(86,Population,"{D001,Total:}",d001)
(87,Population,"{D002,Total:,""Not Hispanic or Latino:""}",d002)
```

Instead of erroring out, the preceding example returns the canonical representation of a lu_fact_type data type. Looking at the first record: 86 is the fact_type_id, Popula tion is the category, and {D001,Total:} is the fact_subcats property, which happens to be an array. Composites can serve as input to several useful functions, among which are array_agg and hstore (a function packaged with the hstore extension that converts a row into a key-value hstore object).

If you are using version 9.2 or higher and are building Ajax applications, you can take advantage of the built-in JSON (*http://json.org/*) support and use a combination of array_agg and array_to_json to output a query as a single JSON object. We demonstrate this in Example 7-16.

Example 7-16. Query to JSON output

```
SELECT array_to_json(array_agg(f)) As cat ❶
FROM (
    SELECT MAX(fact_type_id) As max_type, category ❷
    FROM census.lu_fact_types
    GROUP BY category
) As f;
```

This will give you an output of:

```
cats
-------------------------------------------------
[{"max_type":102,"category":"Population"},
{"max_type":153,"category":"Housing"}]
```

❶   Collects all these f rows into one composite array of fs.

❷   Defines a subquery with name f. f can then be used to reference each row in the subquery.

In version 9.3, the json_agg function chains together array_to_json and array_agg, offering both convenience and speed. In Example 7-17, we repeat Example 7-16 using json_agg. Example 7-17 will have the same output as Example 7-16.

Example 7-17. Query to JSON using json_agg

```
SELECT json_agg(f) As cats
FROM (
    SELECT MAX(fact_type_id) As max_type, category
    FROM census.lu_fact_types
    GROUP BY category
) As f;
```

DO

The DO command allows you to inject a piece of procedural code into your SQL on the fly. As an example, we'll load the data collected in Example 3-7 into production tables from our staging table. We'll use PL/pgSQL for our procedural snippet, but you're free to use other languages.

Example 7-18 generates a series of INSERT INTO SELECT statements. The SQL also performs an unpivot operation to convert columnar data into rows.

Example 7-18 is only a partial listing of code needed to build lu_fact_types. For full code, refer to the *building_census_tables.sql* file that is part of the book code and data download.

Example 7-18. Using DO to generate dynamic SQL

```
set search_path=census;
DROP TABLE IF EXISTS lu_fact_types;
CREATE TABLE lu_fact_types (
    fact_type_id serial,
    category varchar(100),
    fact_subcats varchar(255)[],
    short_name varchar(50),
    CONSTRAINT pk_lu_fact_types PRIMARY KEY (fact_type_id)
);

DO language plpgsql
$$
DECLARE var_sql text;
BEGIN
    var_sql := string_agg(
        'INSERT INTO lu_fact_types(category, fact_subcats, short_name)
        SELECT
            ''Housing'',
            array_agg(s' || lpad(i::text,2,'0') || ') As fact_subcats,
            ' || quote_literal('s' || lpad(i::text,2,'0')) || ' As short_name
        FROM staging.factfinder_import
        WHERE s' || lpad(I::text,2,'0') || ' ~ ''^[a-zA-Z]+'' ', ';'
    )
    FROM generate_series(1,51) As I; ❶
```

```
       EXECUTE var_sql;  ❷
END
$$;
```

❶ Use `string_agg` to form a set of SQL statements as a single string of the form
    `INSERT INTO lu_fact_type(...) SELECT ... WHERE s01 ~ '[a-zA-Z]+';`

❷ Execute the SQL.

FILTER Clause for Aggregates

New in version 9.4 is the `FILTER` clause for aggregates, recently standardized in ANSI
SQL. This replaces the standard `CASE WHEN` clause for reducing the number of rows
included in an aggregation. For example, suppose you used `CASE WHEN` to break out
average test scores by student, as shown in Example 7-19.

Example 7-19. CASE WHEN used in AVG

```
SELECT student,
    AVG(CASE WHEN subject ='algebra' THEN score ELSE NULL END) As algebra,
    AVG(CASE WHEN subject ='physics' THEN score ELSE NULL END) As physics
FROM test_scores
GROUP BY student;
```

The `FILTER` clause equivalent for Example 7-19 is shown in Example 7-20.

Example 7-20. FILTER used with AVG aggregate

```
SELECT student,
    AVG(score) FILTER (WHERE subject ='algebra') As algebra,
    AVG(score) FILTER (WHERE subject ='physics') As physics
FROM test_scores
GROUP BY student;
```

In the case of averages and sums and many other aggregates, the `CASE` and `FILTER` are
equivalent. The benefit is that `FILTER` is a little clearer in purpose and for large datasets
is faster. However, there are some aggregates—such as `array_agg`, which considers
NULLs—where the `CASE` statement gives you extra `NULL` values you don't want. In
Example 7-21 we try to get the list of scores for each subject of interest for each student
using the `CASE .. WHEN..` approach.

Example 7-21. CASE WHEN used in array_agg

```
SELECT student,
    array_agg(CASE WHEN subject ='algebra' THEN score ELSE NULL END) As algebra,
    array_agg(CASE WHEN subject ='physics' THEN score ELSE NULL END) As physics
FROM test_scores
GROUP BY student;
 student |         algebra          |         physics
---------+--------------------------+---------------------------------
```

```
jojo   | {74,NULL,NULL,NULL,74,..} | {NULL,83,NULL,NULL,NULL,79,..}
jdoe   | {75,NULL,NULL,NULL,78,..} | {NULL,72,NULL,NULL,NULL,72..}
robe   | {68,NULL,NULL,NULL,77,..} | {NULL,83,NULL,NULL,NULL,85,..}
lhsu   | {84,NULL,NULL,NULL,80,..} | {NULL,72,NULL,NULL,NULL,72,..}
(4 rows)
```

Observe that in Example 7-21 we get a bunch of NULLs in our arrays. We could work around this issue with some clever use of subselects, but most of those will be more verbose and slower than the FILTER alternative shown in Example 7-22.

Example 7-22. FILTER used with array_agg

```
SELECT student,
    array_agg(score) FILTER (WHERE subject ='algebra') As algebra,
    array_agg(score) FILTER (WHERE subject ='physics') As physics
FROM test_scores
GROUP BY student;

 student | algebra | physics
---------+---------+---------
 jojo    | {74,74} | {83,79}
 jdoe    | {75,78} | {72,72}
 robe    | {68,77} | {83,85}
 lhsu    | {84,80} | {72,72}
```

The FILTER clause works for all aggregate functions, not just aggregate functions built into PostgreSQL.

Window Functions

Window functions are a common ANSI SQL feature supported in PostgreSQL since version 8.4. A window function has the prescience to see and use data beyond the current row; hence the term *window*. A window defines which other rows need to be considered in addition to the current row. Windows let you add aggregate information to each row of your output where the aggregation involves other rows in the same window. Window functions such as row_number and rank are useful for ordering your data in sophisticated ways that use rows outside the selected results but within a window.

Without window functions, you'd have to resort to using joins and subqueries to poll neighboring rows. On the surface, window functions violate the set-based principle of SQL, but we mollify the purist by claiming that they are merely shorthand. You can find more details and examples in Window Functions (*http://bit.ly/1yUcnhM*).

Example 7-23 gives you a quick start. Using a window function, we can obtain both the detail data and the average value for all records with fact_type_id of 86 in one single SELECT. Note that the WHERE clause is always evaluated *before* the window function.

Example 7-23. The basic window

```
SELECT tract_id, val, AVG(val) OVER () as val_avg
FROM census.facts
WHERE fact_type_id = 86;

  tract_id   |    val    |        val_avg
------------+-----------+-----------------------
25001010100 |  2942.000 | 4430.0602165087956698
25001010206 |  2750.000 | 4430.0602165087956698
25001010208 |  2003.000 | 4430.0602165087956698
25001010304 |  2421.000 | 4430.0602165087956698
:
```

The OVER sets the boundary of the window. In this example, because the parentheses contain no constraint, the window covers all the rows in our WHERE. So the average is average across all rows with fact_type_id = 86. The clause also morphed our conventional AVG aggregate function into a window aggregate function. For each row, PostgreSQL submits all the rows in the window to the AVG aggregation and outputs the value as part of the row. Because our window has multiple rows, the result of the aggregation is repeated. Notice that with window functions, we were able to perform an aggregation without GROUP BY. Furthermore, we were able to rejoin the aggregated result back with the other variables without using a formal join.

You can use all SQL aggregate functions as window functions. In addition, you'll find ROW, RANK, LEAD, and others listed in Window Functions (*http://bit.ly/1FUiJ2d*).

PARTITION BY

You can run a window function over rows containing particular values instead of using the whole table. This requries the addition of a PARTITION BY clause, which instructs PostgreSQL to take the aggregate over the indicated rows. In Example 7-24, we repeat what we did in Example 7-23 but partition our window by county code, which is always the first five characters of the tract_id column.

Example 7-24. Partition our window by county code

```
SELECT tract_id, val, AVG(val) OVER (PARTITION BY left(tract_id,5)) As val_avg_coun
ty
FROM census.facts WHERE fact_type_id = 2 ORDER BY tract_id;

  tract_id   |    val    |     val_avg_county
------------+-----------+-----------------------
25001010100 |  1765.000 | 1709.9107142857142857
25001010206 |  1366.000 | 1709.9107142857142857
25001010208 |   984.000 | 1709.9107142857142857
:
25003900100 |  1920.000 | 1438.2307692307692308
25003900200 |  1968.000 | 1438.2307692307692308
```

```
25003900300 | 1211.000 | 1438.2307692307692308
:
```

ORDER BY

Window functions also allow an ORDER BY in the OVER clause. Without getting too abstruse, the best way to think about this is that all the rows in the window will be ordered as indicated by ORDER BY, and the window function will consider only rows that range from the first row in the window up to and including the current row in the window or partition. The classic example uses the ROW_NUMBER function to sequentially number rows. In Example 7-25, we demonstrate how to number our census tracts in alphabetical order. To arrive at the row number, ROW_NUMBER counts all rows up to and including current row based on the order dictated by the ORDER BY.

Example 7-25. Numbering using ROW_NUMBER window function

```
SELECT ROW_NUMBER() OVER (ORDER BY tract_name) As rnum, tract_name
FROM census.lu_tracts
ORDER BY rnum LIMIT 4;

rnum |                     tract_name
-----+------------------------------------------------------
1    | Census Tract 1, Suffolk County, Massachusetts
2    | Census Tract 1001, Suffolk County, Massachusetts
3    | Census Tract 1002, Suffolk County, Massachusetts
4    | Census Tract 1003, Suffolk County, Massachusetts
```

In Example 7-25, we also have an ORDER BY for the entire query. Don't get confused between this and the ORDER BY that's specific to the window function.

You can combine ORDER BY with PARTITION BY, restarting the ordering for each partition. Example 7-26 returns to our example of county codes.

Example 7-26. Combining PARTITION BY and ORDER BY

```
SELECT tract_id, val,
    SUM(val) OVER (PARTITION BY left(tract_id,5) ORDER BY val) As sum_county_ordered
FROM census.facts
WHERE fact_type_id = 2
ORDER BY left(tract_id,5), val;

   tract_id  |   val    | sum_county_ordered
-------------+----------+--------------------
 25001014100 | 226.000  |            226.000
 25001011700 | 971.000  |           1197.000
 25001010208 | 984.000  |           2181.000
 :
 25003933200 | 564.000  |            564.000
 25003934200 | 593.000  |           1157.000
 25003931300 | 606.000  |           1763.000
 :
```

The key observation to make in the output is how the sum changes from row to row. The ORDER BY clause means that the sum will be taken only from the beginning of the partition to the current row, giving you a running total, where the location of the current row in the list is dictated by the ORDER BY. For instance, if your row is in the fifth row in the third partition, the sum will cover only the first five rows in the third partition. We put an ORDER BY left(tract_id,5), val at the end of the query so you could easily see the pattern, but keep in mind that the ORDER BY of the query is independent of the ORDER BY in each OVER clause.

You can explicitly control the rows under consideration by adding a RANGE or ROWS clause: ROWS BETWEEN CURRENT ROW AND 5 FOLLOWING.

PostgreSQL also supports window naming, which is useful if you have the same window for each of your window columns. Example 7-27 demonstrates how to name windows, as well as how to use the LEAD and LAG window functions to show a record value before and after for a given partition.

Example 7-27. Naming windows, demonstrating LEAD and LAG

```
SELECT * FROM (
    SELECT
        ROW_NUMBER() OVER( wt ) As rnum, ❶
        substring(tract_id,1, 5) As county_code,
        tract_id,
        LAG(tract_id,2) OVER wt As tract_2_before,
        LEAD(tract_id) OVER wt As tract_after
    FROM census.lu_tracts
    WINDOW wt AS (PARTITION BY substring(tract_id,1, 5) ORDER BY tract_id) ❷
) As x
WHERE rnum BETWEEN 2 and 3 AND county_code IN ('25007','25025')
ORDER BY county_code, rnum;
```

```
rnum | county_code |  tract_id   | tract_2_before | tract_after
-----+-------------+-------------+----------------+-------------
2    | 25007       | 25007200200 |                | 25007200300
3    | 25007       | 25007200300 | 25007200100    | 25007200400
2    | 25025       | 25025000201 |                | 25025000202
3    | 25025       | 25025000202 | 25025000100    | 25025000301
```

❷   Naming our window wt window.

❶   Using our window name instead of retyping.

Both LEAD and LAG take an optional step argument that defines how many rows to skip forward or backward; the step can be positive or negative. LEAD and LAG return NULL when trying to retrieve rows outside the window partition. This is a possibility that you always have to account for.

In PostgreSQL, any aggregate function you create can be used as a window function. Other databases tend to limit window functions to using built-in aggregates such as AVG, SUM, MIN, and MAX.

Common Table Expressions

Essentially, common table expressions (CTEs) allow you to define a query that can be reused in a larger query. PostgreSQL has supported this feature since version 8.4 and expanded the feature in version 9.1 with the introduction of writable CTEs. CTEs act as temporary tables defined within the scope of the statement; they're gone once the enclosing statement has finished execution.

There are three ways to use CTEs:

Basic CTE
> This is your plain-vanilla CTE, used to make your SQL more readable or to encourage the planner to materialize a costly intermediate result for better performance.

Writable CTE
> This is an extension of the basic CTE with UPDATE, INSERT, and DELETE commands. A common final step in the CTE is to return changed rows.

Recursive CTE
> This puts an entirely new whirl on standard CTE. The rows returned by a recursive CTE vary during the execution of the query.

PostgreSQL allows you to have a CTE that is both writable and recursive.

Basic CTEs

The basic CTE looks like Example 7-28. The WITH keyword introduces the CTE.

Example 7-28. Basic CTE

```
WITH cte AS (
    SELECT
        tract_id, substring(tract_id,1, 5) As county_code,
        COUNT(*) OVER(PARTITION BY substring(tract_id,1, 5)) As cnt_tracts
    FROM census.lu_tracts
)
SELECT MAX(tract_id) As last_tract, county_code, cnt_tracts
FROM cte
WHERE cnt_tracts > 100
GROUP BY county_code, cnt_tracts;
```

cte is the name of the CTE in Example 7-28, defined using a SELECT statement to contain three columns: tract_id, county_code, and cnt_tracts. The main SELECT refers to the CTE.

You can stuff as many CTEs as you like, separated by commas, in the WITH clause, as shown in Example 7-29. The order of the CTEs matters in that CTEs defined later can call CTEs defined earlier, but not vice versa.

Example 7-29. Multiple CTEs

```
WITH
    cte1 AS (
        SELECT
            tract_id,
            substring(tract_id,1, 5) As county_code,
            COUNT(*) OVER (PARTITION BY substring(tract_id,1,5)) As cnt_tracts
        FROM census.lu_tracts
    ),
    cte2 AS (
        SELECT
            MAX(tract_id) As last_tract,
            county_code,
            cnt_tracts
        FROM cte1
        WHERE cnt_tracts < 8 GROUP BY county_code, cnt_tracts
    )
SELECT c.last_tract, f.fact_type_id, f.val
FROM census.facts As f INNER JOIN cte2 c ON f.tract_id = c.last_tract;
```

Writable CTEs

The writable CTE was introduced in version 9.1 and extends the CTE to allow for update, delete, and insert statements. We'll revisit our logs tables that we created in Example 6-2, adding another child table and populating it:

```
CREATE TABLE logs_2011_01_02 (
    PRIMARY KEY (log_id),
    CONSTRAINT chk
        CHECK (log_ts >= '2011-01-01' AND log_ts < '2011-03-01')
)
INHERITS (logs_2011);
```

In Example 7-30, we move data from our parent 2011 table to our new child Jan-Feb 2011 table. The ONLY keyword is described in "Restricting DELETE, UPDATE, SELECT from Inherited Tables" on page 129 and the RETURNING keyword in "Returning Affected Records to the User" on page 130.

Example 7-30. Writable CTE moving data from one branch to another

```
WITH t AS (
    DELETE FROM ONLY logs_2011 WHERE log_ts < '2011-03-01' RETURNING *
```

```
)
INSERT INTO logs_2011_01_02 SELECT * FROM t;
```

Recursive CTE

The official documentation for PostgreSQL (*http://www.postgresql.org/docs/current/interactive/queries-with.html*) describes it best: "The optional RECURSIVE modifier changes CTE from a mere syntactic convenience into a feature that accomplishes things not otherwise possible in standard SQL." A more interesting CTE is one that uses a recursively defining construct to build an expression. PostgreSQL recursive CTEs utilize UNION ALL to combine tables, a kind of combination that can be done repeatedly as the query adds the tables over and over.

To turn a basic CTE to a recursive one, add the RECURSIVE modifier after the WITH. WITH RECURSIVE can contain a mix of recursive and nonrecursive table expressions. In most other databases, the RECURSIVE keyword is not necessary to denote recursion.

A common use of recursive CTEs is to represent message threads and other tree-like structures. We have an example of this in Recursive CTE to Display Tree Structures (*http://bit.ly/1yx9ggR*).

In Example 7-31, we query the system catalog to list the cascading table relationships we have in our database.

Example 7-31. Recursive CTE

```
WITH RECURSIVE tbls AS (
    SELECT
        c.oid As tableoid,
        n.nspname AS schemaname,
        c.relname AS tablename ❶
    FROM
        pg_class c LEFT JOIN
        pg_namespace n ON n.oid = c.relnamespace LEFT JOIN
        pg_tablespace t ON t.oid = c.reltablespace LEFT JOIN
        pg_inherits As th ON th.inhrelid = c.oid
    WHERE
        th.inhrelid IS NULL AND
        c.relkind = 'r'::"char" AND c.relhassubclass
    UNION ALL
    SELECT
        c.oid As tableoid,
        n.nspname AS schemaname,
        tbls.tablename || '->' || c.relname AS tablename  ❷ ❸
    FROM
        tbls INNER JOIN
        pg_inherits As th ON th.inhparent = tbls.tableoid INNER JOIN
        pg_class c ON th.inhrelid = c.oid LEFT JOIN
        pg_namespace n ON n.oid = c.relnamespace LEFT JOIN
    pg_tablespace t ON t.oid = c.reltablespace
```

```
)
SELECT * FROM tbls ORDER BY tablename; ❹

tableoid | schemaname |          tablename
---------+------------+-----------------------------------
3152249 | public     | logs
3152260 | public     | logs->logs_2011
3152272 | public     | logs->logs_2011->logs_2011_01_02
```

❶   Get a list of all tables that have child tables but no parent table.

❷   This is the recursive part; it gets all children of tables in `tbls`.

❸   The names of the child tables start with the parental name.

❹   Return parents and all child tables. Because we sort by the table name, which
    prepends the parent name, all child tables will follow their parents in their
    output.

Lateral Joins

LATERAL is a new ANSI SQL construction in version 9.3. Here's the motivation behind
it: suppose you perform joins on two tables or subqueries; normally, the pair partici-
pating in the join are independent units and can't read data from each other. For example,
the following interaction would generate an error because `l.year = 2011` is not a column in righthand side of the join:

```
SELECT *
    FROM
        census.facts L
        INNER JOIN
        (SELECT *
            FROM census.lu_fact_types
            WHERE category =
                CASE WHEN L.yr = 2011 THEN 'Housing' ELSE category END
        ) R
    ON L.fact_type_id = R.fact_type_id;
```

Now add the LATERAL keyword, and the error is gone:

```
SELECT * FROM census.facts L INNER JOIN LATERAL
    (SELECT * FROM census.lu_fact_types
      WHERE category = CASE WHEN L.yr = 2011 THEN 'Housing' ELSE category END) R
    ON L.fact_type_id = R.fact_type_id;
```

LATERAL lets you share data in columns across two tables in a FROM clause. However, it
works only in one direction: the righthand side can draw from the left side, but not vice
versa.

There are situations when you should avail yourself of LATERAL to avoid extremely convoluted syntax. In Example 7-32, a column in the left side serves as a parameter in the generate_series function of the right side:

```
CREATE TABLE interval_periods(i_type interval);
INSERT INTO interval_periods (i_type)
VALUES ('5 months'), ('132 days'), ('4862 hours');
```

Example 7-32. Using LATERAL with generate_series

```
SELECT i_type, dt
FROM
    interval_periods CROSS JOIN LATERAL
    generate_series('2012-01-01'::date, '2012-12-31'::date, i_type) AS dt
WHERE NOT (dt = '2012-01-01' AND i_type = '132 days'::interval);
```

```
 i_type     |           dt
------------+------------------------
 5 mons     | 2012-01-01 00:00:00-05
 5 mons     | 2012-06-01 00:00:00-04
 5 mons     | 2012-11-01 00:00:00-04
 132 days   | 2012-05-12 00:00:00-04
 132 days   | 2012-09-21 00:00:00-04
 4862:00:00 | 2012-01-01 00:00:00-05
 4862:00:00 | 2012-07-21 15:00:00-04
```

Lateral is also helpful for using values from the lefthand side to limit the number of rows returned from the righthand side. Example 7-33 uses LATERAL to return, for each superuser who has used our site within the last 100 days, the last five logins and what they were up to. Tables used in this example were created in "TYPE OF" on page 111 and "Basic Table Creation" on page 109.

Example 7-33. Using LATERAL to limit rows from a joined table.

```
SELECT u.user_name, l.description, l.log_ts
FROM
    super_users AS u CROSS JOIN LATERAL (
    SELECT description, log_ts
    FROM logs
    WHERE
        log_ts > CURRENT_TIMESTAMP - interval '100 days' AND
        logs.user_name = u.user_name
    ORDER BY log_ts DESC LIMIT 5
    ) AS l;
```

Although you can achieve the same results by using window functions, lateral joins yield faster results with a more succinct syntax.

You can use multiple lateral joins in your SQL and even chain them in sequence as you would when joining more than two subqueries. You can sometimes get away with omitting the LATERAL keyword; the query parser is smart enough to figure out a lateral join if you have a correlated expression. But we advise that you always include the keyword for the sake of clarity. Also, you'll get an errors if you write your statement assuming the use of a lateral join but run the statement on a prelateral version PostgreSQL. Without the keyword, PostgreSQL might end up performing a join with unintended results.

Other database products also offer lateral joins, although they don't abide by the ANSI moniker. In Oracle, you'd use a table pipeline construct. In SQL Server, you'd use CROSS APPLY or OUTER APPLY.

## CHAPTER 8

Writing Functions

With most databases, you can string a series of SQL statements together and treat them as a unit. PostgreSQL is no exception. Different databases ascribe different names for this unit: stored procedures, user-defined functions, and so on. PostgreSQL simply refers to them as *functions*.

Aside from marshalling SQL statements, functions often add the capability to control the execution of the SQL using procedural languages (PLs). In PostgreSQL, you have your choice of languages when it comes to writing functions. SQL, C, PL/pgSQL, PL/Perl, and PL/Python are often packaged with installers. As of version 9.2, you'll also find PL/V8 (*http://code.google.com/p/plv8js/*), which allows you to write procedural functions in JavaScript. PL/V8 should be an exciting addition for web developers and a darling companion to the built-in json and jsonb data types covered in "JSON" on page 98.

You can always install additional languages such as PL/R (*http://bit.ly/12sf8v9*), PL/Java (*http://bit.ly/1vUsHxX*), PL/sh (*http://bit.ly/1yUcwll*), PL/TSQL (*http://bit.ly/1q2gCHA*), and even experimental ones geared for high-end processing and artificial intelligence, such as PL/Scheme (*http://bit.ly/1Iam4hw*) or PL/OpenCL (*http://bit.ly/1q2gFDe*). You can find a listing of available languages in Procedural Languages (*http://bit.ly/1vUsHxX*).

Anatomy of PostgreSQL Functions

Function Basics

Regardless of which languages you choose for writing functions, all functions share a similar structure, shown in Example 8-1.

Example 8-1. Basic function structure

```
CREATE OR REPLACE FUNCTION func_name(arg1 arg1_datatype DEFAULT arg1_default)
RETURNS some type | set of some type | TABLE (..) AS
$$
BODY of function
$$
LANGUAGE language_of_function
```

Argument names are optional, but if the arguments are not named, you cannot call them using the arg1 := ... argument syntax. Arguments can also take a default value, which makes the argument optional. Optional arguments should be positioned after nonoptional arguments.

Functional definitions often include additional qualifiers to optimize execution and to enforce security:

LANGUAGE

The language must be one installed in your database. Obtain a list with the SELECT lanname FROM pg_language; query.

VOLATILITY

This setting clues the query planner into whether outputs can be cached and used across multiple calls. Your choices are:

IMMUTABLE

The function will always return the same output for the same input.

STABLE

The function will return the same value for the same inputs within the same query.

VOLATILE

The function can return different values with each call, even with the same inputs. Functions that change data or depend on environment settings like system time should be marked as VOLATILE. This is the default.

Keep in mind that the volatility setting is merely a hint to the planner. The default value of VOLATILE ensures that the planner will always recompute the plan. If you use one of the other values, the planner can still choose to forgo caching if it decides that recomputing is more cost-effective.

STRICT

A strict function will always return NULL if any inputs are NULL, and the planner in that case will skip evaluating the function altogether. Unless the function is adorned with the STRICT qualifier, the query planner deems it not to be strict. When writing SQL functions, be careful when using STRICT, because it could prevent the planner from taking advantage of indexes. Read our aticle STRICT on SQL Functions (*http://bit.ly/1rX26C5*) for more details.

COST

This is a relative measure of computational intensiveness. SQL and PL/pgSQL functions default to 100 and C functions to 1. This affects the order that the planner will follow when evaluating functions in a WHERE clause, and the likelihood of caching. The higher you set the cost, the more computation the planner will assume the function needs.

ROWS

Applies only to functions returning sets of records. This value provides an estimate of how many rows will be returned. The planner will take this value into consideration when coming up with the best strategy.

SECURITY DEFINER

This causes execution to take place within the security context of the owner of the function. If omitted, the function executes under the context of the user calling the function. This qualifier is useful for giving people rights to update a table via a function when they do not have direct update privileges.

Triggers and Trigger Functions

No database of merit should lack triggers, which automatically detect and handle changes in data. PostgreSQL allows you to attach triggers to both tables and views.

Triggers can actuate at both the statement level and the row level. Statement triggers run once per SQL statement, whereas row triggers run for each row affected by the SQL. For example, if you execute an UPDATE statement that affects 1,500 rows, a statement-level update trigger will fire only once, whereas the row-level trigger can fire up to 1,500 times.

You can further refine the timing of the trigger by making a distinction between BEFORE, AFTER, and INSTEAD OF triggers. A BEFORE trigger fires prior to the execution of the statement, giving you a chance to cancel or back up data before the change. An AFTER trigger fires after statement execution, giving you a chance to retrieve the new data values. AFTER triggers are often used for logging or replication purposes. INSTEAD OF triggers execute in lieu of the statement. You can attach BEFORE and AFTER triggers only to tables, and INSTEAD OF triggers only to views.

You can also adorn a trigger with a WHEN condition to control which rows being updated will fire the trigger, or an UPDATE OF columns_list clause to have the trigger fire only if certain columns are updated. To gain a more nuanced understanding of the interplay between triggers and the underlying statement, see the official documentation: Overview of Trigger Behavior (*http://bit.ly/1vUsXgq*). We also demonstrated a view-based trigger in Example 7-4.

PostgreSQL offers specialized functions to handle triggers. These are called *trigger functions* and behave like any other function and have the same basic structure. Where they differ is in the input parameter and the output type. A trigger function never takes an argument, because internally the function already has access to the data and can modify it.

A trigger function always outputs a data type called a `trigger`. Because PostgreSQL trigger functions are no different from any other function, you can reuse the same trigger function across different triggers. This is usually not the case for other databases, in which each trigger has its own nonreusable handler code.

In PostgreSQL, each trigger must have exactly one associated triggering function to handle the firing. To apply multiple triggering functions, you must create multiple triggers against the same event. The alphabetical order of the trigger name determines the order of firing. Each trigger will have access to the revised data from the previous trigger. Triggers themselves do not constitute separate transactions. If any trigger issues a rollback, all data amended by earlier triggers fired by the same event will roll back.

You can use almost any language to create trigger functions, with SQL being the notable exception. PL/pgSQL is by far the most popular language. We demonstrate writing trigger functions using PL/pgSQL in "Writing Trigger Functions in PL/pgSQL" on page 154.

Aggregates

Most other databases limit you to ANSI SQL built-in aggregate functions such as `MIN`, `MAX`, `AVG`, `SUM`, and `COUNT`. In PostgreSQL, you don't have this limit. If you need a more esoteric aggregate function, you're welcome to write your own. Because you can use any aggregate function in PostgreSQL as a window function (see "Window Functions" on page 134), you can get twice the use out of any aggregate function that you author.

You can write aggregates in almost any language, SQL included. An aggregate is generally composed of one or more functions. It must have at least a state transition function to perform the computation; usually this function runs repeatedly to create a single output from two input rows. You can also specify optional functions to manage initial and final states. You can also use a different language for each of the subfunctions. We have various examples of building aggregates using PL/pgSQL, PL/Python, and SQL in the article PostgreSQL Aggregates (*http://bit.ly/1CNAd3Y*).

Regardless of which language you use to code the functions, the glue that brings them all together is the `CREATE AGGREGATE` command:

```
CREATE AGGREGATE my_agg (input data type) (
SFUNC=state function name,
STYPE=state type,
FINALFUNC=final function name,
INITCOND=initial state value, SORTOP=sort_operator
);
```

The final function is optional, but if specified, it must take as input the result of the state function. The state function always takes a data type as the input along with the result of the last call to the state function. Sometimes this result is what you want as the result of the aggregate function, and sometimes you want to run a final function to massage the result. The initial condition is also optional. When it is present, the command uses it to initialize the state value.

The optional sort operator can serve as the associated sort operator for a MIN- or MAX-like aggregate. It is used to take advantage of indexes. It is just an operator name such as > and <. It should be used only when the two following statements are equivalent:

```
SELECT agg(col) FROM sometable;
```

```
SELECT col FROM sometable ORDER BY col USING sortop LIMIT 1;
```

 The PostgreSQL 9.4 CREATE AGGREGATE structure was expanded to include support for creating moving aggregates, which are useful with window functions that move the window. See PostgreSQL 9.4: CREATE AGGREGATE (*http://bit.ly/12IFIRA*) for details.

Aggregates need not depend on a single column. If you need more than one column for your aggregate (an example is a built-in covariance function), see How to Create Multi-Column Aggregates (*http://bit.ly/1s2pEQD*) for guidance.

SQL language functions are easy to write. You don't have fancy control flow commands to worry about, and you probably have a good grasp of SQL to begin with. When it comes to writing aggregates, you can get pretty far with the SQL language alone. We demonstrate aggregates in "Writing SQL Aggregate Functions" on page 152.

Trusted and Untrusted Languages

Function languages are characterized by trust level: trusted versus untrusted. Many—but not all—languages offer both a trusted and untrusted version. The term *trusted* connotes that the language can do no harm to the underlying operating system:

Trusted

A trusted language lacks access to the server's file system beyond the data cluster. It therefore cannot execute OS commands. Users of any level can create functions in a trusted language. Languages such as SQL, PL/pgSQL, and PL/Perl are trusted.

Untrusted

An untrusted language can interact with the OS. It can execute OS functions and call web services. Only superusers have the privilege of authoring functions in an untrusted language. However, a superuser can grant permission to another role to run an untrusted function. By convention, languages that are untrusted end in the letter U (PL/PerlU, PL/PythonU, etc.).

Writing Functions with SQL

Although SQL is mostly a language for issuing queries, it can also be used to write functions that run against the database. In PostgreSQL, doing so is fast and easy. Take your existing SQL statements, add a functional header and footer, and you're done. The ease comes at a price. You won't have fancy control languages to create conditional execution branches. More restrictively, you can't run dynamic SQL statements that you assemble on the fly depending on the arguments passed into the function.

On the positive side, the query planner can peek into an SQL function and optimize execution depending on what it sees, a process called *inlining*. Planners treat other languages as black boxes. Inlining lets SQL functions take advantage of indexes and collapse repetitive computations.

Basic SQL Function

Example 8-2 shows a primitive SQL function that inserts a row into a table and returns a scalar value.

Example 8-2. SQL function that returns the identifier of inserted record

```
CREATE OR REPLACE FUNCTION write_to_log(param_user_name varchar, param_description text)
RETURNS integer AS
$$
INSERT INTO logs(user_name, description) VALUES($1, $2)
RETURNING log_id;
$$
LANGUAGE 'sql' VOLATILE;
```

To call the function, execute something like:

```
SELECT write_to_log('alejandro', 'Woke up at noon.') As new_id;
```

Similarly, you can update data with an SQL function and return a scalar or void, as shown in Example 8-3.

Example 8-3. SQL function to update a record

```
CREATE OR REPLACE FUNCTION
update_logs(log_id int, param_user_name varchar, param_description text)
RETURNS void AS
$$
UPDATE logs SET user_name = $2, description = $3
 , log_ts = CURRENT_TIMESTAMP WHERE log_id = $1;
$$
LANGUAGE 'sql' VOLATILE;
```

To execute:

```
SELECT update_logs(12, 'alejandro', 'Fell back asleep.');
```

 Prior to version 9.2, SQL functions could use only the ordinal position of the input arguments in the body of the function. From version 9.2 onward, you have the option of using named arguments. For example, you can write param_1, param_2 instead of $1, $2. Languages other than SQL did not have this limitation before version 9.2.

Functions in almost all languages can return sets. SQL functions are no exception. There are three common approaches to do this: the ANSI SQL standard RETURNS TABLE syntax, OUT parameters, and composite data types. The RETURNS TABLE approach requires at least version 8.3 and is closest to what you'll find in other database products. In Example 8-4, we demonstrate how to write the same function three ways.

Example 8-4. Examples of function returning sets

Using RETURNS TABLE:

```
CREATE OR REPLACE FUNCTION select_logs_rt(param_user_name varchar)
RETURNS TABLE (log_id int, user_name varchar(50), description text, log_ts time
stamptz) AS
$$
SELECT log_id, user_name, description, log_ts FROM logs WHERE user_name = $1;
$$
LANGUAGE 'sql' STABLE;
```

Using OUT parameters:

```
CREATE OR REPLACE FUNCTION select_logs_out(param_user_name varchar, OUT log_id int
, OUT user_name varchar, OUT description text, OUT log_ts timestamptz)
RETURNS SETOF record AS
$$
SELECT * FROM logs WHERE user_name = $1;
$$
LANGUAGE 'sql' STABLE;
```

Using a composite type:

```
CREATE OR REPLACE FUNCTION select_logs_so(param_user_name varchar)
RETURNS SETOF logs AS
$$
SELECT * FROM logs WHERE user_name = $1;
$$
LANGUAGE 'sql' STABLE;
```

Call all these functions using:

```
SELECT * FROM select_logs_xxx('alejandro');
```

Writing SQL Aggregate Functions

This section demonstrates how to create a geometric mean aggregate function with SQL. A *geometric mean* (*http://www.buzzardsbay.org/geomean.htm*) is the *n*th root of a product of *n* positive numbers ($(x1*x2*x3...xn)^{(1/n)}$). It has various uses in finance, economics, and statistics. A geometric mean substitutes for the more common arithmetic mean when the numbers range across vastly different scales. A more suitable computational formula uses logarithms to transform a multiplicative process to an additive one ($EXP(SUM(LN(x))/n)$). We'll be using this method in our example.

For our geometric mean aggregate, we'll use two subfunctions: a state transition function to sum the logs (see Example 8-5) and a final function to exponentiate the logs. We'll also specify an initial condition of zero when we put everything together.

Example 8-5. Geometric mean aggregate: state function

```
CREATE OR REPLACE FUNCTION geom_mean_state(prev numeric[2], next numeric)
RETURNS numeric[2] AS
$$
SELECT
  CASE
    WHEN $2 IS NULL OR $2 = 0 THEN $1
    ELSE ARRAY[COALESCE($1[1],0) + ln($2), $1[2] + 1]
  END;
$$
LANGUAGE sql IMMUTABLE;
```

Our state transition function takes two inputs: the previous state passed in as an array with two elements, and the next addend in the summation. If the next argument evaluates to NULL or zero, the state function returns the prior state. Otherwise, it returns a new array in which the first element is the sum of the logs and the second element is the running count.

We also need a final function, shown in Example 8-6, that divides the sum from the state transition by the count.

Example 8-6. Geometric mean aggregate: final function

```
CREATE OR REPLACE FUNCTION geom_mean_final(numeric[2])
RETURNS numeric AS
$$
SELECT CASE WHEN $1[2] > 0 THEN exp($1[1]/$1[2]) ELSE 0 END;
$$
LANGUAGE sql IMMUTABLE;
```

Now we stitch all the subfunctions together in our aggregate definition, as shown in Example 8-7. (Note that our aggregate has an initial condition that is the same data type as what is returned by our state function.)

Example 8-7. Geometric mean aggregate: assembling the pieces

```
CREATE AGGREGATE geom_mean(numeric) (
SFUNC=geom_mean_state,
STYPE=numeric[],
FINALFUNC=geom_mean_final,
INITCOND='{0,0}'
);
```

Let's take our geom_mean function for a test drive. In Example 8-8, we compute a heuristic rating for racial diversity and list the top five most racially diverse counties in Massachusetts.

Example 8-8. Top five most racially diverse counties using geometric mean

```
SELECT left(tract_id,5) As county, geom_mean(val) As div_county
FROM census.vw_facts
WHERE category = 'Population' AND short_name != 'white_alone'
GROUP BY county
ORDER BY div_county DESC LIMIT 5;
```

```
county |     div_county
-------+--------------------
25025  | 85.1549046212833364
25013  | 79.5972921427888918
25017  | 74.7697097102419689
25021  | 73.8824162064128504
25027  | 73.5955049035237656
```

Let's put things into overdrive and try our new aggregate function as a window aggregate, as shown in Example 8-9.

Example 8-9. Top five most racially diverse census tracts with averages

```
WITH X AS (SELECT
  tract_id,
  left(tract_id,5) As county,
  geom_mean(val) OVER (PARTITION BY tract_id) As div_tract,
  ROW_NUMBER() OVER (PARTITION BY tract_id) As rn,
  geom_mean(val) OVER(PARTITION BY left(tract_id,5)) As div_county
FROM census.vw_facts WHERE category = 'Population' AND short_name != 'white_alone'
)
SELECT tract_id, county, div_tract, div_county
FROM X
WHERE rn = 1
ORDER BY div_tract DESC, div_county DESC LIMIT 5;
```

```
tract_id   | county |     div_tract      |     div_county
-----------+--------+--------------------+--------------------
25025160101 | 25025 | 302.6815688785928786 | 85.1549046212833364
25027731900 | 25027 | 265.6136902148147729 | 73.5955049035237656
25021416200 | 25021 | 261.9351057509603296 | 73.8824162064128504
25025130406 | 25025 | 260.3241378371627137 | 85.1549046212833364
25017342500 | 25017 | 257.4671462282508267 | 74.7697097102419689
```

Writing PL/pgSQL Functions

When your functional needs outgrow SQL, turning to PL/pgSQL is a common practice. PL/pgSQL surpasses SQL in that you can declare local variables using DECLARE and you can incorporate control flow.

Basic PL/pgSQL Function

To demonstrate syntax differences from SQL, in Example 8-10 we rewrite Example 8-4 as a PL/pgSQL function.

Example 8-10. Function to return a table using PL/pgSQL

```
CREATE FUNCTION select_logs_rt(param_user_name varchar)
RETURNS TABLE (log_id int, user_name varchar(50), description text, log_ts time
stamptz) AS
$$
BEGIN RETURN QUERY
    SELECT log_id, user_name, description, log_ts FROM logs
     WHERE user_name = param_user_name;
END;
$$
LANGUAGE 'plpgsql' STABLE;
```

Writing Trigger Functions in PL/pgSQL

Because you can't write trigger functions in SQL, PL/pgSQL is your next-best bet. In this section, we'll demonstrate how to write a basic trigger function in PL/pgSQL.

We proceed in two steps. First, we write the trigger function. Second, we explicitly attach the trigger function to the appropriate trigger. The second step is a powerful feature of PostgreSQL that decouples the function handling the trigger from the trigger itself. You can attach the same trigger function to multiple triggers, adding another level of reuse not found in other databases. Because each trigger function can stand on its own, you have your choice of languages, and mixing is completely OK. For a single triggering event, you can set up multiple triggers, each with functions written in a different language. For example, you can have a trigger email a client written in PL/PythonU or PL/PerlU and another trigger write to a log file with plPgSQL.

A basic trigger function and accompanying trigger is demonstrated in Example 8-11.

Example 8-11. Trigger function to timestamp new and changed records

```
CREATE OR REPLACE FUNCTION trig_time_stamper() RETURNS trigger AS ❶
$$
BEGIN
    NEW.upd_ts := CURRENT_TIMESTAMP;
    RETURN NEW;
END;
```

```
$$
LANGUAGE plpgsql VOLATILE;

CREATE TRIGGER trig_1
BEFORE INSERT OR UPDATE OF session_state, session_id ❷
ON web_sessions
FOR EACH ROW EXECUTE PROCEDURE trig_time_stamper();
```

❶ Defines the trigger function. This function can be used on any table that has a
upd_ts column. It updates the upd_ts field to the current time before returning
the changed record. Trigger functions that change values of a row should be
called only in the BEFORE event, because in the AFTER event, all updates to the
NEW record will be ignored.

❷ This is a new feature introduced in version 9.0 that allows us to limit the firing
of the trigger so it happens only if specified columns have changed. Prior to
version 9.0, the trigger would fire on any update and you would need to perform
a column-wise comparison using OLD.some_column and NEW.some_column to
determine what changed. (This feature is not supported for INSTEAD OF triggers.)

Writing PL/Python Functions

Python is a slick language with a vast number of available libraries. PostgreSQL is the
only database we know of that'll let you compose functions using Python. Since version
9.0, PostgreSQL supports both Python 2 and Python 3.

Although you can install both plpython2u and plpython3u in the
same database, you can't use both during the same session. This
means that you can't write a query that calls both plpython2u and
plpython3u functions. You may encounter a third extension called
plpythonu; this is an alias for plpython2u and left around for backward compatibility.)

In order to use PL/Python, you first need to install Python on your server. For Windows
and Mac, Python installers are available at *http://www.python.org/download/*. For
Linux/Unix systems, Python binaries are usually available via the various distributions.
For details, see PL/Python (*http://bit.ly/1zvCawf*). After installing Python, install the
PostgreSQL Python extension:

```
CREATE EXTENSION plpython2u;
CREATE EXTENSION plpython3u;
```

Make absolutely sure that you have Python properly running on your server before
attempting to install the extension or else you will run into errors that could be difficult
to troubleshoot.

The extensions are compiled against a specific minor version of Python. You should install the minor version of Python that matches what your plpythonu extensions were compiled against. For example, if your plpython2u was compiled against Python 2.7, you should install Python 2.7.

Basic Python Function

PostgreSQL automatically converts PostgreSQL data types to Python data types and back. PL/Python is capable of returning arrays and composite types. You can use PL/Python to write triggers and create aggregate functions. We've demonstrated some of these in the Postgres OnLine Journal, in PL/Python Examples (*http://bit.ly/12IG0rC*).

Python allows you to perform feats that aren't possible in PL/pgSQL. In Example 8-12, we demonstrate how to write a PL/Python function to do a text search of the online PostgreSQL document site.

Example 8-12. Searching PostgreSQL documents using PL/Python

```
CREATE OR REPLACE FUNCTION postgresql_help_search(param_search text)
RETURNS text AS
$$
import urllib, re ❶
response = urllib.urlopen(
  'http://www.postgresql.org/search/?u=%2Fdocs%2Fcurrent%2F&q=' + param_search
) ❷
raw_html = response.read() ❸
result = raw_html[raw_html.find("<!-- docbot goes here -->") : raw_html.find("<!--
pgContentWrap -->") - 1] ❹
result = re.sub('<[^<]+?>', '', result).strip() ❺
return result ❻
$$
LANGUAGE plpython2u SECURITY DEFINER STABLE;
```

❶   Imports the libraries we'll be using.

❷   Performs a search after concatenating the search term.

❸   Reads the response and saves the retrieved HTML to a variable called raw_html.

❹   Saves the part of the raw_html that starts with <!-- docbot goes here --> and ends just before the beginning of <!-- pgContentWrap --> into a new variable called result.

❺   Removes leading and trailing HTML symbols and whitespace.

❻   Returns result.

Calling Python functions is no different from calling functions written in other languages. In Example 8-13, we use the function we created in Example 8-12 to output the result with three search terms.

Example 8-13. Using Python function in a query

```
SELECT search_term, left(postgresql_help_search(search_term), 125) As result
FROM (VALUES ('regexp_match'),('pg_trgm'),('tsvector')) As x(search_term);
```

Recall that PL/Python is an untrusted language, without a trusted counterpart. This means only superusers can write functions using PL/Python, and the function can interact with the file system of the OS. Example 8-14 takes advantage of the untrusted nature of PL/Python to retrieve file listings from a directory. Keep in mind that from the perspective of the OS, a PL/Python function runs under the context of the post gres user account created during installation, so you need to be sure that this account has adequate access to the relevant directories.

Example 8-14. List files in directories

```
CREATE OR REPLACE FUNCTION list_incoming_files()
RETURNS SETOF text AS
$$
import os
return os.listdir('/incoming')
$$
LANGUAGE 'plpython2u' VOLATILE SECURITY DEFINER;
```

Run the function in Example 8-14 with the following query:

```
SELECT filename
FROM list_incoming_files() As filename
WHERE filename ILIKE '%.csv'
```

Writing PL/V8, PL/CoffeeScript, and PL/LiveScript Functions

PL/V8 (*http://code.google.com/p/plv8js/wiki/PLV8*) (aka PL/JavaScript) is a trusted language built atop the Google V8 (*http://code.google.com/p/v8/*) engine. It allows you to write functions in JavaScript and interface with the JSON data type. It is not part of the core PostgreSQL offering, so you won't find it in most popular PostgreSQL distributions except Heroku. You can always compile it from source. For Windows, we've built PL/V8 extension windows binaries (*http://bit.ly/1u09x5B*). You can download them from our Postgres OnLine site for PostgreSQL 9.2 (*http://bit.ly/1q2h6xo*), and from our Postgres OnLine site for PostgreSQL 9.3 (*http://bit.ly/1IamTXq*) (both 32-bit and 64-bit).

Although you can compile PL/V8 version 9.1, we strongly suggest that you upgrade to 9.2, with native JSON support, instead.

When you add PL/V8 binaries to your PostgreSQL setup, you get not one, but three JavaScript-related languages:

PL/V8 (plv8)

This is the basic language that serves as the basis for the other two JavaScript languages.

PL/CoffeeScript (plcoffee)

This language lets you write functions in CoffeeScript (*http://coffeescript.org/*). CoffeeScript is JavaScript with a more succinct syntax structure that resembles Python. Like Python, it relies on indentation to impart context but does away with annoying curly braces.

PL/LiveScript (plls)

PL/LiveScript allows you to write functions in LiveScript (*http://livescript.net/*), a fork of CoffeeScript. LiveScript is similar to CoffeeScript but with some added syntactic condiments. This article promotes LiveScript as a superior alternative to CoffeeScript: 10 Reasons to Switch from CoffeeScript to LiveScript (*http://bit.ly/1BltJrs*). If anything, LiveScript does have more Python, F#, and Haskell features than CoffeeScript. If you're looking for a language with a lighter footprint than PL/Python and that is trusted, you might want to give LiveScript a try.

PL/CoffeeScript and PL/LiveScript are compiled using the same PL/V8 library. Their functionality is therefore identical to that of PL/V8. In fact, you can easily convert back to PL/V8 if they don't suit your taste buds. All three languages are trusted. This means they can't access OS file systems, but they can be used by nonsuperusers to create functions.

Example 8-15 has the commands to install the three languages using extensions. For each database where you'd like to install the support, you must run these lines. You need not install all three if you choose not to.

Example 8-15. Installing all PL/V8 family of languages

```
CREATE EXTENSION plv8;
CREATE EXTENSION plcoffee;
CREATE EXTENSION plls;
```

The PL/V8 family of languages has many key qualities that make them stand apart from PL/pgSQL, some of which you'll only find in other high-end procedural languages like PL/R:

- Generally faster numeric processing than SQL and PL/pgSQL.
- The ability to create window functions. You can't do this using SQL, PL/pgSQL, or PL/Python. (You can in PL/R and C, though.)
- The ability to create triggers and aggregate functions.
- Support for prepared statements, subtransactions, inner functions, classes, and try-catch error handling.

- The ability to dynamically generate executable code using an `eval` function.

- JSON support, allowing for looping over and filtering of JSON objects.

- Access to functions from `DO` commands.

- Node.js (*http://nodejs.org*) users, and other users who want to use Javascript for building network applications, will appreciate that PL/V8 and Node.js are built on the same Google V8 engine and that many of the libraries available for Node.js will work largely unchanged when used in PL/V8. There is an extension called `plv8x` (*https://github.com/clkao/plv8x*) that makes using Node.js modules and modules you build easier to reuse in PL/V8.

You can find several examples on our site of PL/V8 use, some even involving copying fairly large bodies of JavaScript code that we pulled from the Web and wrapping them in a PL/V8 wrapper, as detailed in Using PLV8 to build JSON Selectors (*http://bit.ly/1Blrkgm*). The PL/V8 family mates perfectly with web applications because much of the same client-side JavaScript logic can be reused. More important, it makes a great all-purpose language for developing numeric functions, updating data, and so on.

Basic Functions

One of the great benefits of PL/V8 is that you can use any JavaScript function in your PL/V8 functions with minimal change. For example, you'll find many JavaScript examples on the Web to validate email address. We arbitrarily picked one and made a PL/V8 out of it in Example 8-16.

Example 8-16. Using PL/V8 to validate email address

```
CREATE OR REPLACE FUNCTION
validate_email(email text) returns boolean as
$$
 var re = /\S+@\S+\.\S+/;
 return re.test(email);
$$ LANGUAGE plv8 IMMUTABLE STRICT;
```

Our code uses a JavaScript regex object to check the email address. To use the function, see Example 8-17.

Example 8-17. Calling PL/V8 email validator

```
SELECT email, validate_email(email) AS is_valid
 FROM (VALUES ('alexgomezq@gmail.com')
 ,('alexgomezqgmail.com'),('alexgomezq@gmailcom')) AS x (email);
```

which outputs:

```
      email        | is_valid
---------------------+----------
 alexgomezq@gmail.com | t
```

```
alexgomezqgmail.com   | f
alexgomezq@gmailcom   | f
```

Although you can code the same function using the PL/pgSQL and PostgreSQL's own regular expression support, we guiltlessly poached someone else's time-tested code and wasted no time of our own. If you're a web developer and find yourself having to validate data on both the client side and the database side, using PL/V8 could halve your development efforts, pretty much by cutting and pasting.

You can store a whole set of these validation functions in a modules table. You can then inject results onto the page but also use the validation functions directly in the database, as described in Andrew Dunstan's "Loading Useful Modules in PLV8" (*http://bit.ly/1q2htrz*). This is possible because the `eval` function is part of the PL/V8 JavaScript language. The built-in function allows you to compile functions at startup for later use.

We fed Example 8-17 through an online converter (*js2coffee.org*), and added a `return` statement to generate its CoffeeScript counterpart in Example 8-18.

Example 8-18. PL/Coffee validate email function

```
CREATE OR REPLACE FUNCTION
validate_email(email text) returns boolean as
$$
    re = /\S+@\S+\.\S+/
    return re.test email
$$
LANGUAGE plcoffee IMMUTABLE STRICT;
```

CoffeeScript doesn't look all that different from JavaScript, except for the lack of parentheses, curly braces, and semicolons. The LiveScript version looks exactly like the CoffeeScript except with a `LANGUAGE plls` specifier.

Writing Aggregate Functions with PL/V8

In Example 8-19, using PL/V8, we redo the geometric mean aggregate function ("Writing SQL Aggregate Functions" on page 152).

Example 8-19. PL/V8 geometric mean aggregate: state transition function

```
CREATE OR REPLACE FUNCTION geom_mean_state(prev numeric[2], next numeric)
RETURNS numeric[2] AS
$$
    return (next == null || next == 0) ? prev :
    [(prev[0] == null)? 0: prev[0] + Math.log(next), prev[1] + 1];
$$
LANGUAGE plv8 IMMUTABLE;
```

Example 8-20. PL/V8 geometric mean aggregate: final function

```
CREATE OR REPLACE FUNCTION geom_mean_final(in_num numeric[2])
RETURNS numeric AS
$$
  return in_num[1] > 0 ? Math.exp(in_num[0]/in_num[1]) : 0;
$$
LANGUAGE plv8 IMMUTABLE;
```

The final `CREATE AGGREGATE` puts all the pieces together and looks more or less the same in all languages. Our PL/V8 variant is shown in Example 8-21.

Example 8-21. PL/V8 geometric mean aggregate: putting all the pieces together

```
CREATE AGGREGATE geom_mean(numeric) (
  SFUNC=geom_mean_state,
  STYPE=numeric[],
  FINALFUNC=geom_mean_final,
  INITCOND='{0,0}'
);
```

When you run Example 8-9, calling to our new PL/V8 function, you get the same answers, but the PL/V8 version is two to three times faster. For mathematical operations, you'll find that PL/V8 functions are 10 to 20 times faster than their SQL counterparts in many cases.

## CHAPTER 9

Query Performance Tuning

Sooner or later, we'll all face a query that takes just a bit longer to execute than we have patience for. The best and easiest fix is to perfect the underlying SQL, followed by adding indexes and updating planner statistics. To guide you in these pursuits, PostgreSQL comes with a built-in explainer that informs you how the query planner is going to execute your SQL. Armed with your knack for writing flawless SQL, your instinct to sniff out useful indexes, and the insight of the explainer, you should have no trouble getting your queries to run as fast as your hardware budget will allow.

EXPLAIN

The easiest tool for targeting query performance problems is use of the EXPLAIN and EXPLAIN (ANALYZE) commands. These have been around ever since the early years of PostgreSQL. Since then it has matured into a full-blown tool capable of reporting highly detailed information about the query execution. Along the way, it added more output formats. Since version 9.0, you can even dump the output to XML, JSON, or YAML.

Perhaps the most exciting enhancement for the casual user came several years back when pgAdmin introduced graphical EXPLAIN. With a hard and long stare, you can identify where the bottlenecks are in your query, which tables are missing indexes, and whether the path of execution took an unexpected turn.

EXPLAIN Options

To use the nongraphical version of EXPLAIN, simply preface your SQL with the words EXPLAIN or EXPLAIN (ANALYZE).

EXPLAIN by itself will give you just an idea of how the planner intends to execute the query without running it. Adding the ANALYZE argument, as in EXPLAIN (ANALYZE), will execute the query and give you a comparative analysis of expected versus actual.

Adding the VERBOSE argument, as in EXPLAIN (VERBOSE), will report down to the columnar level. Adding the BUFFERS argument, which must be used in conjunction with ANALYZE, as in EXPLAIN (ANALYZE, BUFFERS), will report *share hits*. The higher this number, the more records were already in memory from prior queries, meaning that the planner did not have to go back to disk to reretrieve them.

An EXPLAIN that provides all details, including timing, output of columns, and buffers, would look something like EXPLAIN (ANALYZE, VERBOSE, BUFFERS) *your_query_here*;.

It goes without saying that to use graphical EXPLAIN, you need a GUI such as pgAdmin. After launching graphical EXPLAIN via pgAdmin, compose the query as usual, but instead of executing it, choose EXPLAIN or EXPLAIN (ANALYZE) from the drop-down menu. To those of you who pride yourself on being self-sufficient using only the command-line, all we can say is: good for you!

If you use EXPLAIN (ANALYZE) on a data-changing statement such as UPDATE or INSERT and you want to see the plan without making the actual data change, wrap the statement in a transaction that you abort: place BEGIN before the statement and ROLLBACK after it.

Sample Runs and Output

Let's try an example. First we'll use the EXPLAIN (ANALYZE) command with a table we created in Example 4-1 and Example 4-2.

In order to ensure that the planner doesn't use an index, we first drop the primary key from our table:

```
ALTER TABLE census.hisp_pop DROP CONSTRAINT IF EXISTS hisp_pop_pkey;
```

This is so that by running the query in Example 9-1, we can see the most basic of plans in action, the sequential scan strategy.

Example 9-1. EXPLAIN (ANALYZE) of a sequential scan

```
EXPLAIN (ANALYZE) SELECT tract_id, hispanic_or_latino
FROM census.hisp_pop
WHERE tract_id = '25025010103';
```

Example 9-2 shows the output of Example 9-1.

Example 9-2. EXPLAIN (ANALYZE) output

```
Seq Scan on hisp_pop
    (cost=0.00..33.48 rows=1 width=16)
    (actual time=0.205..0.339 rows=1 loops=1)
    Filter: ((tract_id)::text = '25025010103'::text)
    Rows Removed by Filter: 1477
Total runtime: 0.360 ms
```

In almost all EXPLAIN plans, you'll see a breakdown by steps, and each step can have have child steps. Each step will have a reported cost that looks something like cost=0.00..33.48, as shown in Example 9-2. The first number, 0.00, is the estimated startup cost, and the second number, 33.48, is the total estimated cost of the step. The startup is the time before retrieval of data and could include scanning of indexes, joins of tables, etc. For sequential scan steps, the startup cost is zero because the planner mindlessly pulls all data so retrieval begins right away.

Keep in mind that the cost measure is reported in arbitrary units, which vary based on hardware and are largely controlled by planner cost constants. As such, it makes sense to use only as an estimate when comparing different plans on same server. The planner's job is to pick the plan with the lowest estimated overall costs.

Because we opted to include the ANALYZE argument in Example 9-1, the planner will run the query, and we're blessed with the actual timings as well.

From the plan in Example 9-2, we can see that the planner elected a sequential scan because it couldn't find any indexes. The additional tidbit of information Rows Removed by Filter: 1477 is the number of rows that the planner examined before excluding them from the output.

In PostgreSQL 9.4, the output makes a distinction between planning time and execution time. Planning time is the amount of time it takes for the planner to come up with the execution plan, whereas the execution time is everything that follows. The output in version 9.4 would look as shown in Example 9-3.

Example 9-3. EXPLAIN (ANALYZE) output in version 9.4

```
Seq Scan on hisp_pop
    (cost=0.00..33.48 rows=1 width=16) (actual time=0.213..0.346 rows=1 loops=1)
    Filter: ((tract_id)::text = '25025010103'::text)
    Rows Removed by Filter: 1477
Planning time: 0.095 ms
Execution time: 0.381 ms
```

Let's now add back our primary key:

```
ALTER TABLE census.hisp_pop ADD CONSTRAINT hisp_pop_pkey PRIMARY KEY(tract_id);
```

Repeating Example 9-1, we now see the plan output in Example 9-4 (PostgreSQL 9.4 style).

Example 9-4. EXPLAIN (ANALYZE) output of index strategy plan

```
Index Scan using idx_hisp_pop_tract_id_pat on hisp_pop
    (cost=0.28..8.29 rows=1 width=16) (actual time=0.018..0.019 rows=1 loops=1)
    Index Cond: ((tract_id)::text = '25025010103'::text)
Planning time: 0.110 ms
Execution time: 0.046 ms
```

The planner concludes that using the index is cheaper than a sequential scan and switches to an index scan. The estimated overall cost dropped from 33.48 to 8.29. The startup cost is no longer zero, because the planner first scans the index, then pulls the matching records from data pages (or from memory if in shared buffers already). You'll also notice that the planner no longer needed to scan 1,477 records. This greatly reduced the cost.

More complex queries, such as Example 9-5, include more child steps. The final step is always listed first, and its total cost and time equals the sum of all its child steps. The output indents the child steps.

Example 9-5. EXPLAIN (ANALYZE) with GROUP BY and SUM

```
EXPLAIN (ANALYZE)
SELECT left(tract_id,5) AS county_code, SUM(white_alone) As w
FROM census.hisp_pop
WHERE tract_id BETWEEN '25025000000' AND '25025999999'
GROUP BY county_code;
```

The accompanying output of Example 9-5 is shown in Example 9-6, showing a grouping and sum.

Example 9-6. EXPLAIN (ANALYZE) output of HashAggregate strategy plan

```
HashAggregate
    (cost=29.57..32.45 rows=192 width=16) (actual time=0.664..0.664 rows=1 loops=1)
    Group Key: "left"((tract_id)::text, 5)
    -> Bitmap Heap Scan on hisp_pop
        (cost=10.25..28.61 rows=192 width=16) (actual time=0.441..0.550 rows=204
loops=1)
      Recheck Cond:
        (((tract_id)::text >= '25025000000'::text) AND
        ((tract_id)::text <= '25025999999'::text))
      Heap Blocks: exact=15
      -> Bitmap Index Scan on hisp_pop_pkey
          (cost=0.00..10.20 rows=192 width=0) (actual time=0.421..0.421 rows=204
loops=1)
        Index Cond:
          (((tract_id)::text >= '25025000000'::text) AND
          ((tract_id)::text <= '25025999999'::text))
Planning time: 4.835 ms
Execution time: 0.732 ms
```

The parent step of Example 9-6 is the Hash Aggregate. It contains a child step of Bitmap Heap Scan, which in turn contains a child step of Bitmap Index Scan. In this example, because this is the first time we're running this query, our planning time greatly overshadows the execution time. However, PostgreSQL caches plans, so if we were to run this query or a similar one, we should be rewarded with a much reduced planning time.

Graphical Outputs

If reading the output is giving you a headache, see Figure 9-1 for the graphical EXPLAIN (ANALYZE).

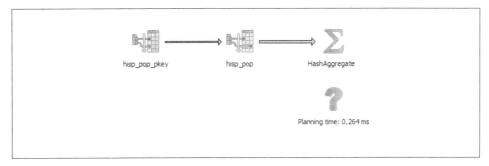

Figure 9-1. Graphical EXPLAIN output

You can get more detailed information about each part by mousing over the node in the display.

Before wrapping up this section, we must pay homage to the tabular explain plan (*http://explain.depesz.com*) created by Hubert Lubaczewski. Using his site, you can copy and paste the text output of your EXPLAIN output, and it will show you a beautifully formatted table, as shown in Figure 9-2.

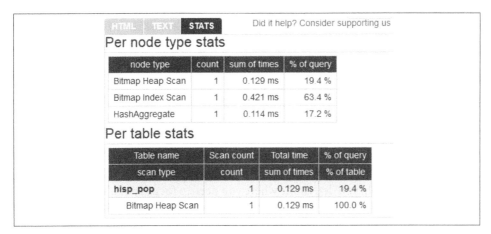

Figure 9-2. Online EXPLAIN stats

In the HTML tab, you'll see a nicely reformatted color-coded table of the plan, with problem areas highlighted in vibrant colors, as shown in Figure 9-3. It has columns for exclusive time (time consumed by the parent step) and inclusive time (the time of the parent step plus its child steps).

#	exclusive	inclusive	rows x	rows	loops	node
1.	0.114	0.664	↑ 192.0	1	1	→ HashAggregate (cost=29.57..32.45 rows=192 width=16) (actual time=0.664..0.664 rows=1 loops=1) Group Key: "left"((tract_id)::text, 5)
2.	0.129	0.550	↓ 1.1	204	1	→ Bitmap Heap Scan on hisp_pop (cost=10.25..28.61 rows=192 width=16) (actual time=0.441..0.550 rows=204 loops=1) Recheck Cond: (((tract_id)::text >= '25025000000'::text) AND ((tract_id)::text <= '25025999999'::text)) Heap Blocks: exact=15
3.	0.421	0.421	↓ 1.1	204	1	→ Bitmap Index Scan on hisp_pop_pkey (cost=0.00..10.20 rows=192 width=0) (actual time=0.421..0.421 rows=204 loops=1) Index Cond: (((tract_id)::text >= '25025000000'::text) AND ((tract_id)::text <= '25025999999'::text))

Figure 9-3. Tabular explain output

Although the HTML table in Figure 9-3 provides much the same information as our plain-text output, the color coding and breakout of numbers makes it easier to see where our estimates are off. For example, yellow, brown, and red highlight areas where you should focus.

The *rows x* column is the expected number of rows, while the *rows* column shows the actual number. This reveals that although our final step was expecting 192 records, it received just one, and the bitmap scan returned 203 false positives caught by the recheck. Bad row estimates often stem from out-of-date table statistics. It's always a good idea to run an analysis on tables before a long query to update the statistics.

Gathering Statistics on Statements

The first step in optimizing performance is to determine which queries are bottlenecks. One monitoring extension useful for getting a handle on your most costly queries is pg_stat_statements (*http://bit.ly/1IanI2K*). This extension provides metrics on running queries: which are the most frequently run queries and how long each takes. Studying these metrics will help you determine where you need to focus your query optimization efforts.

pg_stat_statements comes packaged with most PostgreSQL distributions but must be preloaded on startup to initiate its data-collection process:

1. In *postgresql.conf*, change `shared_preload_libraries = ''` to `shared_pre load_libraries = 'pg_stat_statements'`.

2. In the customized options section of *postgresql.conf*, add the lines:

```
        pg_stat_statements.max = 10000
        pg_stat_statements.track = all
```

3. Restart your `postgresql` service.

4. In any database you want to use for monitoring, enter `CREATE EXTENSION pg_stat_statements;`.

The extension provides two key features:

- A view called `pg_stat_statements`, which shows all the databases to which the currently connected user has access.

- A function called `pg_stat_statements_reset`, which flushes the query log. This function can be run only by superusers.

The query in Example 9-7 lists the top five most costly queries in the `post gresql_book` database.

Example 9-7. Expensive queries in specific database

```
SELECT
    query, calls, total_time, rows,
    100.0*shared_blks_hit/nullif(shared_blks_hit+shared_blks_read,0) AS hit_percent
FROM pg_stat_statements As s INNER JOIN pg_database As d On d.oid = s.dbid
WHERE d.datname = 'postgresql_book'
ORDER BY total_time DESC LIMIT 5;
```

Guiding the Query Planner

The planner's behavior is driven by the presence of indexes, cost settings, strategy settings, and its general perception of the distribution of data. In this section, we'll go over various approaches for optimizing the planner's behavior.

Strategy Settings

Although the PostgreSQL query planner doesn't accept index hints as some other database products do, you can disable various strategy settings on a per-query or permanent basis to dissuade the planner from going down an unproductive path. All planner optimizing settings are documented in the section Planner Method Configuration (*http://www.postgresql.org/docs/current/static/runtime-config-query.html*) of the manual. By default, all strategy settings are enabled, arming the planner for maximum flexibility. You can disable various strategies if you have some prior knowledge of the data. Keep in mind that disabling doesn't necessarily mean that the planner will be barred from using the strategy. You're only making a polite request to the planner to avoid it.

Two settings that we occasionally disable are the `enable_nestloop` and `enable_seqs can`. The reason is that these two strategies tend to be the slowest and should be used only as a last resort. Although you can disable them, the planner can still use them when it has no viable alternative. When you do see them being used, it's a good idea to double-check that the planner is using them out of necessity, not out of ignorance. One quick way to check is to disable them.

How Useful Is Your Index?

When the planner decides to perform a sequential scan, it plans to loop through all the rows of a table. It opts for this route when it finds no index that could satisfy a query condition, or it concludes that using an index is more costly than scanning the table. If you disable the sequential scan strategy, and the planner still insists on using it, this means that indexes are missing or that the planner thinks that the indexes you have in place won't be helpful for the particular query. Two common mistakes people make are to leave useful indexes out of their tables or to put in indexes that can't be used by their queries. An easy way to check whether your indexes are used is to query the `pg_stat_user_indexes` and `pg_stat_user_tables` views using the `pg_stat_state ments` extension described in "Gathering Statistics on Statements" on page 168.

Let's start off with a query against the table we created in Example 7-18. We'll add a GIN index on the array column. GIN indexes are among the few indexes you can use to index arrays:

```
CREATE INDEX idx_lu_fact_types ON census.lu_fact_types USING gin (fact_subcats);
```

To test our index, we'll execute a query to find all rows with subcats containing "White alone" or "Asian alone." We explicitly enabled sequential scan even though it's the default setting, just to be sure. The accompanying EXPLAIN output is shown in Example 9-8.

Example 9-8. Allow planner choose sequential scan

```
set enable_seqscan = true;
EXPLAIN (ANALYZE)
SELECT *
FROM census.lu_fact_types
WHERE fact_subcats && '{White alone, Black alone}'::varchar[];

Seq Scan on lu_fact_types
    (cost=0.00..2.85 rows=2 width=200) (actual time=0.066..0.076 rows=2 loops=1)
Filter: (fact_subcats && '{"White alone","Black alone"}'::character varying[]) Rows
Removed by Filter: 66
Planning time: 0.182 ms
Execution time: 0.108 ms
```

Observe that when `enable_seqscan` is enabled, our index is not being used and the planner has chosen to do a sequential scan. This could be because our table is so small or because the index we have is no good for this query. If we repeat the query but turn off sequential scan beforehand, as shown in Example 9-9, we can see that we have succeeded in forcing the planner to use the index.

Example 9-9. Disable sequential scan, coerce index use

```
set enable_seqscan = false;
EXPLAIN (ANALYZE)
SELECT *
FROM census.lu_fact_types
WHERE fact_subcats && '{White alone, Black alone}'::varchar[];
```

```
Bitmap Heap Scan on lu_fact_types (cost=12.02..14.04 rows=2 width=200) (actual
time=0.058..0.058 rows=2 loops=1) Recheck Cond: (fact_subcats && '{"White
alone","Black alone"}'::character varying[]) Heap Blocks: exact=1 -> Bitmap Index
Scan on idx_lu_fact_types
        (cost=0.00..12.02 rows=2 width=0) (actual time=0.048..0.048 rows=2 loops=1)
          Index Cond: (fact_subcats && '{"White alone","Black alone"}'::character
varying[])
Planning time: 0.230 ms
Execution time: 0.119 ms
```

From this plan, we learn that our index can be used, but because the estimated cost is more than doing a sequential scan, the planner under normal circumstances will opt for the sequential scan. The planner was right in its assessment because our index execution time turns out to be a little more than a sequential scan. As we add more data to our table, we'll probably find that the planner changes strategies to an index scan.

In contrast to the previous example, suppose we were to write a query of the form:

```
SELECT * FROM census.lu_fact_types WHERE 'White alone' = ANY(fact_subcats);
```

We would discover that, regardless of how we set enable_seqscan, the planner will always perform a sequential scan because the index we have in place can't service this query. So it is important to consider which indexes will be useful and to write queries to take advantage of them. And experiment, experiment, experiment!

Table Statistics

Despite what you might think or hope, the query planner is not a magician. Its decisions follow prescribed logic that's far beyond the scope of this book. The rules that the planner follows depend heavily on the current state of the data. The planner can't possibly scan all the tables and rows prior to formulating its plan. That would be self-defeating. Instead, it relies on aggregated statistics about the data.

Having accurate and current stats is crucial for the planner to make the right decision. If stats differ greatly from reality, the planner will often come up with bad plans, the most detrimental of these being unnecessary sequential table scans. Generally, only about 20 percent of the entire table is sampled to produce stats. This percentage could be even lower for very large tables. You can control the number of rows sampled on a column-by-column basis by setting the STATISTICS value.

To get a sense of what the planner uses, query the `pg_stats` table, as illustrated in Example 9-10:

```
SELECT
    attname As colname,
    n_distinct,
    most_common_vals AS common_vals,
    most_common_freqs As dist_freq
FROM pg_stats
WHERE tablename = 'facts'
ORDER BY schemaname, tablename, attname;
```

Example 9-10. Data distribution histogram

```
colname       | n_distinct | common_vals       | dist_freq
--------------+------------+-------------------+-----------------
fact_type_id  |         68 | {135,113...       | {0.0157,0.0156333,...
perc          |        985 | {0.00,...         | {0.1845,0.0579333,0.056...
tract_id      |       1478 | {25025090300...   | {0.00116667,0.00106667,0.0...
val           |       3391 | {0.000,1.000,2...| {0.2116,0.0681333,0...
yr            |          2 | {2011,2010}       | {0.748933,0.251067}
```

`pg_stats` gives the planner a sense of how actual values are dispersed within a given column and lets it plan accordingly. The `pg_stats` table is constantly updated as a background process. After a large data load or a major deletion, you should manually update the stats by executing VACUUM ANALYZE. VACUUM permanently removes deleted rows from tables; ANALYZE updates the stats.

For columns that participate often in joins and are used heavily in WHERE clauses, you should consider increasing sampled rows.

```
ALTER TABLE census.facts ALTER COLUMN fact_type_id SET STATISTICS 1000;
```

Random Page Cost and Quality of Drives

Another setting that influences the planner is the `random_page_cost` (RPC) ratio, which is the relative cost of the disk in retrieving a record using a sequential read versus using random access. Generally, the faster (and more expensive) the physical disk, the lower the ratio. The default value for RPC is 4, which works well for most mechanical hard drives on the market today. The use of solid-state drives (SSDs), high-end storage area networks (SANs), or cloud storage makes it worth tweaking this value.

You can set the RPC ratio per database, per server, or per tablespace. At the server level, it makes most sense to set the ratio in the *postgresql.conf* file. If you have different kinds of disks, you can set the values at the `tablespace` level using the ALTER TABLESPACE (*http://bit.ly/1AvAsf1*) command:

```
ALTER TABLESPACE pg_default SET (random_page_cost=2);
```

Details about this setting can be found at Random Page Cost Revisited (*http://bit.ly/ 15SZdrT*). The article suggests the following settings:

- High-end NAS/SAN: 2.5 or 3.0
- Amazon EBS and Heroku: 2.0
- iSCSI and other mediocre SANs: 6.0, but varies widely
- SSDs: 2.0 to 2.5
- NvRAM (or NAND): 1.5

Caching

If you execute a complex query that takes a while to run, subsequent runs are often much faster. Thank caching. If the same query executes in sequence, by the same user or different users, and no changes have been made to the underlying data, you should get back the same result. As long as there's space in memory to cache the data, the planner can skip replanning or reretrieving. Using common table expressions and immutable functions in your queries encourages caching.

How do you check what's in the current cache? If you are running PostgreSQL 9.1 or later, you can install the pg_buffercache extension:

```
CREATE EXTENSION pg_buffercache;
```

You can then run a query against the pg_buffercache view, as shown in Example 9-11.

Example 9-11. Are my table rows in buffer cache?

```
SELECT
    C.relname,
    COUNT(CASE WHEN B.isdirty THEN 1 ELSE NULL END) As dirty_buffers,
    COUNT(*) As num_buffers
FROM
    pg_class AS C INNER JOIN
    pg_buffercache B ON C.relfilenode = B.relfilenode INNER JOIN
    pg_database D ON B.reldatabase = D.oid AND D.datname = current_database()
WHERE C.relname IN ('facts','lu_fact_types')
GROUP BY C.relname;
```

Example 9-11 returns the number of buffered pages of the facts and lu_fact_types tables. Of course, to actually see buffered rows, you need to run a query. Try this one:

```
SELECT T.fact_subcats[2], COUNT(*) As num_fact
FROM census.facts As F INNER JOIN census.lu_fact_types AS T ON F.fact_type_id =
T.fact_type_id
GROUP BY T.fact_subcats[2];
```

The second time you run the query, you should notice at least a 10% performance speed increase and should see the following cached in the buffer:

```
    relname    | dirty_buffers | num_buffers
---------------+---------------+-------------
    facts      |             0 |         736
  lu_fact_types |             0 |           4
```

The more onboard memory you have dedicated to the cache, the more room you'll have to cache data. You can set the amount of dedicated memory by changing the `shared_buf fers` setting in *postgresql.conf*. Don't go overboard; raising `shared_buffers` too much will bloat your cache, leading to more time wasted scanning the cache.

Nowadays, there's no shortage of onboard memory. You can take advantage of this by precaching commonly used tables using an extension called pg_prewarm, now packaged as part of PostgreSQL 9.4 (*http://bit.ly/1rX2Rey*). pg_prewarm lets you prime your PostgreSQL by loading data from commonly used tables into memory so that the first user to hit the database can experience the same performance boost offered by caching as later users. A good article that describes this feature is Prewarming relational data (*http://bit.ly/1FUkmNa*).

Writing Better Queries

The best and easiest way to improve query performance is to start with well-written queries. Four out of five queries we encounter are not written as efficiently as they could be.

There appear to be two primary causes for all this bad querying. First, we see people reuse SQL patterns without thinking. For example, if they successfully write a query using a left join, they will continue to use left join when incorporating more tables instead of considering the sometimes more appropriate inner join. Unlike other programming languages, the SQL language does not lend itself well to blind reuse.

Second, people don't tend to keep up with the latest developments in their dialect of SQL. If a PostgreSQL user is still writing SQL as if he still had an early version, he would be oblivious to all the syntax-saving (and sanity-saving) addenda that have come along.

Writing efficient SQL takes practice. There's no such thing as a wrong query as long as you get the expected result, but there is such a thing as a slow query. In this section, we point out some of the common mistakes we see people make. Although this book is about PostgreSQL, our recommendations are applicable to other relational databases as well.

Overusing Subqueries in SELECT

A classic newbie mistake is to think of subqueries as independent entities. Unlike conventional programming languages, SQL doesn't take kindly to the idea of black-boxing —writing a bunch of subqueries independently and then assembling them mindlessly to get the final result. You have to treat each query holistically. How you piece together data from different views and tables is every bit as important as how you go about retrieving the data in the first place.

The unnecessary use of subqueries, as shown in Example 9-12, is a common symptom of piecemeal thinking.

Example 9-12. Overusing subqueries

```
SELECT tract_id,
    (SELECT COUNT(*) FROM census.facts As F WHERE F.tract_id = T.tract_id) As
num_facts,
    (SELECT COUNT(*)
    FROM census.lu_fact_types As Y
    WHERE Y.fact_type_id IN (
        SELECT fact_type_id
        FROM census.facts F
        WHERE F.tract_id = T.tract_id
    )
    ) As num_fact_types
FROM census.lu_tracts As T;
```

Example 9-12 can be more efficiently written as shown in Example 9-13. This query, consolidating selects and using a join, is not only shorter than the prior one, but faster. If you have a larger dataset or weaker hardware, the difference could be even more pronounced.

Example 9-13. Overused subqueries simplified

```
SELECT T.tract_id,
    COUNT(f.fact_type_id) As num_facts,
    COUNT(DISTINCT fact_type_id) As num_fact_types
FROM census.lu_tracts As T LEFT JOIN census.facts As F ON T.tract_id = F.tract_id
GROUP BY T.tract_id;
```

Figure 9-4 shows the graphical plan for Example 9-12 (we'll save you the eyesore of seeing the gnarled output of the text EXPLAIN), while Figure 9-5 shows the tabular output from *http://explain.depesz.com*, revealing a great deal of inefficiency.

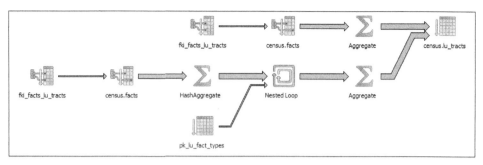

Figure 9-4. Graphical plan of overusing subqueries

exclusive	inclusive	rows x	rows	loops	node
10.709	1292.135	↑ 1.0	1478	1	➡ Seq Scan on lu_tracts t (cost=0.00..615535.37 rows=1478 width=12) (actual time
					SubPlan (forSeq Scan)
63.554	264.562	↑ 1.0	1	1478	➡ Aggregate (cost=207.86..207.87 rows=1 width=0) (ac
153.712	201.008	↑ 1.0	68	1478	➡ Bitmap Heap Scan on facts f (cost=4.79..207.69 rows=68 width=0) (actual time
					Recheck Cond: ((tract_id)::text = (t.tract_id)::text)
47.296	47.296	↑ 1.0	68	1478	➡ Bitmap Index Scan on fki_facts_lu_tracts (cost=0.00..4.78 rows=68 width=0) (actual tim
					Index Cond: ((tract_id)::text = (t.tract_id)::text)
59.120	1016.864	↑ 1.0	1	1478	➡ Aggregate (cost=208.56..208.57 rows=1 width=0) (ac
314.814	957.744	↑ 1.0	68	1478	➡ Nested Loop (cost=207.86..208.39 rows=68 width=0) (actual ti
155.190	341.418	↓ 68.0	68	1478	➡ HashAggregate (cost=207.86..207.87 rows=1 width=4) (actua
141.888	186.228	↑ 1.0	68	1478	➡ Bitmap Heap Scan on facts f (cost=4.79..207.69 rows=68 width=4) (act
					Recheck Cond: ((tract_id)::text = (t.tract_i
44.340	44.340	↑ 1.0	68	1478	➡ Bitmap Index Scan on fki_facts_lu_trac (cost=0.00..4.78 rows=68 width=0) (ac
					Index Cond: ((tract_id)::text = (t.tract_i
301.512	301.512	↑ 1.0	1	100504	➡ Index Scan using pk_lu_fact_types on lu_fact (cost=0.00..0.50 rows=1 width=4) (actual time
					Index Cond: (fact_type_id = f.fact_type_id)

Figure 9-5. Tabular plan of overusing subqueries

Figure 9-6 shows the graphical plan of Example 9-13, demonstrating how much less work goes on in it.

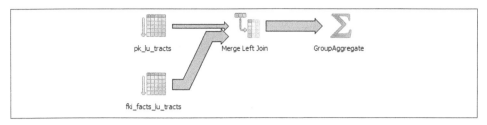

Figure 9-6. Graphical plan of removing subqueries

Keep in mind that we're not asking you to avoid subqueries entirely. We're only asking you to use them judiciously. When you do use them, pay extra attention to how you incorporate them into the main query. Finally, remember that a subquery should work with the the main query, not independently of it.

Avoid SELECT *

SELECT * is wasteful. It's akin to printing out a 1,000-page document when you need only 10 pages. Besides the obvious downside of adding to network traffic, there are two other drawbacks that you might not think of.

First, PostgreSQL stores large blob and text objects using TOAST (The Oversized-Attribute Storage Technique). TOAST maintains side tables for PostgreSQL to store this extra data. So retrieving a large field means that TOAST must assemble the data from rows across different tables. Imagine the extra processing if your table contains text data the size of *War and Peace* and you perform an unnecessary SELECT *.

Second, when you define views, you often will include more columns than you'll need. You might even go so far as to use SELECT * inside a view. This is understandable and perfectly fine. PostgreSQL is smart enough to let you request all the columns you want in your view definition and even include complex calculations or joins without incurring penalty, as long as no user runs a query referring to the columns.

To drive home our point, let's wrap our census in a view and use the slow subquery example from Example 9-12:

```
CREATE OR REPLACE VIEW vw_stats AS
SELECT tract_id,
    (SELECT COUNT(*) FROM census.facts As F WHERE F.tract_id = T.tract_id) As
num_facts,
    (SELECT COUNT(*)
    FROM census.lu_fact_types As Y
    WHERE Y.fact_type_id IN (
        SELECT fact_type_id
        FROM census.facts F
        WHERE F.tract_id = T.tract_id
    )
```

```
        ) As num_fact_types
    FROM census.lu_tracts As T;
```

Now, if we query our view with this query:

```
SELECT tract_id FROM vw_stats;
```

execution time is about 21 ms on our server because it doesn't run any computation for certain field such as num_facts and num_fact_types, fields we did not ask for. If you looked at the plan, you may be startled to find that it never even touches the facts table because it's smart enough to know it doesn't need to. But if we use:

```
SELECT * FROM vw_stats;
```

our execution time skyrockets to 681 ms, and the plan is just as we had in Figure 9-4. Although our results in this example suffer the loss of just milliseconds, imagine tables with tens of millions of rows and hundreds of columns. Those milliseconds could translate into overtime at the office waiting for a query to finish.

Make Good Use of CASE

We're always surprised how frequently people forget about using the ANSI SQL CASE expression. In many aggregate situations, a CASE can obviate the need for inefficient subqueries. We'll demonstrate the point with two equivalent queries and their corresponding plans. Example 9-14 uses subqueries.

Example 9-14. Using subqueries instead of CASE

```
SELECT T.tract_id, COUNT(*) As tot, type_1.tot AS type_1
FROM
    census.lu_tracts AS T LEFT JOIN
    (SELECT tract_id, COUNT(*) As tot
        FROM census.facts
        WHERE fact_type_id = 131
        GROUP BY tract_id
    ) As type_1 ON T.tract_id = type_1.tract_id LEFT JOIN
    census.facts AS F ON T.tract_id = F.tract_id
GROUP BY T.tract_id, type_1.tot;
```

Figure 9-7 shows the graphical plan of Example 9-14.

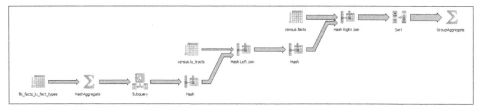

Figure 9-7. Graphical plan of using subqueries instead of CASE

We now rewrite the query using CASE. You'll find that the economized query, shown in Example 9-15, is generally faster and much easier to read.

Example 9-15. Using CASE instead of subqueries

```
SELECT T.tract_id, COUNT(*) As tot,
    COUNT(CASE WHEN F.fact_type_id = 131 THEN 1 ELSE NULL END) AS type_1
FROM census.lu_tracts AS T LEFT JOIN census.facts AS F
ON T.tract_id = F.tract_id
GROUP BY T.tract_id;
```

Figure 9-8 shows the graphical plan of Example 9-15.

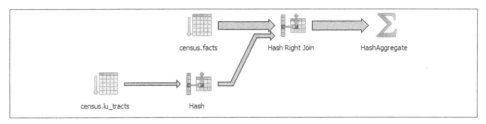

Figure 9-8. Graphical EXPLAIN of using CASE instead

Even though our rewritten query still doesn't use the fact_type index, it's faster than using subqueries because the planner scans the facts table only once. A shorter plan is generally not only easier to comprehend but also often performs better than a longer one, although not always.

Using Filter Instead of CASE

PostgreSQL 9.4 offers the new FILTER construct, which we introduced in "FILTER Clause for Aggregates" on page 133. FILTER can often replace CASE in aggregate expressions. Not only is this syntax pleasanter to look at, but in many cases performs better. We repeat Example 9-15 with the equivalent filter version in Example 9-16.

Example 9-16. Using CASE instead of subqueries

```
SELECT T.tract_id, COUNT(*) As tot,
    COUNT(*) FILTER(WHERE F.fact_type_id = 131) AS type_1
FROM census.lu_tracts AS T LEFT JOIN census.facts AS F
ON T.tract_id = F.tract_id
GROUP BY T.tract_id;
```

For this particular example, the FILTER performance is only about a millisecond faster than our CASE version, and the plans are more or less the same.

CHAPTER 10
Replication and External Data

PostgreSQL has a number of options for sharing data with external servers or data sources. The first option is the built-in replication options of PostgreSQL, which allows you to create a copy of your server ready to run on another PostgreSQL server. The second option is to use third-party add-ons, many of which are freely available and time-tested. The third option, unveiled in version 9.1, is to use *foreign data wrappers* (FDW). FDWs gives you the flexibility to query from a wide array of external data sources. Since version 9.3, some FDWs such as `postgres_fdw` (*http://bit.ly/1z3iIIZ*) and `hadoop_fdw` (*http://bit.ly/1yxbFIn*) also permit updating.

Replication Overview

The seemingly countless reasons for the need to replicate your databases all distill down to two: availability and scalability. If your main server goes down, you want another to immediately assume its role. For small databases, you could just make sure you have another physical server ready and restore the database onto it. But for large databases (in the terabytes), the restore itself could take many hours. To avoid downtime, you'll need to replicate. The other main reason is scalability. You set up a database to breed fancy elephant shrews (*http://en.wikipedia.org/wiki/elephant_shrew*) for profit. After a few years of breeding, you now have thousands of shrews. People all over the world come to your site to gawk and purchase. You're overwhelmed by the traffic. Replication comes to your aid; you set up a read-only slave server to replicate with your main server. You direct the countless gawkers to the slave, and only let serious buyers onto the master server to finalize their purchases.

Replication Jargon

Before we get too carried away with replication, we had better introduce some common lingo used in connection with it:

Master

The master server is the database server sourcing the data being replicated and where all updates happen. You're allowed only one master when using the built-in replication features of PostgreSQL. Plans are in place to support multimaster replication scenarios. Watch for it in future releases.

Slave

A slave server consumes the replicated data and provides a replica of the master. More aesthetically pleasing terms such as *subscriber* and *agent* have been bandied about, but *slave* is still the most apropos. PostgreSQL built-in replication supports only read-only slaves at this time.

Write-ahead log (WAL)

WAL is the log that keeps track of all transactions, often referred to as the *transaction log* in other database products. To stage replication, PostgreSQL simply makes the logs available to the slaves. Once slaves have pulled the logs, they just need to execute the transactions therein.

Synchronous

A transaction on the master will not be considered complete until at least one slave is updated. If you have multiple synchronous slaves, they do not all need to respond for success.

Asynchronous

A transaction on the master will commit even if slaves haven't been updated. This is useful in the case of distant servers where you don't want transactions to wait because of network latency, but the downside is that your dataset on the slave might lag behind, and the slave might miss some transactions in the event of transmission failure.

Streaming

The streaming replication model was introduced in PostgreSQL 9.0. Unlike prior versions, it does not require direct file access between master and slaves. Instead, it relies on the PostgreSQL connection protocol to transmit the WALs.

Cascading replication

Starting with version 9.2, slaves can receive logs from nearby slaves instead of directly from the master. This allows a slave to also behave like a master for replication purposes. The slave remains read-only. When a slave acts as both a receiver and a sender, it is called a *cascading standby*.

Remastering

Remastering is the process whereby you promote a slave to be the master. Up to and including version 9.2, this was a process that required using WAL file archiving instead of streaming replication. It also required all slaves to be recloned. Version 9.3 introduced streaming-only remastering, which means remastering no longer needs access to a WAL archive; it can be done via streaming, and slaves no longer need to be recloned. As of version 9.4, a restart is still required though. This may change in future releases.

 Unlogged tables don't participate in replication.

Evolution of PostgreSQL Replication

PostgreSQL's stock replication relies on WAL shipping. In versions prior to 9.3, streaming replication slaves must be running the same architecture to ensure faithful execution of the received log stream. Streaming replication in version 9.3 and later is now architecture-independent but still requires all servers to run the same version of PostgreSQL.

Support for built-in replication improved over the following PostgreSQL releases:

1. Prior to version 9.0, PostgreSQL offered only asynchronous warm slaves. A warm slave retrieved the WAL and kept itself in sync but was not be available for queries. It acted only as a standby.

2. Version 9.0 introduced asynchronous hot slaves as well as streaming replication, whereby users can execute read-only queries against the slave and replication can happen without direct file access between the servers (using database connections for shipping logs instead).

3. With version 9.1, synchronous replication became possible.

4. Version 9.2 introduced *cascading streaming replication*. The main benefit is reductions in latency. It's much faster for a slave to receive updates from a nearby slave than from a master far, far away.

Third-Party Replication Options

As alternatives to PostgreSQL's built-in replication, common third-party options abound. Slony (*http://slony.info/*) and Bucardo (*http://bucardo.org/wiki/Bucardo*) are two of the most popular open source ones. Although PostgreSQL is improving replication with each new release, Slony, Bucardo, and other third-party replication options still offer more flexibility. Slony and Bucardo allow you to replicate individual databases or even tables instead of the entire server. They also don't require that all masters and slaves be of the same PostgreSQL version and OS. Both also support multimaster scenarios. However, both rely on additional triggers to initiate the replication and often don't support DDL commands for actions such as creating new tables, installing extensions, and so on. This makes them more invasive than merely shipping logs.

Postgres-XC (*http://postgres-xc.sourceforge.net*), still in beta, is starting to gain an audience. The raison d'être of Postgres-XC is not replication but distributed query processing. It is designed with scalability in mind rather than high availability. Postgres-XC is not an add-on to PostgreSQL but a completely separate fork focused on providing a write-scalable, multimaster symmetric cluster very similar in purpose to Oracle RAC (*http://bit.ly/1z3iT6S*).

We urge you to consult a comparison matrix of popular third-party options (*http://bit.ly/1vUu5AP*) before deciding what to use.

Setting Up Replication

Let's go over the steps to set up replication. We'll take advantage of streaming introduced in version 9.0, which requires connections only at the PostgreSQL database level between the master and slaves. We will also use features introduced in version 9.1 that allow you to easily set up authentication accounts specifically for replication.

Configuring the Master

The basic steps for setting up the master server are:

1. Create a replication account:

   ```
   CREATE ROLE pgrepuser REPLICATION LOGIN PASSWORD 'woohoo';
   ```

2. Alter the following configuration settings in *postgresql.conf*:

   ```
   listen_addresses = *
   wal_level = hot_standby
   archive_mode = on
   max_wal_senders = 2
   wal_keep_segments = 10
   ```

   These settings are described in Server Configuration: Replication (*http://bit.ly/1z3iXUq*).

3. Add the archive_command configuration directive to *postgresql.conf* to indicate where the WAL will be saved. With streaming, you're free to choose any directory. More details on this setting can be found at the PostgreSQL PGStandby (*http://bit.ly/1yxbOvw*) documentation.

   On Linux/Unix, your archive_command line should look something like:

   ```
   archive_command = 'cp %p ../archive/%f'
   ```

   You can also use rsync instead of cp if you want to archive to a different server:

   ```
   archive_command = 'rsync -av %p postgres@192.168.0.10:archive/%f'
   ```

On Windows:

```
archive_command = 'copy %p ..\\archive\\%f'
```

4. The *pg_hba.conf* file should include a rule allowing the slaves to act as replication agents. As an example, the following rule will allow a PostgreSQL account named `pgrepuser` on a server on my private network with an IP address in the range 192.168.0.1 to 192.168.0.254 to replicate using an md5 password:

```
host replication pgrepuser 192.168.0.0/24 md5
```

5. Shut down the PostgreSQL service and copy all the files in the *data* folder except the *pg_xlog* and *pg_log* folders to the slaves. Make sure that *pg_xlog* and *pg_log* folders are both present on the slaves but devoid of any files.

If you have a large database cluster and can't afford a shutdown for the duration of the copy, you can use the `pg_basebackup` (*http://www.postgresql.org/docs/current/interactive/app-pgbasebackup.html*) utility, found in the *bin* folder of your PostgreSQL installation. This will create a copy of the data cluster files in the specified directory and allow you to do a base backup while the `postgres` service is running.

Configuring the Slaves

To minimize headaches, slaves should have the same configuration as the master, especially if you'll be using them for failover. In order for the server to be a slave, it must be able to play back the WAL transactions of the master. The steps for creating a slave are:

1. Create a new instance of PostgreSQL with the same version (preferably even microversions) as your master server and the same OS at the same patch level. Keeping servers identical is not a requirement, and you're welcome to experiment and see how far you can deviate.

2. Shut down PostgreSQL on the new slave.

3. Overwrite the data folder files with those you copied from the master.

4. Add the following configuration setting to the *postgresql.conf* file:

```
hot_standby = on
```

5. You don't need to run the slaves on the same port as the master, so you can optionally change the port either via *postgresql.conf* or via some other OS-specific startup script that sets the `PGPORT` environment variable before startup. Any startup script will override the setting you have in *postgresql.conf*.

6. Create a new file in the *data* folder called *recovery.conf* that contains the following lines, and substitute the actual host name, IP address, and port of your master on the second line:

```
standby_mode = 'on'
primary_conninfo = 'host=192.168.0.1 port=5432 user=pgrepuser password=woo-
hoo'
trigger_file = 'failover.now'
```

7. If you find that the slave can't play back WALs fast enough, you can specify a location for caching. In that case, add to the *recovery.conf* file a line such as the following, which varies depending on the OS:

On Linux/Unix
```
restore_command = 'cp %p ../archive/%f'
```

On Windows
```
restore_command = 'copy %p ..\\archive\\%f'
```

In this example, the *archive* folder is where we're caching.

Initiating the Replication Process

It's a good idea to start up the `postgres` service on all the slaves before starting it on the master. Otherwise, the master might start writing data or altering the database before the slaves can capture and replicate the changes. When you start up each slave server, you'll get an error in logs saying that it can't connect to the master. Ignore the message. Once the slaves have started, start up the `postgres` service on the master.

You should now be able to connect to both servers. Any changes you make on the master, even structural changes such as installing extensions or creating tables, should trickle down to the slaves. You should also be able to query the slaves.

When and if the time comes to liberate a chosen slave, create a blank file called *fail over.now* in the data folder of the slave. PostgreSQL will then complete playback of WAL and rename the *recovery.conf* file to *recover.done*. At that point, your slave will be unshackled from the master and continue life on its own with all the data from the last WAL. Once the slave has tasted freedom, there's no going back. In order to make it a slave again, you'll need to go through the whole process from the beginning.

Foreign Data Wrappers

Foreign data wrappers (FDWs) are an extensible, standard-complaint method for your PostgreSQL server to query other data sources: other PostgreSQL servers, and many types of non-PostgreSQL data sources. FDW was first introduced in PostgreSQL 9.1. At the center of the concept is a *foreign table*, a table that you can query like one in your PostgreSQL database but that resides in another data source, perhaps even on another physical server. Once you put in the effort to establish foreign tables, they persist in your database and you're forever free from having to worry about the intricate protocols of communicating with alien data sources. You can find a catalog of FDWs for PostgreSQL at PGXN FDW (*http://pgxn.org/tag/fdw/*) and PGXN Foreign Data Wrapper (*http://bit.ly/1z3j9D3*). You can also find examples of usage in PostgreSQL Wiki FDW (*http://wiki.postgresql.org/wiki/Foreign_data_wrappers*).

At this time, the FDW extension automatically installs two wrappers by default: `file_fdw` (*http://www.postgresql.org/docs/current/interactive/file-fdw.html*) and `postgres_fdw` (*http://www.postgresql.org/docs/current/interactive/postgres-fdw.html*). If you need to to wrap foreign data sources, start by visiting these two links to see whether someone has already done the work of creating wrappers. If not, try creating one yourself. If you succeed, be sure to share it with others.

In PostgreSQL 9.1 and 9.2, you're limited to `SELECT` queries against the FDW. PostgreSQL 9.3 introduced an API feature to update foreign tables. `postgres_fdw` is the only FDW shipped with PostgreSQL that supports this new feature.

In this section, we'll demonstrate how to register foreign servers, foreign users, and foreign tables, and finally, how to query foreign tables. Although we use SQL to create and delete objects in our examples, you can perform the exact same commands using pgAdmin III.

Querying Flat Files

The `file_fdw` wrapper is packaged as an extension. To install, use the SQL:

```
CREATE EXTENSION file_fdw;
```

Although `file_fdw` can read only from file paths accessible by your local server, you still need to define a server for it for the sake of consistency. Issue the following command to create a "faux" foreign server in your database:

```
CREATE SERVER my_server FOREIGN DATA WRAPPER file_fdw;
```

Next, you must register the tables. You can place foreign tables in any schema you want. We usually create a separate schema to house foreign data. For this example, we'll use our staging schema, as shown in Example 10-1.

Example 10-1. Make a foreign table from a delimited file

```
CREATE FOREIGN TABLE staging.devs (developer VARCHAR(150), company VARCHAR(150))
SERVER my_server
OPTIONS (format 'csv', header 'true', filename '/postgresql_book/ch10/devs.psv',
    delimiter '|', null ''
);
```

In our example, even though we're registering a pipe-delimited file, we still use the `csv` option. A CSV file, as far as FDW is concerned, represents any file delimited by specified characters, regardless of delimiter.

When the setup is finished, you can finally query your pipe-delimited file directly:

```
SELECT * FROM staging.devs WHERE developer LIKE 'T%';
```

Once you no longer need our foreign table, you can drop it:

```
DROP FOREIGN TABLE staging.devs;
```

Querying a Flat File as Jagged Arrays

Often, flat-file data sources have a different number of columns in each line and contain multiple header rows and footer rows. These kinds of files tend to be prevalent when the flat files originated as spreadsheets. Our favorite flat-file FDW for handling these unstructured flat files is `file_textarray_fdw`. This wrapper can handle any kind of delimited flat file, even if the number of elements in each row is inconsistent. It brings in each row as a text array (`text[]`).

Unfortunately, `file_textarray_fdw` is not part of the core PostgreSQL offering, so you'll need to compile it yourself. First, install PostgreSQL with PostgreSQL development headers. Then download the `file_textarray_fdw` source code from the Adunstan GitHub site (*https://github.com/adunstan/file_text_array_fdw*). There is a different branch for each version of PostgreSQL, so make sure to pick the right branch. Once you've compiled the code, install it as an extension, as you would any other FDW.

If you are on Linux/Unix, it's an easy compile if you have the `postgresql-dev` package installed. We did the work of compiling for Windows; you can download our binaries from Windows-32 9.1 FDWs (*http://bit.ly/1FUkLPQ*), Windows-32 9.2 FDWs (*http://bit.ly/1yn35Z6*), Windows-64 9.2 FDWs (*http://bit.ly/1u0c0NF*), Windows-32 9.3 FDWs (*http://bit.ly/1rX3aG7*), and Windows-64 9.3 FDWs (*http://bit.ly/1yn3cne*).

The first step to perform after you have installed an FDW is to create an extension in your database:

```
CREATE EXTENSION file_textarray_fdw;
```

Then create a a foreign server as you would with any FDW:

```
CREATE SERVER file_taserver FOREIGN DATA WRAPPER file_textarray_fdw;
```

Next, register the tables. You can place foreign tables in any schema you want. In Example 10-2, we use our staging schema again.

Example 10-2. Make a file text array foreign table from delimited file

```
CREATE FOREIGN TABLE staging.factfinder_array (x text[])
SERVER file_taserver
OPTIONS (format 'csv', filename '/postgresql_book/ch10/
DEC_10_SF1_QTH1_with_ann.csv',
header 'false', delimiter ',', quote '"', encoding 'latin1', null ''
);
```

Our example CSV begins with eight header rows and has more columns than we care to count. When the setup is finished, you can finally query our delimited file directly. This following query will give us the names of the header rows where the first column header is GEO.id:

```
SELECT unnest(x) FROM staging.factfinder_array WHERE x[1] = 'GEO.id'
```

This next query will give us the first two columns of our data:

```
SELECT x[1] As geo_id, x[2] As tract_id FROM staging.factfinder_array WHERE
x[1] ~ '[0-9]+';
```

When you no longer need the foreign table, you can drop it:

```
DROP FOREIGN TABLE staging.factfinder_array;
```

Querying Other PostgreSQL Servers

The PostgreSQL FDW, postgres_fdw (*http://bit.ly/1z3iIIZ*), is packaged with most distributions of PostgreSQL 9.3. This FDW allows you to read as well as push updates to other PostgreSQL servers, even different versions.

Start by installing the FDW for the PostgreSQL server in a new database:

```
CREATE EXTENSION postgres_fdw;
```

Next, create a foreign server:

```
CREATE SERVER book_server
FOREIGN DATA WRAPPER postgres_fdw
OPTIONS (host 'localhost', port '5432', dbname 'postgresql_book');
```

If you need to change or add connection options to the foreign server after creation, you can use the ALTER SERVER command. For example, if you needed to change the server you are pointing to, you could do:

```
ALTER SERVER book_server OPTIONS (SET host 'prod');
```

 Changes to connection settings such as the host, port, and database do not take effect until a new session is created. This is because the connection is opened on first use and is kept open.

Next, create a user, mapping its public role to a single role on the foreign server:

```
CREATE USER MAPPING FOR public SERVER book_server
OPTIONS (user 'role_on_foreign', password 'your_password');
```

Anyone who can connect to your database will be able to access the foreign server as well. The role you map to must exist on the foreign server and have login rights.

Now you are ready to create a foreign table. This table can have a subset or full set of columns of the table it connects to. In Example 10-3, we create a foreign table that maps to the census.facts table.

Example 10-3. Defining a PostgreSQL foreign table

```
CREATE FOREIGN TABLE ft_facts (
    fact_type_id int NOT NULL, tract_id varchar(11),
    yr int, val numeric(12,3), perc numeric(6,2))
SERVER book_server OPTIONS (schema_name 'census', table_name 'facts');
```

This example includes only the most basic options for the foreign table. By default, all PostgreSQL foreign tables are editable/updatable, unless of course the remote account you used doesn't have update access to that table. The updatable setting is a Boolean setting that can be changed at the foreign table or the foreign server definition. For example, to make your table read-only, execute:

```
ALTER FOREIGN TABLE ft_facts OPTIONS (ADD updatable 'false');
```

You can set the table back to updatable by running:

```
ALTER FOREIGN TABLE ft_facts OPTIONS (SET updatable 'true');
```

The updatable property at the table level overrides the foreign server setting.

In addition to changing OPTIONS, you can also add and drop columns with the ALTER FOREIGN TABLE statement. The statement is covered in PostgreSQL Manual ALTER FOREIGN TABLE (*http://bit.ly/1yUdsGw*).

Querying Nonconventional Data Sources

The database world does not appear to be getting more homogeneous. Exotic databases are sprouting up faster than we can keep tabs on. Some are fads and quickly drown in their own hype. Some aspire to dethrone relational databases altogether. Some could hardly be considered databases. The introduction of FDWs is in part a response to the growing diversity. FDW assimilates without compromising the PosgreSQL core.

In this next example, we'll demonstrate how to use the www_fdw FDW to query web services. We borrowed the example from www_fdw Examples (*http://bit.ly/12sggyN*).

The www_fdw FDW is not generally packaged with PostgreSQL. If you are on Linux/ Unix, it's an easy compile if you have the postgresql-dev package installed and can download the latest source (*https://github.com/cyga/www_fdw*). We did the work of compiling for some Windows platforms; you can download our binaries from Windows-32 9.1 FDWs (*http://bit.ly/1FUkLPQ*) and Windows-64 9.3 FDWs (*http:// bit.ly/1yn3cne*).

Now create an extension to hold the FDW:

```
CREATE EXTENSION www_fdw;
```

Then create your Google foreign data server:

```
CREATE SERVER www_fdw_server_google_search
FOREIGN DATA WRAPPER www_fdw
OPTIONS (uri 'http://ajax.googleapis.com/ajax/services/search/web?v=1.0');
```

The default format supported by www_fdw is JSON, so we didn't need to include it in the OPTIONS modifier. The other supported format is XML. For details on additional parameters that you can set, refer to the www_fdw documentation (*https://github.com/cyga/ www_fdw/wiki/Documentation*). Each FDW is different and comes with its own API settings.

Next, establish at least one user for your FDW. All users that connect to your server should be able to access the Google search server, so here we create one for the entire public group:

```
CREATE USER MAPPING FOR public SERVER www_fdw_server_google_search;
```

Now create your foreign table, as shown in Example 10-4.

Example 10-4. Make a foreign table from Google

```
CREATE FOREIGN TABLE www_fdw_google_search (
    q text,
    GsearchResultClass text,
    unescapedUrl text,
    url text,
    visibleUrl text,
    cacheUrl text,
    title text,
    content text
) SERVER www_fdw_server_google_search;
```

The user mapping doesn't assign any rights. You still need to grant rights before being able to query the foreign table:

```
GRANT SELECT ON TABLE www_fdw_google_search TO public;
```

Now comes the fun part. We search with the term New in PostgreSQL 9.4 and mix in a bit of regular expression goodness to strip off HTML tags:

```
SELECT regexp_replace(title, E'(?x)(< [^>]*? >)', '', 'g') As title
FROM www_fdw_google_search where q='New in PostgreSQL 9.4'
LIMIT 2;
```

Voilà! We have our response:

```
title
-------------------------------------------------
What's new in PostgreSQL 9.4 - PostgreSQL wiki
PostgreSQL: PostgreSQL 9.4 Beta 1 Released
(2 rows)
```

Installing PostgreSQL

Windows, Desktop Linux

EnterpriseDB (*http://www.EnterpriseDB.com*) builds installers for Windows and desktop versions of Linux. For Windows users, this is the preferred installer to use.

The installers are easy to use. They come packaged with PgAdmin and a stack builder from which you can install add-ons like JDBC, .NET drivers, Ruby, PostGIS, phpPgAdmin, and pgAgent.

EnterpriseDB has two PostgreSQL offerings: the official, open source edition of PostgreSQL, dubbed the Community Edition; and its proprietary edition, called Advanced Plus. The proprietary fork offers Oracle compatibility and enhanced management features. Don't get confused between the two when you download installers. In this book, we focused on the official PostgreSQL, not Postgres Plus Advanced Server; however, much of the material applies to Postgres Plus Advanced Server.

 If you want to try out different versions of PostgreSQL on the same machine or want to run it from a USB device, EnterpriseDB also offers binaries. Read Starting PostgreSQL in Windows without Install (*http://bit.ly/1yxcuAY*) for guidance.

CentOS, Fedora, Red Hat, Scientific Linux

Most Linux/Unix distributions offer PostgreSQL in their main repositories, though the version might be outdated. To compensate, many people use backports, which are alternative package repositories offering newer versions.

For adventurous Linux users, download the latest PostgreSQL, including the developmental versions, by going to the PostgreSQL Yum repository (*http://yum.post*

gresql.org). Not only will you find the core server, but you can also retrieve popular add-ons. PostgreSQL developers maintain this repository and release patches and updates as soon as they are available. At the time of writing, PostgreSQL Yum repository is available for Fedora 14-20, Red Hat Enterprise Linux 4-6, CentOS 4-6, and Scientific Linux 5-6. If you have older versions of the OS or still need PostgreSQL 8.3, check the documentation to see what the repository still maintains. For detailed installation instructions using YUM, refer to the Yum section (*http://www.postgresonline.com/journal/categories/53-yum*) of our PostgresOnLine journal site.

Debian, Ubuntu

Ubuntu stays up to date with latest versions of PostgreSQL. Debian tends to be a bit slower. You can install the latest PostgreSQL with:

```
sudo apt-get install postgresql-9.3
```

If you plan to compile add-ons generally not packaged with PostgreSQL, such as PostGIS or R, then you'll want to install the development libraries:

```
sudo apt-get install postgresql-server-dev-9.3
```

If your repository doesn't have the latest version of PostgreSQL, try visiting the Apt PostgreSQL packages (*http://apt.postgresql.org*) for the latest stable and beta releases. They also offer additional packages such as PL/V8 and PostGIS. At last check, they have packages for Debian 6-7 and Ubuntu 10-14.

FreeBSD

FreeBSD is a popular platform for PostgreSQL. However, many people who use FreeBSD tend to compile their own directly from source rather than using a packaged distribution. You can find the latest beta versions of PostgreSQL at FreeBSD (*http://www.freebsd.org/ports/databases.html*).

Mac OS X

We've seen a variety of ways to install PostgreSQL on Macs. EnterpriseDB offers an installer. The Homebrew is gaining popularity and attracts advanced Mac users. Kyng-Chaos is suitable for folks looking for an up-to-date and complete open source GIS experience. Postgres.app is a newcomer geared for the novice. The long-standing Mac-Ports and Fink distributions are still around. We do advise against mixing installers for Mac users. For instance, if you installed PostgreSQL using KyngChaos, don't go to EnterpriseDB to get add-ons:

- EnterpriseDB (*http://www.EnterpriseDB.com*) maintains an easy-to-use, one-step installer for Mac OS X. PgAdmin comes as part of the installer. For add-ons, EnterpriseDB offers a stack builder program, from which you can install popular extensions, drivers, languages, and administration tools.

- Homebrew (*http://brew.sh*) is a Mac OS package manager for many things PostgreSQL. Russ Brooks dishes out step-by-step instructions (*http://bit.ly/12IJA59*) for installing PostgreSQL 9 on Homebrew. You can follow these steps for later versions of PostgreSQL, as little has changed in the way of installation procedures. Upgrading from 9.2 to 9.3 with Brew (*http://bit.ly/1vwKw7y*) provides instructions for upgrading an older install. You'll find plenty of useful articles at the Homebrew PostgreSQL Wiki (*https://wiki.postgresql.org/wiki/Homebrew*).

- Postgres.app (*http://postgresapp.com/*) distributed by Heroku is a free desktop distribution touted as the easiest way to get started with PostgreSQL on the Mac. It usually maintains the latest version of PostgreSQL bundled with popular extensions such as PostGIS, PL/Python, and PLV8. Postgres.app runs as a standalone application that you can stop and start as needed, making it suitable for development or single users.

- KyngChaos PostgreSQL + GIS (*http://www.kyngchaos.com/software:postgres*) has the latest release package of PostgreSQL geared toward GIS users. PostGIS, pgRouting, R, and QGIS come standard.

- MacPorts (*http://www.macports.org*) is a Mac OS X package distribution for compiling, installing, and upgrading many open source packages. It's the oldest of the Mac OS distributions systems that carries PostgreSQL. At time of writing, PostgreSQL 9.3 is the latest version.

- Fink (*http://www.finkproject.org*) is a Mac OS X package distribution based on the Debian apt-get installation framework. As the time of writing, it offers version 9.2 and trails behind other Mac distributions.

APPENDIX B
PostgreSQL Packaged Command-Line Tools

This appendix summarizes indispensable command-line tools packaged with PostgreSQL server. We discussed them at length in the book. Here we list their help messages. We hope to save you a bit of time with their inclusion and perhaps make this book a not-so-strange bedfellow.

Database Backup Using pg_dump

Use pg_dump (*http://www.postgresql.org/docs/current/interactive/app-pgdump.html*) to back up all or part of a database. Backup file formats available are TAR, compressed (PostgreSQL custom format), plain text, and plain-text SQL. Plain-text backup can copy psql-specific commands; therefore, restore by running the file within psql. Plain-text SQL backup is merely a file with standard SQL CREATE and INSERT commands. To restore, you can run the file using psql or pgAdmin. Example B-1 shows the pg_dump help output. For full covereage of pg_dump usage, see "Selective Backup Using pg_dump" on page 38.

Example B-1. pg_dump help

```
pg_dump --help

pg_dump dumps a database as a text file or to other formats.
Usage:
pg_dump [OPTION]... [DBNAME]

General options:
-f, --file=FILENAME        output file or directory name
-F, --format=c|d|t|p       output file format (custom, directory, tar, plain
text)
-j, --jobs=NUM             use this many parallel jobs to dump ❶
-v, --verbose              verbose mode
-Z, --compress=0-9         compression level for compressed formats
--lock-wait-timeout=TIMEOUT fail after waiting TIMEOUT for a table lock
```

197

```
--help                        show this help, then exit
--version                     output version information, then exit
Options controlling the output content:
-a, --data-only               dump only the data, not the schema
-b, --blobs                   include large objects in dump
-c, --clean                   clean (drop) database objects before recreating
-C, --create                  include commands to create database in dump
-E, --encoding=ENCODING       dump the data in encoding ENCODING
-n, --schema=SCHEMA           dump the named schema(s) only
-N, --exclude-schema=SCHEMA   do NOT dump the named schema(s)
-o, --oids                    include OIDs in dump
-O, --no-owner                skip restoration of object ownership in
plain-text format
-s, --schema-only             dump only the schema, no data
-S, --superuser=NAME          superuser user name to use in plain-text format
-t, --table=TABLE             dump the named table(s) only
-T, --exclude-table=TABLE     do NOT dump the named table(s)
-x, --no-privileges           do not dump privileges (grant/revoke)
--binary-upgrade              for use by upgrade utilities only
--column-inserts              dump data as INSERT commands with column names
--disable-dollar-quoting      disable dollar quoting, use SQL standard quoting
--disable-triggers            disable triggers during data-only restore
--exclude-table-data=TABLE    do NOT dump data for the named table(s) ❷
--if-exists                   use IF EXISTS when dropping objects ❸
--inserts                     dump data as INSERT commands, rather than COPY
--no-security-labels          do not dump security label assignments
--no-synchronized-snapshots   do not use synchronized snapshots in parallel jobs ❹
--no-tablespaces              do not dump tablespace assignments
--no-unlogged-table-data      do not dump unlogged table data
--quote-all-identifiers       quote all identifiers, even if not key words
--section=SECTION             dump named section (pre-data, data, or post-data) ❺
--serializable-deferrable     wait until the dump can run without anomalies
--use-set-session-authorization
use SET SESSION AUTHORIZATION commands instead of
ALTER OWNER commands to set ownership
Connection options:
-d, --dbname=DBNAME           database to dump ❻
-h, --host=HOSTNAME           database server host or socket directory
-p, --port=PORT               database server port number
-U, --username=NAME           connect as specified database user
-w, --no-password             never prompt for password
-W, --password                force password prompt (should happen automatically)
--role=ROLENAME               do SET ROLE before dump
```

❶ ❹ New features introduced in PostgreSQL 9.3.
❻

❸   New features introduced in PostgreSQL 9.4.

❷ ❺ New features introduced in PostgreSQL 9.2.

Server Backup: pg_dumpall

Use pg_dump_all (*http://bit.ly/1q2iRdW*) to back up all databases on your server onto a single plain-text or plain-text SQL file. The backup routine will automatically include server-level objects such as roles and tablespaces. Example B-2 shows the pg_dumpall help output. See "Systemwide Backup Using pg_dumpall" on page 40 for the full discussion.

Example B-2. pg_dumpall help

```
pg_dumpall --help

pg_dumpall extracts a PostgreSQL database cluster into an SQL script file.
Usage:
pg_dumpall [OPTION]...

General options:
-f, --file=FILENAME        output file name
--lock-wait-timeout=TIMEOUT fail after waiting TIMEOUT for a table lock
--help                     show this help, then exit
--version                  output version information, then exit

Options controlling the output content:
 -a, --data-only           dump only the data, not the schema
 -c, --clean               clean (drop) databases before recreating
 -g, --globals-only        dump only global objects, no databases
 -o, --oids                include OIDs in dump
 -O, --no-owner            skip restoration of object ownership
 -r, --roles-only          dump only roles, no databases or tablespaces
 -s, --schema-only         dump only the schema, no data
 -S, --superuser=NAME      superuser user name to use in the dump
 -t, --tablespaces-only    dump only tablespaces, no databases or roles
 -x, --no-privileges       do not dump privileges (grant/revoke)
 --binary-upgrade          for use by upgrade utilities only
 --column-inserts          dump data as INSERT commands with column names
 --disable-dollar-quoting  disable dollar quoting, use SQL standard quoting
 --disable-triggers        disable triggers during data-only restore
 --inserts                 dump data as INSERT commands, rather than COPY
 --no-security-labels      do not dump security label assignments
 --no-tablespaces          do not dump tablespace assignments
 --no-unlogged-table-data  do not dump unlogged table data
 --quote-all-identifiers   quote all identifiers, even if not key words
 --use-set-session-authorization
use SET SESSION AUTHORIZATION commands instead o
ALTER OWNER commands to set ownership

Connection options:
 -d, --dbname=CONNSTR      connect using connection string ❶
 -h, --host=HOSTNAME       database server host or socket directory
 -l, --database=DBNAME     alternative default database
 -p, --port=PORT           database server port number
 -U, --username=NAME       connect as specified database user
```

```
-w, --no-password           never prompt for password
-W, --password              force password prompt (should happen automatically)
--role=ROLENAME             do SET ROLE before dump
```

If -f/--file is not used, then the SQL script will be written to the standard output.

❶   New in PostgreSQL 9.3

Database Restore: pg_restore

Use pg_restore to restore backup files in tar, custom, or directory formats created using pg_dump. Example B-3 shows the pg_restore help output. See "Restore" on page 40 for more examples.

Example B-3. pg_restore help

```
pg_restore --help

pg_restore restores a PostgreSQL database from an archive created by pg_dump.
Usage:
  pg_restore [OPTION]... [FILE]

General options:
  -d, --dbname=NAME         connect to database name
  -f, --file=FILENAME       output file name
  -F, --format=c|d|t        backup file format (should be automatic)
  -l, --list                print summarized TOC of the archive
  -v, --verbose             verbose mode
  -V, --version             output version information, then exit
  -?, --help                show this help, then exit

Options controlling the restore:
  -a, --data-only           restore only the data, no schema
  -c, --clean               clean (drop) database objects before recreating
  -C, --create              create the target database
  -e, --exit-on-error       exit on error, default is to continue
  -I, --index=NAME          restore named index
  -j, --jobs=NUM            use this many parallel jobs to restore
  -L, --use-list=FILENAME   use table of contents from this file for
                            selecting/ordering output
  -n, --schema=NAME         restore only objects in this schema
  -O, --no-owner            skip restoration of object ownership
  -P, --function=NAME(args) restore named function
  -s, --schema-only         restore only the schema, no data
  -S, --superuser=NAME      superuser user name to use for disabling triggers
  -t, --table=NAME          restore named table(s)
  -T, --trigger=NAME        restore named trigger
  -x, --no-privileges       skip restoration of access privileges (grant/revoke)
  -1, --single-transaction  restore as a single transaction
  --disable-triggers        disable triggers during data-only restore
```

```
    --no-data-for-failed-tables  do not restore data of tables that could not be
                                 created
    --no-security-labels         do not restore security labels
    --no-tablespaces             do not restore tablespace assignments
    --section=SECTION             restore named section (pre-data, data, or post-data)
❶
    --use-set-session-authorization
                                 use SET SESSION AUTHORIZATION commands instead of
                                 ALTER OWNER commands to set ownership

Connection options:
  -h, --host=HOSTNAME       database server host or socket directory
  -p, --port=PORT           database server port number
  -U, --username=NAME       connect as specified database user
  -w, --no-password         never prompt for password
  -W, --password            force password prompt (should happen automatically)
      --role=ROLENAME       do SET ROLE before restore
```

❶ New features introduced in PostgreSQL 9.2.

psql Interactive Commands

Example B-4 lists commands available in psql when you launch an interactive session. For examples of usage, see "Environment Variables" on page 47 and "Interactive versus Noninteractive psql" on page 48.

Example B-4. Getting list of interactive psql commands

```
\?
General
  \copyright          show PostgreSQL usage and distribution terms
  \g [FILE] or ;      execute query (and send results to file or |pipe)
  \gset [PREFIX]      execute query and store results in psql variables ❶
  \h [NAME]           help on syntax of SQL commands, * for all commands
  \q                  quit psql
  \watch [SEC]        execute query every SEC seconds ❷
Query Buffer
  \e [FILE] [LINE]    edit the query buffer (or file) with external editor
  \ef [FUNCNAME [LINE]] edit function definition with external editor
  \p                  show the contents of the query buffer
  \r                  reset (clear) the query buffer
  \w FILE             write query buffer to file
Input/Output
  \copy ...           perform SQL COPY with data stream to the client host
  \echo [STRING]      write string to standard output
  \i FILE             execute commands from file
 \ir FILE             as \i, but relative to location of current script ❸
  \o [FILE]           send all query results to file or |pipe
  \qecho [STRING]     write string to query output stream (see \o)
Informational
```

```
(options: S = show system objects, + = additional detail)
\d[S+]                  list tables, views, and sequences
\d[S+]    NAME          describe table, view, sequence, or index
\da[S]   [PATTERN]      list aggregates
\db[+]   [PATTERN]      list tablespaces
\dc[S]   [PATTERN]      list conversions
\dC      [PATTERN]      list casts
\dd[S]   [PATTERN]      show comments on objects
\ddp     [PATTERN]      list default privileges
\dD[S]   [PATTERN]      list domains
\det[+]  [PATTERN]      list foreign tables
\des[+]  [PATTERN]      list foreign servers
\deu[+]  [PATTERN]      list user mappings
\dew[+]  [PATTERN]      list foreign-data wrappers
\df[antw][S+] [PATRN]   list [only agg/normal/trigger/window] functions
\dF[+]   [PATTERN]      list text search configurations
\dFd[+]  [PATTERN]      list text search dictionaries
\dFp[+]  [PATTERN]      list text search parsers
\dFt[+]  [PATTERN]      list text search templates
\dg[+]   [PATTERN]      list roles
\di[S+]  [PATTERN]      list indexes
\dl                     list large objects, same as \lo_list
\dL[S+]  [PATTERN]      list procedural languages
\dm[S+]  [PATTERN]      list materialized views  ❹
\dn[S+]  [PATTERN]      list schemas
\do[S]   [PATTERN]      list operators
\dO[S+]  [PATTERN]      list collations
\dp      [PATTERN]      list table, view, and sequence access privileges
\drds [PATRN1 [PATRN2]] list per-database role settings
\ds[S+]  [PATTERN]      list sequences
\dt[S+]  [PATTERN]      list tables
\dT[S+]  [PATTERN]      list data types
\du[+]   [PATTERN]      list roles
\dv[S+]  [PATTERN]      list views
\dE[S+]  [PATTERN]      list foreign tables
\dx[+]   [PATTERN]      list extensions
\dy      [PATTERN]      list event triggers  ❺
\l[+]                   list databases
\sf[+] FUNCNAME         show a function's definition
\z       [PATTERN]      same as \dp
Formatting
\a                      toggle between unaligned and aligned output mode
\C [STRING]             set table title, or unset if none
\f [STRING]             show or set field separator for unaligned query output
\H                      toggle HTML output mode (currently off)
\pset NAME [VALUE]      set table output option
                        (NAME := {format|border|expanded|fieldsep|fieldsep_zero ❻
| footer|null|
              numericlocale|recordsep|tuples_only|title|tableattr|pager}) ❼
\t [on|off]             show only rows (currently off)
\T [STRING]             set HTML <table> tag attributes, or unset if none
\x [on|off]             toggle expanded output (currently off)
```

```
Connection
  \c[onnect] [DBNAME|- USER|- HOST|- PORT|-]
                          connect to new database (currently "postgres")
  \encoding [ENCODING]    show or set client encoding
  \password [USERNAME]    securely change the password for a user
  \conninfo               display information about current connection
Operating System
  \cd [DIR]               change the current working directory
\setenv NAME [VALUE]    set or unset environment variable ❽
  \timing [on|off]        toggle timing of commands (currently off)
  \! [COMMAND]            execute command in shell or start interactive shell
```

❶ ❷ New features introduced in PostgreSQL 9.3.
❹ ❺

❸ ❻ New features introduced in PostgreSQL 9.2.
❽

❼   New feature introduced in PostgreSQL 9.4. You can use \pset without any arguments and it will output all the options you can set and what the current values are set to.

psql Noninteractive Commands

Example B-5 shows the noninteractive commands help screen. Examples of their usage are covered in "Interactive versus Noninteractive psql" on page 48.

Example B-5. psql basic help screen

```
psql --help

psql is the PostgreSQL interactive terminal.
Usage:
psql [OPTION]... [DBNAME [USERNAME]]

General options:
-c, --command=COMMAND    run only single command (SQL or internal) and exit
-d, --dbname=DBNAME      database name to connect to
-f, --file=FILENAME      execute commands from file, then exit
-l, --list               list available databases, then exit
-v, --set=, --variable=NAME=VALUE
set psql variable NAME to VALUE
-X, --no-psqlrc          do not read startup file (~/.psqlrc)
-1 ("one"), --single-transaction
execute command file as a single transaction
--help                   show this help, then exit
--version                output version information, then exit

Input and output options:
-a, --echo-all           echo all input from script
-e, --echo-queries       echo commands sent to server
```

```
-E, --echo-hidden       display queries that internal commands generate
-L, --log-file=FILENAME  send session log to file
-n, --no-readline       disable enhanced command-line editing (readline)
-o, --output=FILENAME   send query results to file (or |pipe)
-q, --quiet             run quietly (no messages, only query output)
-s, --single-step       single-step mode (confirm each query)
-S, --single-line       single-line mode (end of line terminates SQL command)


Output format options:
-A, --no-align          unaligned table output mode
-F, --field-separator=STRING
set field separator (default: "|")
-H, --html              HTML table output mode
-P, --pset=VAR[=ARG]    set printing option VAR to ARG (see \pset command)
-R, --record-separator=STRING
set record separator (default: newline)
-t, --tuples-only       print rows only
-T, --table-attr=TEXT   set HTML table tag attributes (e.g., width, border)
-x, --expanded          turn on expanded table output
-z, --field-separator-zero ❶
                        set field separator to zero byte
-0, --record-separator-zero ❷
                        set record separator to zero byte


Connection options:
-h, --host=HOSTNAME     database server host or socket directory
-p, --port=PORT         database server port (default: "5432")
-U, --username=USERNAME database user name
-w, --no-password       never prompt for password
-W, --password          force password prompt (should happen automatically)
```

For more information, type "\?" (for internal commands) or "\help" (for SQL commands) from within psql, or consult the psql section in the PostgreSQL documentation.

❶ ❷ These items are new features introduced in PostgreSQL 9.2.

Index

Symbols

#> operator, 100
#>> operator, 100
&& (overlap) operator, 98, 114
-> operator, 100
->> operator, 100
: (colon), 51
<@ (contained) operator, 98, 103
= (equality) operator, 103
? (key exists) operator, 103
@> (contains) operator, 98, 103
|| (concatenation) operator, 84, 93
~ (similar to) operator, 86

A

Adminer tool, 3
administration tools, 1–4
adminpack extension, 63
aggregates
    FILTER clause and, 133–134
    PL/V8 and, 160
    window functions, 134–138
ALTER DATABASE command, 29, 42
ALTER DEFAULT PRIVILEGES command, 31
ALTER SEQUENCE command, 82
ALTER SYSTEM command, 17, 20
ALTER TABLE command, 42, 113
ALTER TABLESPACE command, 43, 172

ALTER TYPE command, 112
archive_command configuration directive, 184
array function, 92
arrays
    about, 92
    creating, 92
    JSON starting number, 101
    referencing elements in, 93
    slicing and splicing, 93
    splitting strings into, 84
    unnesting to rows, 94
array_agg function, 93, 101
array_to_json function, 101
array_upper function, 93
asynchronous transactions, 182
authentication methods, 21–23
autocommit commands, 51

B

B-Tree indexes, 115, 117
B-Tree-GIN indexes, 116
B-Tree-GiST indexes, 116
back-referencing, 85
backup and restore
    pgAdmin tool, 69–71
    pg_dump tool, 38–40, 69, 70, 197–198
    pg_dumpall tool, 38, 40, 70, 199
    pg_restore tool, 40–42, 69, 200
basic CTEs, 138

We'd like to hear your suggestions for improving our indexes. Send email to index@oreilly.com.

batch jobs, pgAgent and, 75
BETWEEN operator, 90
Big SQL technology, 16
bigserial data type, 82
bitmap index scan, 119
btree_gin extension, 36
btree_gist extension, 36, 114
btrim function, 84

C

caching, 173
canonical form, 96
cascading replication, 182, 183
CASE expression, 178
case sensitivity, 128
casts, 8, 128
catalogs, 5
\cd command, 63
char data type, 83
characters and strings
    about, 83
    pattern matching and, 85–86
    regular expressions and, 85–86
    splitting strings, 84
    string functions, 84
check constraints, 113
colon (:), 51
columns view, 5
command-line tools
    fetching output from, 55
    packaged, 197–204
    retrieving prior commands, 52
common table expressions (CTEs)
    about, 138
    basic, 138
    recursive, 140
    writable, 139
composite data types, 105, 130–131
concatenation operator, 84, 93
configuration files, 17–23, 63
\connect command, 50
connections
    managing, 23–24
    to servers, 60
constraints
    about, 109, 112
    check, 113
    exclusion, 114
    foreign key, 112

unique, 113
constructor range functions, 97
contained (<@) operator, 98, 103
contains (@>) operator, 98, 103
continuous range types, 95
contribs (see extensions)
Coordinated Universal Time (UTC), 87
\copy command, 54–56, 66
CREATE DATABASE command, 27, 30, 41
CREATE EXTENSION command, xi, 7, 35, 63
CREATE GROUP command, 25
CREATE MATERIALIZED VIEW command, 125
CREATE PRODCEDURAL LANGUAGE command, 7
CREATE ROLE command, 25, 25, 30
CREATE SCHEMA command, 29
CREATE SEQUENCE command, 82
CREATE TABLE command, 99
CREATE TABLESPACE command, 42
CREATE TYPE command, 111
CREATE UNIQUE INDEX command, 125
CREATE USER command, 25
CREATEDB rights, 27
crontab command, 75
CTEs (common table expressions)
    about, 138
    basic, 138
    recursive, 140
    writable, 139
custom data types
    building, 106
    building operators and functions for, 107
    tables as, 105

D

daemons (services)
    about, 4
    pgAgent tool and, 75
data definition language (DDL), 8
data types
    about, 7, 81
    arrays, 92–95
    characters and strings, 83–86
    custom and composite, 105–108
    json, 98–103
    jsonb, 99, 101–103
    numerics, 81–83
    range types, 95–98

temporals, 86–92
xml, 103–105
database administration
    backup and restore, 38–42, 70–71, 197–201
    common mistakes, 43–45
    configuration files, 17–23
    creating assets, 64
    database creation, 27
    extensions and, 32–38
    managing connections, 23–24
    managing disk storage, 42
    privileges and, 29–32, 64–66
    roles and, 24–26
    services and, 4
database drivers, 14
database objects, 4–9
date data type, 87
daterange data type, 96
datetime operators and functions, 90
date_part function, 91
daylight saving time (DST), 87
dblink extension, 37
DDL (data definition language), 8
Debian platform, 194
default privileges, 31
DELETE USING command, 130
delimiters, 55, 67
discrete range types, 95
DISTINCT ON clause, 127
DO command, 132
Document Type Definition (DTD), 103
DROP MATERIALIZED VIEW command, 126
DST (daylight saving time), 87
DTD (Document Type Definition), 103
Dunstan Andrew, 160

E

effective_cache_size network setting, 20
enable_nestloop setting, 169
enable_seqscan setting, 169
end-of-life (EOL) support, 9
EnterpriseDB, 193–195
environment variables, 47
EOL (end-of-life) support, 9
equality (=) operator, 103
exclusion constraints, 114
EXPLAIN ANALYZE command, 163
EXPLAIN ANALYZE VERBOSE command, 51
EXPLAIN command, 163

exporting data
    pgAdmin and, 67–68
    psql and, 54–55
extensions
    about, 6, 32–34
    classic, 37
    common, 36–38
    downloading, 34
    getting information about, 33
    installing, 32–36
    popular, 36
    upgrading to new model, 35

F

FDWs (foreign data wrappers)
    about, 6, 181, 186
    querying flat files, 187–189
    querying foreign servers, 189
    querying nonconventional data sources, 190
Fedora platform, 193
file_fdw wrapper, 187
FILTER clause, 133–134, 179
filtered indexes, 118
flat files, querying, 187–189
foreign data wrappers (FDWs)
    about, 6, 181, 186
    querying flat files, 187–189
    querying foreign servers, 189
    querying nonconventional data sources, 190
foreign key constraints, 112
foreign servers, querying, 189
foreign tables, 6
forking, 15
FreeBSD platform, 194
functional indexes, 118
functions
    about, 7, 81
    anatomy of, 145–150
    building for custom data types, 107
    datetime, 90
    PL/CoffeeScript, 157–161
    PL/LiveScript, 157–161
    PL/plSQL, 154–155
    PL/Python, 155–157
    PL/V8, 157–161
    returning, 129
    string, 84
    window, 134–138
    writing in SQL, 150–153

fuzzystrmatch extension, 37

G

Generalized Inverted Index (GIN) indexes, 115
Generalized Search Tree (GiST) indexes, 115
generate_series function, 91, 129
geocoding, pgScript and, 72
GIN (Generalized Inverted Index) indexes, 115
GiST (Generalized Search Tree) indexes, 115
GRANT command, 26, 30
Grant Wizard, 65
graphical explain plan, 74
group login roles, 25
group roles
    about, 24
    creating, 25–26
    inheriting rights from, 26

H

hash indexes, 116
hstore extension, 37, 131
HTML format, 56–58, 67

I

\i command, 63
ident authentication method, 23
ILIKE operator, 37, 128
importing data
    pgAdmin and, 66
    psql and, 54–56
indexes
    about, 109, 114
    bitmap index scan, 119
    determining usefulness of, 170–171
    filtered, 118
    functional, 118
    multicolumn, 119
    operator classes and, 116–118
    partial, 118
    troubleshooting, 118
information_schema catalog, 5, 62
inheriting
    rights from group roles, 26
    tables, 110, 129
INSERT command, 99
INSTEAD OF triggers, 121, 123
int4range data type, 96

int8range data type, 96
interval data type, 87–88

J

Java language, 14
JavaScript language, 98
job scheduling, 75–78
joins, lateral, 141–143
json data type
    about, 98
    inserting data, 99
    outputting data, 101
    queries and, 99–101
jsonb data type, 99, 101–103
jsonb_array_element function, 101
jsonb_array_length function, 103
jsonb_each function, 102
jsonb_extract_path_text function, 102
jsonb_object_field function, 101
json_agg function, 101
json_array_elements function, 99
json_array_length function, 100, 103
json_each function, 102
json_extract_path function, 99, 100
json_extract_path_text function, 99, 102

K

key exists (?) operator, 103

L

LAG function, 137
LATERAL keyword, 141–143
LEAD function, 137
LibreOffice office suite, 14
LIKE operator, 37, 117, 128
LIMIT clause, 127
Linux platform
    crontab command, 75
    installing PostgreSQL, 193
    psql tool and, 49
listen_addresses network setting, 19
lists of objects, 53
login roles, 24–25
lpad function, 84
ltrim function, 84
Lubaczewski, Hubert, 56, 167

M

Mac OS X platform, 194
maintenance_work_mem network setting, 20
master servers, 182, 184
materialized views, 122, 125–126
max_connections network setting, 19
md5 authentication method, 22
multicolumn indexes, 119
multirow constructor, 128

N

navigating pgAdmin tool, 61–62
.NET Framework, 14
Netezza database, 15
Node.js framework, 15
numeric data types, 82
numrange data type, 96

O

ODBC (Open Database Connectivity), 14
OFFSET clause, 127
OLAP (online analytical processing) applications, 125
Open Database Connectivity (ODBC), 14
OpenSCG, 16
operator classes, 116–118
operators
    about, 7, 81
    building for custom data types, 107
    datetime, 90
    json data type, 100
    jsonb data type, 103
    range, 98
    string, 84
ORDER BY clause, 136–138
overlap (&&) operator, 98, 114
overlaps function, 90
OVERLAPS operator (ANSI SQL), 90

P

parentheses, 107
partial indexes, 118
PARTITION BY clause, 135
password authentication method, 23
pattern matching, 85–86
peer authentication method, 23

performance tuning (see query performance tuning)
Perl language, 15
pgAdmin tool
    about, 2–3, 59
    accessing pqsql from, 63
    backup and restore, 69–71
    connecting to servers, 60
    editing configuration files, 63
    exporting data and, 67–68
    features overview, 59–60, 63–71
    graphical explain, 74
    importing data and, 66
    job scheduling and, 75–78
    navigating, 61–62
    pgScript and, 72–74
    privilege settings and, 29
pgAgent tool
    about, 75
    batch jobs and, 75
    installing, 75
    query examples, 78
    scheduling jobs, 76–77
    troubleshooting, 79
pgcrypto extension, 37
PGHOST environment variable, 47
PGPORT environment variable, 47
pgScript tool, 72–74
PGUSER environment variable, 47
pg_buffercache extension, 173
pg_cancel_backend function, 24
pg_catalog catalog, 5, 62
pg_clog folder, 43
pg_ctl reload command, 23
pg_default tablespace, 42
pg_dump tool
    about, 38–40, 197–198
    pgAdmin and, 71
    selective backup and, 70
    version considerations, 69
pg_dumpall tool, 38, 40, 70, 199
pg_global tablespace, 42
pg_hba.conf file, 17, 21–23, 63
pg_ident.conf file, 17
pg_log folder, 21, 43
pg_opclass system table, 117
pg_prewarm extension, 174
pg_restore tool, 40–42, 69, 200
pg_settings view, 18

pg_stat_activity view, 24
pg_stat_statements extension, 168, 170
pg_stat_statements view, 169
pg_stat_statements_reset function, 169
pg_terminate_backend function, 24
pg_trgm (trigram) extension, 37
pg_xlog folder, 43
PHP language, 14
phpPgAdmin tool, 3
PL/CoffeeScript language, 158–161
PL/LiveScript language, 158–161
PL/V8 language, 158–161
PLs (procedural languages), 7
port network setting, 19
postgis extension, 36
postgres service, 22–23, 45
postgres superuser account, 17, 25, 44
Postgres-XC cluster solution, 16, 184
Postgres-XL cluster solution, 16
PostgreSQL
    about, ix
    additional resources, xii
    downloading, 1
    help resources, 15
    installing, 193–195
    reasons for not using, xii
    reasons for using, x–xii
    version enhancements, 9–14
postgresql-dev package, 188
postgresql.conf file, 17–21, 63
postgres_fdw wrapper, 187
postmaster.pid file, 21
primary keys
    B-Tree and, 115
    inheritance and, 110
    naming considerations, 112
    serial data type and, 82, 110
    table constraints, 113
privileges
    about, 29
    default, 31
    getting started, 30
    GRANT command, 30
    idiosyncrasies of, 32
    setting, 64–66
    types of, 30
procedural languages (PLs), 7
psql tool
    about, 2, 47

    accessing from pgAdmin, 63
    autocommit commands, 51
    basic reporting, 56–58
    custom prompts, 50
    customizations, 49–52
    environment variables and, 47
    executing shell commands, 52
    exporting data, 54–55
    importing data, 54–56
    interactive commands, 48, 201–203
    lists and, 53
    noninteractive commands, 48, 203
    restoring data, 40
    retrieving prior commands, 52
    shortcuts for, 51
    timing executions, 51
    watching statements, 52
PSQLRC environment variable, 47
psqlrc.conf file, 49–52
PSQL_HISTORY environment variable, 47
Python language, 14

Q
quality of drives, 172
queries
    composite types in, 130–131
    flat files, 187–189
    foreign servers, 189
    json data type and, 99–101
    lateral joins, 141–143
    nonconventional data sources, 190
    pgAgent and, 78
    writing better, 174–179
    xml data type and, 104
query performance tuning
    about, 163
    gathering statistics on statements, 168
    graphical outputs, 167
    sample runs and output, 164
query planner
    index usefulness, 170–171
    quality of drives, 172
    random page cost and, 172
    strategy settings, 169
    table statistics, 171

R
random page cost (RPC) ratio, 172

range data types
  about, 95
  built-in, 96
  defining ranges, 96
  defining tables with, 97
  discrete versus continuous, 95
  temporals and, 87
range operators, 98
rank function, 134
records (rows)
  about, 8
  converting to JSON objects, 101
  unnesting arrays to, 94
recursive CTEs, 140
Red Hat platform, 193
REFRESH command, 122
REFRESH MATERIALIZED VIEW command,
  125, 126
regexp_matches function, 86
regexp_replace function, 85
regular expressions, 85–86
reloading configuration files, 23
remastering process, 182
replication
  about, 181
  cascading, 182, 183
  common terminology, 181–183
  evolution of, 183
  initiating process, 186
  setting up, 184–186
  third-party options, 183
reports
  export options, 68
  psql and, 56–58
restore (see backup and restore)
RETURNING clause, 106, 130
returning functions, 129
reverse solidus (\), 85
REVOKE command, 31
rights, inheriting from group roles, 26
roles
  about, 24
  backing up, 40
rows (records)
  about, 8
  converting to JSON objects, 101
  unnesting arrays to, 94
row_number function, 134
row_to_json function, 101

rpad function, 84
RPC (random page cost) ratio, 172
rtrim function, 84
Ruby language, 15
rules, 9, 121

S
scheduling jobs, 75–78
schemas, 5, 27–29
searches, case-insensitive, 128
SELECT command, 177
sequences
  about, 8
  serial data types and, 82
serial data type, 82, 110
services (daemons)
  about, 4
  pgAgent tool and, 75
\set command, 50, 51
SET ROLE command, 26
SET SESSION AUTHORIZATION command,
  26
shared_buffers network setting, 20, 21, 44
shell commands, executing, 52
shorthand casting, 128
SHOW ALL command, 19
similar to (~) operators, 86
single table views, 122
slave servers, 182, 185
SP-GIST indexes, 116
split_part function, 85
statistics
  gathering on statements, 168
  table, 171
storage, managing with tablespaces, 42
streaming replication model, 182, 183
strings (see characters and strings)
string_agg function, 84, 98, 133
string_to_array function, 85, 93
subqueries, 175–177, 178
substring function, 84
substrings
  extracting, 84
  splitting strings into, 84
superuser roles, 25
synchronous transactions, 182

T

tab-delimited files, 55
tables
    about, 6, 109
    composite data type and, 111
    creating, 109
    creating using pgScript, 72
    as custom data types, 105
    defining with ranges, 97
    foreign, 6
    inherited, 110, 129
    lateral joins, 141–143
    moving, 42
    populating with pgScript, 73
    single views, 122
    splitting strings into, 84
    statistics and, 171
    types supported, 109
    unlogged, 111, 183
tables view, 5
tablespaces
    about, 7
    backing up, 40
    creating, 42
    managing disk storage with, 42
    moving objects between, 42
tabular explain plan, 167
template database, 27
temporal data types
    about, 86–88
    adding intervals, 90
    datetime operators and functions, 90
    subtracting intervals, 90
text data type, 83, 110
third-party replication options, 183
time data type, 87
time zones
    about, 88–90
    temporals and, 87
timestamp data type, 87, 90
timestamptz data type, 87, 110
timetz data type, 87
\timing command, 51
timing executions (psql), 51
TOAST, 177
to_char function, 91
tPostgres database management system, 16
triggers
    about, 8

INSTEAD OF, 121, 123
    updating views, 123–125
trim function, 84
troubleshooting
    indexes, 118
    pgAgent tool, 79
    pg_hba.conf file, 22
    postgresql.conf file, 21
    temporal data types, 89
trust authentication method, 22
tsearch extension, 37
tsrange data type, 88, 96
tstzrange data type, 88, 96
types (data) (see data types)

U

Ubuntu platform, 194
unique constraints, 113
Unix platform
    crontab command, 75
    installing PostgreSQL, 193
    psql tool and, 49
    retrieving command history, 52
unlogged tables, 111, 183
unnest function, 85, 86, 94, 104
\unset command, 50
UPDATE command, 27, 121
UPDATE OF clause, 8, 147
upper function, 128
UTC (Coordinated Universal Time), 87

V

VACUUM ANALYZE command, 172
VALUES keyword, 128
varchar data type, 83, 110
variables
    about, 5
    environment, 47
    psql shortcuts and, 51
versions
    pgAgent tool, 79
    pg_dump tool, 69
    PostgreSQL 9.1, 13
    PostgreSQL 9.2, 12
    PostgreSQL 9.3, 11
    PostgreSQL 9.4, 10–11
    upgrade recommendations, 9

views
  about, 7, 121
  materialized, 122, 125–126
  single table, 122
  updating with triggers, 123–125
views view, 5

W

WAL (Write-ahead log), 182
\watch command, 52
window functions
  about, 134
  ORDER BY clause, 136–138
  PARTITION BY clause, 135
Windows platform
  installing PostgreSQL, 193
  psql tool and, 49
  retrieving command history, 52
WITH CHECK OPTION modifier, 122
WITH GRANT OPTION, 30

work_mem network setting, 20
writable CTEs, 139
Write-ahead log (WAL), 182

X

xlst_process function, 38
xml data type
  about, 103
  inserting data, 103
  querying data, 104
xml extension, 38
XML format, 67
XML Schema Definition (XSD), 103
xpath function, 104
XSD (XML Schema Definition), 103

Y

Y-M-D format, 91
Yum repository, 194

About the Authors

Regina Obe is a coprincipal of Paragon Corporation, a database consulting company based in Boston. She has more than 15 years of professional experience in various programming languages and database systems, with special focus on spatial databases. She is a member of the PostGIS steering committee and the PostGIS core development team. Regina holds a BS degree in mechanical engineering from the Massachusetts Institute of Technology. She coauthored *PostGIS in Action*.

Leo Hsu is a coprincipal of Paragon Corporation, a database consulting company based in Boston. He has more than 15 years of professional experience developing and thinking about databases for organizations large and small. Leo holds an MS degree in engineering of economic systems from Stanford University and BS degrees in mechanical engineering and economics from the Massachusetts Institute of Technology. He coauthored *PostGIS in Action*.

Colophon

The animal on the cover of *PostgreSQL: Up and Running* is an elephant shrew (*Macroscelides proboscideus*), an insectivorous mammal native to Africa named for its lengthy trunk, which resembles that of an elephant. They are distributed across southern Africa in many types of habitat, from the Namib Desert to boulder-covered terrain in South Africa and thick forests.

The elephant shrew is small and quadrupedal; they resemble rodents and opossums with their scaly tails. Their legs are long for their size, allowing them to move around in a hopping fashion similar to a rabbit. The trunk varies in size depending on species, but are all able to twist around in search of food.

They are diurnal and active, though they are hardly seen due to being wary animals, which makes them difficult to trap. They are well camouflaged and quick at dashing away from threats.

Though elephant shrews are not very social, many of them live in monogamous pairs, sharing and defending their home territory. Female elephant shrews experience a menstrual cycle similar to that of human females; their mating period lasts for several days. Gestation lasts from 45 to 60 days, and the female gives birth to litters of one to three young, which are born fairly developed and remain in the nest for several days before venturing out. This can happen several times a year.

Five days after birth, young elephant shrews add mashed insects—which their mother collects and trasnports in her cheeks—to their milk diet. The young begin their migratory phase after about 15 days, lessening their dependency on the mother. They subsequently establish their own home range and become sexually active within 41 to 46 days.

Adult elephant shrews feed on invertebrates, such as insects, spiders, centipedes, millipedes, and earthworms. Eating larger prey can be somewhat messy. The elephant shrew must pin down the prey using its feet, then chews pieces with its cheek teeth, which can result in many dropped bits. The elephant shrew then uses its tongue to flick small food into its mouth, similar to an anteater. When available, some also eat small amounts of plant matter, such as new leaves, seeds, and small fruits.

Many of the animals on O'Reilly covers are endangered; all of them are important to the world. To learn more about how you can help, go to *animals.oreilly.com*.

The cover image is from *Meyers Kleines Lexicon*. The cover fonts are URW Typewriter and Guardian Sans. The text font is Adobe Minion Pro; the heading font is Adobe Myriad Condensed; and the code font is Dalton Maag's Ubuntu Mono.

Have it your way.

Get even more for your money.

Join the O'Reilly Community, and register the O'Reilly books you own. It's free, and you'll get:

- $4.99 ebook upgrade offer
- 40% upgrade offer on O'Reilly print books
- Membership discounts on books and events
- Free lifetime updates to ebooks and videos
- Multiple ebook formats, DRM FREE
- Participation in the O'Reilly community
- Newsletters
- Account management
- 100% Satisfaction Guarantee

Signing up is easy:

1. Go to: oreilly.com/go/register
2. Create an O'Reilly login.
3. Provide your address.
4. Register your books.

Note: English-language books only

To order books online:
oreilly.com/store

For questions about products or an order:
orders@oreilly.com

To sign up to get topic-specific email announcements and/or news about upcoming books, conferences, special offers, and new technologies:
elists@oreilly.com

For technical questions about book content:
booktech@oreilly.com

To submit new book proposals to our editors:
proposals@oreilly.com

O'Reilly books are available in multiple DRM-free ebook formats. For more information:
oreilly.com/ebooks

Lightning Source UK Ltd.
Milton Keynes UK
UKOW06f2339141214

243129UK00003B/6/P